I WAS
CHURCHILL'S
BODYGUARD

I WAS CHURCHILL'S BODYGUARD

Edmund Murray

W.H. ALLEN · LONDON
1987

Copyright © Edmund Murray, 1987

Typeset by Phoenix Photosetting, Chatham
Printed and bound in Great Britain by
Mackays of Chatham Ltd, Kent
for the Publishers W.H. Allen & Co. Plc
44 Hill Street, London W1X 8LB

British Library Cataloguing in Publication Data

Murray, Edmund
    I was Churchill's bodyguard.
    1. Murray, Edmund   2. Bodyguards
    —Great Britain—Biography
    I. Title
    941.082'092'4   DA566.9.C5

    ISBN 0–491–03395–8

CONTENTS

AUTHOR'S NOTE

This book is dedicated to my dear wife, Beryl, whose unfailing love and devotion have been my salvation throughout forty years now, in the hope that I will be spared to enjoy it for many years to come. I also trust that my many friends inside and outside the French Foreign Legion, will understand how much I have valued their friendship during a life not empty of excitement.

Edmund Murray
COMBE DOWN, BATH
14th July (Bastille Day) 1986

I WAS
CHURCHILL'S
BODYGUARD

1

MY EARLY LIFE

THE GREAT MAN TOOK my hand, responding to the light pressure I had been told to use, inspected me carefully . . . and belched. As I struggled to keep the surprise from my face, a smile, a very friendly smile, suffused those cherubic pink and white features, and a round, deep voice said, 'So you are Sergeant Murray. I trust that we shall get on well together for I have heard much about you. You have had a most interesting life. And I hear you even paint in oils.'

Though I was in fact only a Detective-Constable at the time, thenceforth I was Sergeant Murray, not only to the entire Churchill family, but to many other great names as well, including two Presidents of the United States, a Prime Minister of Australia, a Field Marshal, a President of the Royal Academy, a ballerina and a prima donna.

At this time I was thirty-three years old. What seemed a lifetime of adventure was past. Another lifetime of even greater adventures was just beginning.

It all began on 18 August 1917 when I, Edmund, was born to William Grainger Murray and Margaret Elizabeth Buchanan Wildsmith Murray, at a tiny village called Friarside, in the parish of Tanfield, in County Durham. My father came from a Scottish mining family of four brothers, Eddie, Robert (known as Percy), Joe and Tom, and two sisters, Margaret and Selina (known as Alice). Uncle Tom had been a leading stoker on the HMS *Good Hope* when she was sunk in the Battle of Coronel, 1 November 1914. Von Spee won this battle at negligible cost, but revenge came for the British five weeks later in the Battle of the Falkland Isles – the first one of that name.

Father was born in Jarrow where the famous march of the miners began in the 1920s. His favourite pastimes, besides Saturday night beer, were crossword puzzles, enigmas and brain teasers. He played football and cricket, was a Newcastle United fan and for many years was the gamekeeper of the Friarside Woods along the River Derwent, a tributary of the River Tyne, so was able to provide rabbits not only for the manager of the Tilley seam of the coalmine at Friarside, one Frank Braidford, and the deputy manager, but his own growing family as well. The mine and the woods, together with most of the mines for miles around, were owned by the Bowes-Lyon family, who were of course the family of HM Queen Elizabeth, the Queen Mother.

As a deputy overman, father had great responsibility for the safety of the airways and waterways and tub-ways of the seam, and as a shot-firer had to lay and fire the explosive charges to bring down coal and rocks as required. It was only after his death during the blitz in London, where he had moved after leaving the mines, that we discovered that he had been commended and even decorated for gallant rescues and attempted rescues in the mine.

My brothers, Joe and Tom, worked in the same mine, as a team, with one hewing the coal and the other 'putting', that is shovelling, it into the tubs for dispatching it 'out-bye' for loading into the Bowes-Lyon rail trucks. They worked in appalling conditions with seams only eighteen inches in height and when they washed themselves (Mother washed their backs of course) from top to toe in the large tin basin in front of the coal fire in the kitchen, I could see that their backs were scraped raw by contact with the roof of the seam. I often went just a short way 'in-bye' to collect one of the tiny Shetland ponies which were used to pull the heavy tubs of coal, and take it to the stables for a wash and feed. I just loved those wonderful wee ponies.

My mother was one of the many unsung saints of mining, slaving night and day to ensure that her husband had some of the things he wanted as a just reward for the constant struggle for the money necessary to keep a warm home, a filled garden, children at school, and a few bets on the horses. There were three boys and two girls – there had been a third girl but she had died when only a few months old – and I was right in the middle. Mother never had any of the household appliances with which we are now so familiar. All the washing had to be boiled in tin basins over the kitchen fire, though at the side of the kitchen range there was, on one side, the 'copper' and an oven on the other. The boiling washing was taken off the fire and put into the big wooden tub where it had to be 'possed' with a heavy piece of rounded wood, up and down for hours on end. Then it was boiled once more and hung out to dry, in the garden in summer, in the kitchen in winter, after 'mangling' of course. The mangle was a huge bit of equipment with two yard-wide wooden rollers kept tight together by a pair of adjustable springs. The children were often called on to help with the possing and the mangling. We didn't like it.

Like my older brothers, I was good at school, and won a full scholarship to the Alderman Wood Secondary School at West Stanley, some five or six miles from the village of the Lintz, where the family lived. At the Leaes Council School, between the ages of five and ten, I remember being a bright pupil winning several book prizes. I remember my early days at school with much pleasure, and even more pleasant is the memory of my first 'love', Aileen Durdey, who joined the school during my last year there. We had numerous lessons outside the usual curriculum, including single sticks, a sort of junior model of the Japanese martial art of 'kendo', and gardening in the school garden. It was there that I first learned a most important lesson from the teacher, 'A good gardener never hurries!' I have tried to apply it to my own gardening ever since.

The scholarship meant that my education was free, together with the books, exercise books, pens and ink necessary for my studies, and cheap meals were also available in the dining-room. But clothes were also required. These were not provided and were a very expensive item in the budget of a family in the 1930s, a budget soon to be reduced when my two brothers decided to leave the mines for London, where the streets were supposed to be paved with gold, not only for the Irish, but for the Geordies as well. Father was also soon out of work, and on the dole. They had not forgiven him for working during the strike, even though he considered it his duty to keep the airways and waterways free from obstruction so that as soon as the strike was ended, as end it always must, the men would be able to get straight back to work rather than wait months before returning should the mine be unsafe to work. Not only was he a 'blackleg', but so was I at school.

I was very innocent as far as sex was concerned during my early life, although there was the occasional walk with a couple of the lads from Tanfield Lea to Annfield Plain or Catchgate, two or three miles away, to promenade some of the girls from school with a few kisses and cuddles that never hurt anyone. When I was about thirteen I also remember that three or four girls of the neighbourhood tried to rape me. By sheer weight they forced me to the ground and tried to 'unveil' me so that the eldest girl could have her way with me. By dint of a supreme effort I managed to extricate myself. Somehow I don't think that I would have struggled so a few years later.

Then there was Mary who lived in West Stanley. I saw her one Sunday night promenading up the High Street like dozens of young people did in those days. Up one side, down the other. She smiled at me as we passed and I followed behind till she went home. She was undoubtedly several years my senior, but I loved her dark flashing eyes, her dark hair and the way she smiled. She was a working girl and lived with her father in one of the Stanley side streets. I used to spend hours walking up and down the High Street, or opposite her house, just for a glimpse of her, but a few words when we passed each other in the street was all that ever happened.

My constant companion at this time was Jim Burrows who was a couple of years older than me. We used to play snooker in West Stanley – only a penny for twenty minutes at the time – and it was there one day that I met the greatest gentleman snooker and billiards player of them all, Joe Davis. He was awarded an OBE in 1963 for services to charity and died in 1978, leaving a widow, former actress June Malo.

Teas on Sunday at home were the joy of my life at that time. The dining-table was always laden with wonderful home-made products of my mother though I was frequently banished to the kitchen for laughing or causing the rest of the family to go into fits of laughter. It was always my fault. This does not mean for a moment that I went without food – no member of our family ever did go without – but I would have it later when everyone else had finished.

I am quite sure that my secondary school days would have been much more enjoyable had we been able to afford some better clothes, more like those worn by the sons of business and professional men who formed the majority of the students. I suppose that we either ate or wore fine clothes. We could not do both or my parents would have found a way. However, I carried on at Alderman Wood School for some four years, studying arithmetic under Mr Fewster, a proper old grandmother, French with Miss Butters and Miss Boyd, a lovely young vivacious creature, and Latin under Miss Baxter, a super person well rounded in the right places. Miss Lewis was the music mistress who once caught me looking at a book advertising corsets and gave me a quick rap across the earhole. After geography, I suppose my favourite subject was physics, first taught to me by Dr Livesay, with whom I really worked well and had extremely good marks. When he left he was replaced by a vicious little Welshman, Dr Davies, who on one occasion hit me with a metre ruler. I was not accepting this sort of treatment for I had done nothing wrong as far as I could remember, and grabbed the ruler from the teacher, broke it in two across my knee and threw the pieces out of the open window. When confronted by the Headmaster, Dr Hardy, I explained how I had been struck and I was exonerated. Life with Dr Davies was not too easy afterwards, but teachers are not really the malicious people I sometimes thought them to be.

Billie Ritchie was the English mistress I got on so well with. She was very Scottish with a similar mining background to myself. There was nothing namby-pamby about Billie and quite often there were distinct wet patches on her silk blouse owing to discharges from over-ripe breasts. She married just before I left school. She was always good to me and when we were studying any Shakespeare play, I usually took most of the male parts for I used to put my heart and soul into repaying Miss Ritchie for her kindness.

For quite a time after I had returned from the Far East in 1946, I kept in touch by Christmas cards with Miss Sellers who had been my geography mistress. With her and the Latin mistress, Miss Baxter, I had fun for they seemed to accept my undoubted wit and humorous stories in the spirit in which they were presented. But it was with Joe Binks, the art master, with whom I had the best rapport. I was very good at art and produced numerous artefacts which were exhibited at Open Days. Joe did have one awful habit. He wore a heavy gold ring on the middle finger of his right hand, and when he found anybody transgressing he came quietly up behind and brought his right hand quickly and forcefully upwards from the middle of the back of the transgressor, over the nape of the neck, catching the protruding part of the back of the head with the gold ring as it passed, causing sudden acute pain. But he was a good teacher and if today I still enjoy painting in oils and watercolours, and drawing with pencil and charcoal and pastels, I owe any talent I may have to Joe Binks who so encouraged me.

Schooldays were made up of great joy and excitement, of adolescent love, always unrequited. Mainly it was a world where I was constantly told that I owed everything to everybody and I never willingly accepted patronage. I was perhaps a bit of a rebel but generally just high-spirited. I remember the time when I made gunpowder at home, in order to prove the chemical formula. I took it to school and placed it in a hole in the wall which enclosed the playing fields. Shortly afterwards there was a big bang and the hole was much bigger than before. I was suspected, but was never asked any questions, so the incident died a natural death.

On the whole I was a very good pupil when the subject of the lesson interested me, and the education I received at West Stanley has proved most useful in the life I have led since and I humbly express whenever possible my feeling of gratitude to my teachers of those far-off days.

Things were getting very tight at home in Tanfield Lea and I was allowed to leave school. I remember Mr Hardy's last words in the final report. 'Edmund unfortunately leaves us just before sitting the Oxford Examination in which I know he would have acquitted himself well.'

The mention of Tanfield Lea reminds me of an amusing episode in which I played the major role. I had been in the Scouts for a number of years, in the Peewit Troop as Patrol Leader. Meetings were held in the small schoolhouse in the wee village of Tanfield, a couple of miles from Tantobia, where we lived for a time, and the same distance from Tanfield Lea. A Sunday parade had been organized at Tanfield Church, some two hundred yards from the schoolroom, and I duly marched the two miles from Tanfield Lea to parade at the arranged time, 0700. I waited and waited and then decided to go to church on my own. I was not a frequent visitor to church – it was too far away. I sat down among the twenty or so communicants, listened to the vicar, put my penny in the plate as it was passed round, waited while the others received Holy Communion, helped in the hymns with a loud confident voice, then left, still alone, after the service. The choirmaster met me on the way home. He rather belatedly told me that the original parade had been postponed for a week.

Some days later, I arrived home from school to find that my mother was giving a cup of tea and the usual scone to, of all people, the vicar of the church at Tanfield. I never did find out how he came to be visiting us, for although I suppose we were members of his flock, we only went to church for funerals or the rare wedding, and my own church Scout parades, of course. He was just about to leave, and I listened enthralled as he completed telling my mother, who was quite ignorant of the episode, about the young scout who had paid his penny into the collection bag as it was passed round, but did not go up to receive the Host. (As a matter of fact the young scout had not been confirmed at that time, this only happened in 1946, and was not *au fait* with church ritual.) The following Sunday the vicar, still ignorant of the relevant facts of the case, made Acts of the Apostles, XX, 35, 'How much more blessed it is to give than receive' the subject of his sermon.

For a few weeks after leaving school I attended a Council-sponsored woodwork class in Stanley and learned much about the job of making tables and chairs and other things. My most potent memory of the class, though, was the beautiful voice of one of the other young lads there who brightened the rest periods with 'Oh for the wings, for the wings of a dove' and other songs, rendered in a wonderful treble voice.

One day my Uncle Joe, in Chingford, Essex, invited me to look after his house while he took his wife, Maude, and son, Pritchard, on a cruise to the Dardanelles and the Crimea where he himself had seen much action in the First World War. He was to write two books, *Gallipoli as I Saw It* (Kimber 1965) and *Call to Arms – From Gallipoli to the Western Front* (Kimber 1980), on his experiences later on, and in 1983 he made forty-six half-hour cassettes on his wartime efforts for the Imperial War Museum. A New Zealand TV camera team also spent six hours with him at his home in preparation for a documentary on General Lord Freyberg, VC, KCB, KBE, DSO etc. mainly because he was the sole living survivor of the General's historic swim of 23 April 1915.

He had surrounded the garden of his house with huge railway sleepers and before he left for the cruise he forbade me to have anything to do with the people next door. The Willcocks had apparently been singing or playing the gramophone at the time Aunt Maude was giving birth to Pritchard and when he was born with a slightly deformed leg the blame was put on them. On the eve of the first day that I was there on my own, I decided that I was now a man and could smoke the pipe I had bought locally during the day. I filled it with cheap tobacco and went ahead with devastating effect, for within minutes I was in the garden being as sick as a dog.

Early next morning I went into the garden for some fresh air and I was surprised to hear a pleasant voice inquire after my health from the other side of the railway sleepers. I replied that I felt much better, thank you, and that I thought I must throw the pipe away. The lady next door, for it was Mrs Willcocks, then suggested that I dine with them that evening and I accepted. So began a longish courtship of the elder of the two daughters, Aileen by name, which only ended when Sainsbury's, for whom I was then working, transferred me to the other side of London, to Brondesbury. The long cycle ride from the shop to Chingford, and the slinking into the young lady's home to evade discovery by my uncle when he returned from the Crimea, was not really conducive to a young courting couple, however much we were in love, and one day I decided to give up the affair. I still treasure one photograph of Aileen and myself with our bicycles in Epping Forest on one of our jaunts during those halcyon days.

I remained with Joe Sainsbury's for some eighteen months, when best English new-laid eggs were one shilling and sixpence a dozen. This was also the price of a packet of the very best black label tea. Then I wanted a change and went to another provision merchant for a couple of weeks, but I had been spoiled by the cleanliness and efficiency at Joe Sainsbury's and could not condone the lack of them in the new place; then I went as a packer for I. and M. Steiner of St Bartholomew's Close just behind St Paul's Cathedral, for five weeks only.

This firm sold a multitude of mainly electrical gadgets like pencil torches. Only one thing happened there that was of any interest; this took place just before I left, though there was no connection between the events. About five o'clock one fine day, we were surprised to see a young woman of about twenty-one appear in front of us – we were four men working with the double doors wide open. Lifting up the front of her skirt, she asked us 'what we thought of that?' She then waltzed into the packing-room, followed by Ginger, one of our colleagues, and into the hand-operated lift. Up went the lift to stop between the ground and first floors, and the foreman told us to go home. The next day Ginger told us he had enjoyed himself, and I think that I must have felt rather envious at the time.

Next followed a season with the General Steam Navigation Company as a deck steward on the *Crested Eagle*, a paddle steamer plying every day except Friday, from Tower Pier to Southend and Clacton and back. It was great fun and I thoroughly enjoyed that summer. On the way down the Thames after leaving Tower Pier, we stopped at Greenwich for passengers as well as the drinks that were most essential for the success of trips. In those days wooden crates were used for the beer, lager, cider etc, and they were very heavy to carry. On the down trip the full crates had to be collected from the quayside and brought aboard. The higher the tide, of course, the easier the job, but when the tide was low, the gangway was very steep, making the transport of the drinks really hard work. On the return trip passengers and empties had to be unloaded, and the quicker the work was done, the happier everybody was. There was always a crowd sitting on the quayside, or lounging over the rails, ready to cheer us on our way. One particular young lady whom I saw there very often invited herself to London to have tea with me at a Lyons' Corner House, and another young lady, a beautiful German girl who worked on a German ship anchored there, the *Monte Rose* from Hamburg, asked me on board for a drink with the crew one Friday and I had a most enjoyable time.

The *Crested Eagle* incidentally was one of the small boats that took part in the rescue operation from Dunkirk and was sunk by enemy action.

After that job came a spell of twenty-eight days with the Irish Guards at Caterham, but the family of the young lady I was then courting felt that it was *infra dig* and persuaded me to buy myself out. It cost twelve pounds and I duly recovered the same amount when my military effects were sold at Caterham. I enjoyed army life very much, but it was rather marred by the fact that I was not Irish. In fact the only other non-Irish man there happened to be the Regimental Sergeant-Major, which led the rest of the recruits to suggest that I always received preferential treatment. This was nonsense of course but it caused some disagreement. One of the real Paddies and I came to blows about it. The RSM caught us at it and ordered us to report to the gym that evening at 1900 hours. Word got round and the gym was almost full of soldiers surrounding the boxing ring. The gloves were donned and off we went, with my previous boxing instructions in the north-east showing to my advantage. My opponent had to retire after the second round because of a suspected broken thumb. Off he went to the infirmary to return later with his right hand, except for his fingers, in plaster and on light duties.

Then came Sunday with its Church Parade and the inspection of the detachment by the Commanding Officer, Captain Dawnay. It was always understood that after the inspection on the parade ground, the CO would inspect the barracks and nobody was to go near the place until the inspection was over. My recent opponent, on light duties, had the job of polishing the brass taps in the washrooms as part of his work. On that hot Sunday, I was very, very thirsty and without really thinking, I dashed up to the washroom with my mug to grab a drink of water. The Irishman was there and came very close to shouting that I was to 'bugger off' before he 'did me'. I remarked that he had already failed to do this on the last occasion and all I wanted was a drink. 'Wham' went his right fist, complete with plaster, and out crashed my right to his jaw and there he was flat out on the floor. With the arrival of the inspecting CO and his cohorts I was on my way to the guardroom minutes later, with a very dazed 'Paddy', to appear before Captain Dawnay next morning. Against the advice of the English RSM, I stuck to my story that it was the Irishman's left hand that had been used and we were confined to barracks for eight days. But before the eight days were up, my resignation had been accepted, and I went back to my girlfriend's home in Dagenham, Essex, sporting a lovely black eye.

After a few weeks helping my quasi-father-in-law in his newsagent's business, and a few weeks at Plessey's in Ilford, I joined my eldest brother at the Holborn Restaurant, on the corner of Kingsway, at that time one of the best restaurants in London. Alas, no more, for a bank now stands on that fine site in Holborn. After sweeping carpets and floors and stairs, I was promoted to checking clerk on the balcony where Monsieur Rolland held sway as the chef. My brother Joe was in a similar position as checking clerk in the grill-room.

It was a good steady job, modestly paid, but we were well fed, being allowed to order from the menu, with anything we wanted to drink as well. The restaurant was part of the Holborn–Frascati group and was patronized by many famous people. *Thés dansants* were held and many famous orchestras played there. Bram Martin, who died in 1984, was playing during the time I was there. There was a cricket team and it was most pleasant to travel to various places in London and the Home Counties to play in summer. In winter, Joe and I played football in West London and Middlesex. There were actually occasions when brother Tom, who was in the Metropolitan Police Force, also managed to be free to join us for the cricket.

The chef, Rolland, was a typical Frenchman with a florid face, bright eyes, a beaming smile, an extensive waistline and a great knowledge of cordon bleu cooking, together with a host of wonderful tales of food and the people who enjoy it. I sat at the top of a flight of narrow steps leading from the balcony to the kitchen where Rolland was the master of all he surveyed, checking that the waiters received only the food they ordered and for which chits had been correctly made out. Once ordered the food was mainly cooked by the chef, though most of the vegetables came up to the kitchen in a small hand-operated lift worked by the kitchen porter who also washed the dishes. It was there that I learned the finer points of the art of cooking and I often put the knowledge to use today at home.

The restaurant closed on Sundays. One Saturday, Rolland was having a couple of lamb chops for his lunch at the small table in the balcony kitchen and I had already finished my own lunch at my table at the top of the steps. I approached my friend and said, 'Rolland, should I not be here on Monday morning, will you please tell my brother Joe that I have gone to join the French Foreign Legion.' He jumped up and shouted that I was mad. The Legion was only for rogues and vagabonds. It was no place for a nice young fellow with a good job. Despite his vehement arguments and protestations I repeated my request and he promised to tell my brother — but he hoped I would change my mind and appear for work on the following Monday.

The next day, Sunday 5 May 1937, brother Joe heard me moving about very early in the flat we shared in Gayton Road, Hampstead, and wanted to know what on earth I was up to. I told him, crossing my fingers, that I was going for a row in Regent's Park, and off I went, down to Victoria Station where I bought a cheap day-return ticket to Boulogne-sur-Mer. I was dressed in grey flannel trousers, brown shoes and a grey sports jacket brought back from India where it had been confectioned out of an old army blanket by a local Calcutta tailor.

2

THE FRENCH FOREIGN LEGION

ON ARRIVAL AT BOULOGNE I discovered that the nearest recruiting office for the Foreign Legion was at St Omer, some thirty miles away. My French at that time was the school French taught to me by Miss Butters and Miss Boyd and kept active by M. Rolland at the Holborn Restaurant. It proved quite sufficient when I found that I had a couple of hours to spare before the next bus for St Omer. I decided to have a spot of lunch in a small, clean café on the square from where the bus was to leave later on. I had beefsteak and chips and a cup of coffee.

The *patronne* was a dear and asked me if I would like a bit of company while I waited for the bus and I said that I would be very happy to have someone to talk to. She disappeared for a few minutes and returned with a nice young lady who took a coffee with me. I could afford little else for I only had about five pounds with me. While we had our coffee, I noticed that the *patronne* was removing cardboard boxes from the corner of the room where I had had my meal. Shortly afterwards the young lady invited me to go up the staircase, now revealed, to what I found to be a rather pleasant little bedroom. It then dawned on me what was in the offing. This was the very first time. I was just nineteen years old – or should I say that I was now no longer a virgin at the ripe old age of nineteen, just to amaze the young folk of today? Apart from the time and place and the circumstances, I remember nothing at all about the business, except that I still had a couple of pounds or so left in my pocket and the few francs I received in change from the *patronne*, which I eventually found to be more than sufficient for the bus to St Omer.

I have been through St Omer by car while proceeding between Dover and Switzerland a number of times since 1937, but have never stopped to look for the army barracks where I stayed for a

[12]

couple of days in very pleasant company while they allowed me to reflect on the big step I proposed to take. I am quite sure they were also in touch with Scotland Yard to see if I was wanted for any criminal matter like bank robbery, murder, or what have you. On the third day I was escorted by a *troufion* (a simple soldier) to the railway station where he presented me with a packet containing my lunch, and a railway warrant for Toul. I had grown quite fond of my escort who spoke a few words of English and was very happy to have the opportunity of practising what he knew. As I entered a small empty compartment he wished me *bon voyage*. The train moved off, I waved to him from the open window and took stock of my surroundings.

It was a ten-seater compartment, clean, with the seats just plain benches of two-inch wooden slats. I was alone and dozed uncomfortably as the train carried me through the lovely French countryside while now and again I went back over the past few days to the quiet, humdrum life in London. After a while I began to think that somewhere in the carriage there was a dead rat — or was it a dead elephant? As the temperature of the carriage increased an awful smell, nay stink, began to overwhelm me. Standing up, I looked under the seats and in the corners of the carriage. I sniffed and sniffed with an outraged nose which at last led me to the packet that my French soldier friend had handed to me before leaving me. I opened the parcel and found besides a sort of hard sausage and half a loaf of bread, a round wafer-thin wooden box. Lifting the lid I found where the smell was coming from and, convinced that the contents were definitely 'off', I opened the window and threw the offending package out. Since then I have learned to appreciate Camembert more and it has become one of my favourite cheeses.

When I arrived in the dark industrial city of Toul in north-eastern France, I was met by a huge sergeant of the Legion who marched me to the barracks where I was to remain for a couple more days before entraining with five more recruits for Marseilles, on the Mediterranean.

The old town of Marseilles, which goes back to 600 BC when the Greeks founded it (though the Phoenicians probably had a settlement there even before that), is situated on the Gulf of Lyons on the eastern shore of a bay protected to the south by Cape Croisette but open towards the west. It consisted in 1937 of a labyrinth of the city's life, and as an old port was of course inhabited by a seafaring population. On 24 January 1943, the Germans evacuated the entire district of the port and destroyed it with explosives. When I got there and had time to look around I found that the port was defended to the south by Fort St Nicholas and to the north by Fort St Jean. Not far off, in the sea, is the famous islet of the Château d'If where Dumas's Count of Monte Cristo languished. During my brief spell in St Jean I felt I knew exactly what the Count of Monte Cristo had suffered. We were issued with light khaki uniforms consisting of riding-type breeches, jacket, heavy collarless shirt, army boots, socks, braces, puttees, haversack, belt and forage cap. Some of these fitted me and I was able to exchange some of the things that did not fit with one or two of the two dozen or so fellow recruits. When I looked round at my colleagues, I thought that I had never before seen such a ragged-looking collection of tramps. Our civilian effects were auctioned publicly in the square at the summit of the fort to local merchants and the proceeds handed to us. It all seemed to be quite fair though today I have my doubts.

The hundreds of steps, worn low in the middle by the passage of previous inhabitants over the centuries, seemed to rise from the courtyard at the bottom, practically on the quayside, to the clouds at the top, and from very early morn, after a quick cup of atrocious coffee, a chunk of hard army bread and a piece of chocolate or a bit of smoked, oily sardine, until late afternoon, with a short respite between noon and two o'clock for a meal, we traipsed up and down, up and down, with huge blocks of stone on our shoulders. We were building a new Foyer du Légionnaire (like the British NAAFI) at the very top.

Luckily, after a few days, during which the only way of seeing the town was to bribe the Sergeant of the Guard, a small load of cattle was booked to cross the Mediterranean to Africa in the holds of one of the steamers, the *Gouverneur-Général de Gueyden*. There was enough room for us and off we were dispatched. Two days later we landed at Oran where I met Capitaine Hamilton who was in charge of the Legion depot there. He was the first Englishman that I met in the Legion, one of the very few who, like myself, did not try to desert. The next day we entrained for Sidi-bel-Abbès, some sixty miles to the south. Here we were issued with real uniforms and prepared for the next stage: instruction in the art of being a legionnaire. This was to take place at one of the two main depots, Le Kreider or Saida, some hundred miles or so further south. I was sent to Saida where I was to spend three or four weeks of the hardest, toughest, most soul-destroying military instruction it is possible to conceive. I was lucky for I could understand everything shouted at me by NCOs from Spain, Germany, Italy and France, for orders are given in French, but those who did not understand, and this always included the two or three Englishmen who were there, were really made to suffer.

Life became a horrible round. Reveille at 5.30 am, wash the floors, arrange the beds and the kit that you were going to carry around on your back, polish your boots and leathers, grab a cup of foul black coffee to wash down a bit of hard bread and again a piece of chocolate or a couple of oily sardines, then into the courtyard for instruction on how to carry arms, slope arms, ground arms, salutes and orders. Then a march of five miles or so and back for lunch at noon. As far as I can remember the food was quite good though I remember also being particularly revolted at finding weevils in the reputed First World War biscuits that were issued with the soup. But one was very hungry and soon found out that banging the biscuits hard on the table made the weevils fall out before they got as far as the soup.

Then there was an obligatory siesta until three o'clock. The afternoon programme was like the morning one and you were kept at it until five o'clock. Guard duties, fire-watch duties, village patrols, barrack-cleaning duties. Only after a couple of weeks were you allowed an evening in Saida, a small village.

After the first three or four weeks of hell, I was given a premium of 300 francs, which was a colossal sum considering that our regular pay for a fortnight was fifteen francs – equal to half a penny a day at the time – plus two packets of dry French tobacco every two weeks and two glasses of wine each day. I put the money into my wallet where I kept the few photographs I had brought with me to remind me of that heaven I had left behind, and sat down on the edge of my bed the same evening, surrounded by new-made 'friends'. A few beds away the corporal in charge of the room kept an eye on us. Among us was an Irishman who had confessed to having spent some time in an English prison, a seventeen-year-old English lad from Ilford and a Jewish character who turned out to be the son of a very well-known furniture dealer in London and the Home Counties. There were also a couple of Germans and a Swiss lad, though

[15]

one could never be sure of the nationality of a legionnaire. Many Frenchmen who joined the Legion gave their nationality as English, Swiss, Belgian, Canadian or indeed anything that came into their heads, for they were not allowed to join as French because the regular army was open to them. While talking about the past, I took out the photos and put the wallet beside me on the bed.

A few minutes later the young English lad suddenly arose and left saying that he had to get ready for guard duty . . . a few seconds later the Jewish man, D——, declared that he was off to the toilet . . . I stood up to put the photographs back into my wallet, but it was no longer there on the bed.

The Irishman was still there, and after all, with his past declared history, he had to be the prime suspect – so I grabbed him and marched him across to the corporal to be searched. Nothing was found. I suddenly remembered that one of the trio had left with a very feeble excuse and dashed to the toilets at the back of the barracks. He was not there so I sped to his room where he was talking placidly to some other recruits. The look in his eyes made me feel quite certain that he was the guilty one and I moved threateningly towards him, telling the others to form a circle because I intended to give D—— a hiding for stealing my wallet. This was quickly done for any change in the tough routine of daily life was welcome and he was not the best beloved of his fellows, and I advanced upon him. After a few well-placed fists had felled him, he told me that he might know where the wallet was hidden, though he had not put it there himself – he was of course lying through his teeth – and off we went to the toilets where, behind a loose brick, I found the stolen wallet with my money intact.

No further proceedings were taken against D—— after I had finished with him, but a few days later he was posted as 'medically unfit for further service in the Legion'. I was in no way responsible for this so undoubtedly strings had been pulled in England. A private plane was sent to Oran to pick him up and I don't think it was a bad thing for himself, or the Legion.

But the incident had taught me a good lesson. Photos and letters dealing with one's past life, before the Legion, and clothing issued through official channels, must never be stolen, but money and anything of value that was not considered sentimental were always at risk. Incidentally, I found out later that the seventeen-year-old had also been freed on the grounds that he was under age. After the instruction period ended and I was sent to Sidi-bel-Abbès, I never heard anything at all about the Irishman. I think that he was probably destined for a sticky end.

It was about this time that my father informed me that he was in touch with Anthony Eden with a view to having me released because of my age, but I wrote to him saying that I had put my name at the bottom of a contract for five years, and five years was what it was going to be. It was actually eight years before I finally left the Legion – in the middle of a Chinese jungle.

The French I had learned at school really stood me in good stead and I progressed rapidly and was able to 'keep my nose clean'. The only time I saw the inside of a Legion prison was when I was inside on guard duty and that in itself was enough to ensure that I did my best to do as I was told as quickly as possible. I remember particularly two of my platoon commanders, Lieutenant Millet and Lieutenant Pepin-Lehalleur, who both spoke a little English. When we were out on route marches in the *bled* as the local arid countryside is known, I was always at the head of the section and the company. As soon as we began the return journey towards the barracks, after the gruelling exercises we went through every day, I was called upon to start the singing and the old songs of the First World War, the tunes which were well known to most of the recruits, would soar up into the African air. Then, of course, the Germans would become jealous and burst in with their own marching songs, then the Italians and the Russians and the Belgians until at last there we would be, a few hundred yards from the gates to the barracks, being brought to a halt, squared up and quick-marched with sloped arms through the village of Saida until our dismissal on the barrack square.

Towards the end of the three months' instruction we were called to arms one evening and by ten o'clock, complete with arms, ammunition and iron rations, we were force-marched some sixty miles to surround an Arab village where a European agent had been murdered. We were in place the following afternoon, but after a few shots were exchanged, the Arabs realized that the Legion was there and surrendered. Two or three local *caïds* returned with us to Saida and we heard no more of them, or of revolt, or of murder.

During the time I was at Saida there were quite a number of new men who tried to desert. There was a price on their heads so the Arabs, or *schleux* as they were known, were always on the lookout for deserters and they were all brought back eventually, looking very much the worse for wear, to spend the next thirty days in prison if it was a first attempt, sixty days for a second try and at least three months should they try three times. The whole period was spent at the special Disciplinary Corps Prison at Colomb Bechar, in the real Saharan Region. I went there once on escort duty and all thoughts of desertion were dismissed from my mind.

I must confess that I really enjoyed the life of the Legion. It was very, very hard but there was a great *esprit de corps*. Above all, it was a real man's life.

By August 1938, when I was just twenty years old, I had been transferred to Sidi-bel-Abbès and was a member of the Military Band of the First Regiment of the French Foreign Legion, reputedly the finest Military Band in France. I played, very badly, the tenor saxophone, but spent most of my time in the office of the Band. My friend at the time, also in the office, was known as Jean Vandam, a great baritone who had won a first prize at the Namur Conservatory of Music, and who often participated in the concerts given by the Band on the bandstand opposite the Theatre of Sidi-bel-Abbès. Why he had left Belgium I never did find out.

Other members of the orchestra were Jock Lawrence, a broad Scot, who played trombone in the Military Band and second violin in the orchestra; Jules Dardenne, another Belgian of very good background in his native country, who played the trumpet; Theodor Ulrich from Estonia, who played the violin and bass saxophone. So we were four and we were known as the Musketeers. We spoke English most of the time, used the same *bistros* and generally spent our spare time together. At that time I was absolutely teetotal and never drank the wine issued at mealtimes. I used to exchange it alternately with my grateful friends for their ration of dessert. The main point about going out in a group was really as protection, for often enough single soldiers would be discovered lying dead or badly wounded in back streets having been attacked and robbed by other soldiers or by native Arab gangs.

When I first arrived in Sidi-bel-Abbès, Jock was giving English lessons to quite a number of young students preparing their *baccalauréat*, a scholastic step between England's 'O' and 'A' levels. He passed some of the teaching to me and before long I was giving lessons to numerous officers' children and it was quite profitable and very interesting. Not only did I begin to be invited to meals and parties, but it became increasingly easy to get off ordinary duties either by paying somebody else to replace me or by having a word in the ear of an officer whose children relied on me for their examinations.

Then came great excitement. The Band was ordered to go to Paris for some great celebration and off we went with all the instruments, and the cleaning materials which were in my own charge. It was hard work, but the Parisians were delighted to see the famous Regimental Band and a battalion of the Legion gracing the streets of the capital. After the triumphant march down the Champs Elysées, lasting for hours and hours, we were given a whole day free to attend the various celebrations. My friends and I went to the Place de la Bastille where we found that the wine was free (and lots of other things were free as well). The grandest moment of all for me was when I suddenly found myself in the arms of Marlene Dietrich who was making a number of appearances in Paris during the fêtes. We were only together for a few whirls but sufficient for me to tell her that I was English and to be given a lingering kiss for good luck. Then she was snatched from my arms and was soon lost to my sight in the great throng. The rest of the visit to Paris in 1939 was just anticlimax and we returned to Sidi-bel-Abbès without further incident – but the memory of that kiss remains.

There was a theatre in Sidi-bel-Abbès, and two European cinemas. Occasionally visits were made to the city by the famous, and they always came to visit us in the Quartier Vienot, the headquarters of the French Foreign Legion. I soon achieved a reputation as a guide to the barracks and its museums, firstly with visiting British sailors whose ships were anchored in Oran, then with English and American tourists, and eventually with any well-known personality. It was with great pleasure that I spent a whole afternoon with that wonderful entertainer Josephine Baker who was singing at the local cinema, only a few hundred yards from the barracks. She wanted to visit the barracks and as usual I was detailed to show her round. She thought that it was great fun being taken round the museums and the town by an Englishman. That evening we had dinner together and then I watched her show from the wings. At the end of her performance, she turned towards me and announced to the audience, who appeared to love her almost as much as I did by then, that the next song was for 'le petit anglais' who had been so kind to her during her unforgettable visit to the Legion.

The next important visitor, as far as I was concerned, was the one and only Maurice Chevalier. On this occasion I was not called in to do escort duties by the officer on duty at the gate. When Maurice Chevalier visited that part of the *caserne* occupied by the Band, the orchestra was practising under the direction of its Chef de Musique, Captain Paul Aja, and his manager asked if there were any Englishmen present as he himself was from County Durham. Monsieur Petit, the Deputy Chief, immediately sent for me and introduced me to the manager and Maurice. I was given the day off and acted as escort to Maurice who invited me to tea at the Continental Hotel, just down the road, and the cinema where he was appearing. We had great fun and the manager and I spent a long time talking about our home county.

One day I was called to the front gate where I found an elderly American lady called Gladys Hight, on a tour of North Africa, who said she would like to visit the barracks and the museums. Obtaining the necessary authority I showed her round and accepted her invitation to dinner, again at the Continental, which was the only reasonable hotel in the city. Looking back, I suppose that she was then about forty-five or even fifty years old – she certainly seemed rather ancient, but she was good fun, and enjoyed playing cards. I took a few days' leave and we toured the surrounding countryside by taxi. She gave me a signed photograph which I no longer possess having travelled quite a bit since then, and she told me that she was quite well known in New York where she ran the Gladys Hight School of Dancing. One of her pupils, apparently quite famous even then, was the star of *Singing in the Rain*, Gene Kelly.

A great character in Sidi-bel-Abbès at that time was a very eccentric Scandinavian lady, who lived near the Arab quarters in a rambling bungalow with her aged mother. They were charming ladies going under the name of Neilson, and apparently the daughter's main aim in life was her collection of stray animals. She looked after at least a dozen dogs and just as many cats and she had even begun to collect stray legionnaires, inviting them to meals at the bungalow. She spoke several languages, but as it was just before the war broke out and things were looking rather ominous in Europe, the Intelligence Officer of the Legion called me in and asked me to keep my eyes and ears open where the two ladies were concerned, and to report to him daily. Although I never found out anything detrimental to the two ladies, I have since often wondered what they were really doing in such an out-of-the-way place as Sidi-bel-Abbès, if it wasn't to obtain information useful to the Allies or the enemy.

Shortly before war broke out in 1939, Jock Lawrence came to the end of his engagement and left for Britain. (I think he must have been the stranger who called on my brother Joe in Acton, London, in a rather poor condition in 1939, though we've not heard of him since.) He passed all his students on to me so I had quite a business going. I was very fortunate because I was the orderly in the office of the Band until it was dissolved at the outbreak of war, when the musicians were integrated into the other various units. I was issued with a bicycle and one of my most important jobs was to visit local merchants to enlist their support for the funds of the Band by purchasing advertising space in the programme that I prepared for each concert. There was at least one concert each week in the stand opposite the theatre and as there were several bars and *bistros* in the vicinity, with waiters serving drinks at the dozens of round tables round the bandstand, the concerts were very popular, especially among the Europeans of the district. One of my favourite visits was to the Maison Ayribier, where the family Ayribier produced some of the very well-known aperitifs popular in France and its colonies. So, under the pretext that I was visiting the merchants, I only had to inform the office chief, one Chief Corporal Vilaers, or my friend Vandam, that I was looking for custom and I would be free to come and go as I chose, and my own business prospered.

By this time I was twenty-one years of age and very popular with the young ladies of sixteen or seventeen who were studying English. There were also young men of course, but they were probably more serious than their sisters. One or two of them, in fact, were related to ruling Algerian and Moroccan families, destined for very high diplomatic jobs. The families of my pupils were always courteous in their dealings with the 'petit anglais' and trusted me implicitly to behave correctly with their daughters. I can assure you that it was often very difficult, for most of them were very attractive and, sometimes, rather precocious.

There was the Sananes family who for many years had owned the main furniture shop in the Boulevard de la République. One of the sons and a daughter, Lydia, were among my pupils. They worked very hard but they were never very good at languages although

[21]

many years later Lydia married one of my Legion colleagues who taught her German and they now live in New York. After the French were cast out of Algeria, the remaining Sananes family moved to the south of France and my wife and I were very well received by them there. One son has a restaurant and the other two are still in the furniture business.

Another young lady I used to visit was Elvira Mira. She used to work in a quaint little shop with her father where one could buy perfumes, herbs, pure alcohol, soaps etc. When he died she inherited the shop. She lived with her grandmother who was probably of Spanish origin for Elvira was never allowed out on her own, which made it very difficult indeed for me to court her properly. Her brother was married and worked in one of the banks there. He and I got on very well, but he did make me understand that his sister would be expected to marry a member of the Catholic faith and I did not consider myself to be a Catholic, for although baptised as such shortly after birth, I had always thought of myself as Church of England, probably because the Scout troop attended Tanfield C. of E. meetings, and at the grammar school during religious instruction, the first lesson each day, Catholics and one atheist young lady remained in the corridor outside the classroom, as if they were outcasts.

Then there was the Chenillot family, consisting of mother and father, a son and Lucienne, the daughter. Odile, from Alsace–Lorraine, was the old family retainer. Lucienne was probably my very best pupil. She was tall, well built, pleasant and with a wonderful sense of humour. Her parents were in charge of one of the larger schools of Sidi-bel-Abbès, her father also being a major in the Reserve. On many occasions I was invited to meals by Madame Chenillot and I enjoyed the company. With hindsight I realize that they were hoping that maybe one day there might develop a serious relationship between Lucienne and myself, but I had no thoughts on tying myself down then.

When the General Mobilization came I was issued with a rifle and ammunition, but was still allowed almost as much freedom as before thanks to a special pass signed by the colonel of the regiment, Colonel Azan, who had always been kind and considerate to me, treating me as a sort of special case since I was English and a bit of a character.

One day in June 1940, at about eleven o'clock in the morning, I was walking through the market on my way to the bar for my usual rum and blackcurrant (*rhum-cassis*) when I saw Mme Chenillot approaching. Normally she would have stopped and chatted for a while. I removed my *képi* and said 'Bonjour', but she turned her head and marched on. I turned and gazed after her wondering what on earth could have happened to make her snub me like that. Some yards further on, I saw her also turn her head to look back at me, then she hesitated, and walked back towards me. 'Monsieur Murray,' she said, 'after what happened in Oran this morning, please do not ever speak to me again.' I forgot about my drink and went to buy a newspaper. There in great headlines the newspaper told how, because of the Franco–German armistice, a considerable part of the French fleet had taken refuge at Oran and its naval base of Mers-el-Kabir. After fruitless negotiations by the British, with the object of preventing the vessels from falling into Axis hands, a British naval force had bombarded the French vessels, sinking some and severely damaging others.

I was terribly disappointed by Madame Chenillot's attitude, for after all, how was I to blame? My lessons to Lucienne ceased forthwith.

A week later, I was walking down the boulevard in front of the Continental Hotel when I perceived Major Chenillot coming towards me. As he was in uniform, I brought my open hand up to the brim of my *képi* in a perfect salute. Coming towards me, he replied to my salute, but also stretched out his hand in the familiar way among friends and asked me how it was that I no longer came to the house. I told him that it was because of the Oran incident, that I felt it would be embarrassing for them to receive an Englishman as a guest. He stopped any further argument by ordering me to present myself at his house that evening at 1900 hours, or he would be reporting me to my colonel, now Colonel Robert. That evening I duly appeared to give a lesson to Lucienne, who was delighted to see me, and after the lesson, Madame Chenillot herself came to insist I have dinner with the family. Things were back to normal.

My favourite bar at this time was the Bar de la Légion, just a few hundred yards from the gate, and here I made friends with another Madame Sananes and her two daughters, Marguerite, a bright, beautiful, Spanish-looking nineteen-year-old, and Berthe, a serious, lovely twenty-one-year-old. It was a perfect haven from the martial atmosphere of the barracks and they made me welcome. They were often visited by a cousin who came from Mascara, a wine-making town some sixty miles to the east, where her father was Mayor. Rénée was a beautiful, mature girl the same age I suppose as Berthe, and although very much under the watchful eye of her aunt, we still managed to meet each other in the cinema although we never entered or left the building together. It was all very frustrating yet exciting. When I returned to England in 1946, I wrote to Rénée and even proposed to her. She said that she would have to think about it and would like to visit England before making up her mind. I sent her an engagement ring and about one hundred pounds in French francs and that was the last I ever heard of her.

3

AT WAR

IN LATE 1940 THE Germans, after their success in France, established a Commission in Algiers, to investigate those people in North Africa who were of interest to them, including without a doubt the Jews and anti-Nazi elements in the Legion who had fled the German jack-boot and oppression as well as any Englishman. But the Legion looks after its own, and before Vichy-France and the Nazis could do anything about us, we were on our way as the last detachment to relieve the 5th Regiment in Indochina.

As soon as war was declared I tried every possible way to get to France to be integrated into a British force, but the authorities would not let me go. I wrote to the American chargé d'affaires in Algiers, before the arrival of the Germans, for the Americans were then neutral and were dealing with British matters. There was a reply informing me that no instructions had been issued from London to cover my problem, so I put my name down for Indochina and was accepted.

We were to leave within the week. I went to see all my pupils and friends to say farewell, and last of all to the house of the Chenillots. I had dinner with them and Lucienne accompanied me to the door. There was a pleading look in her eyes as we shook hands and she handed me a letter to be opened, she said, when I was far away. I remember some of the words, even today, for the letter went with me to Indochina where I carried it with me for years, only to lose it eventually during the famous retreat from Hanoi to China in March 1945. '. . . think, if you will, sometimes, that a young girl, very foo-lish indeed, loved you from the very first time we met, and that she fought despairingly against those sentiments which were never reciprocated and that nobody else will ever receive. But do not worry, dear Monsieur Murray, I love life too much to play Juliet of your own Shakespeare. Go, and with you goes all my love and best wishes for happiness . . .'

Many years later I discovered somehow that the family had moved to Belfort, and lived in a converted farm at Essert which was on our route to Switzerland. We dropped in to see them and stayed the night in a wonderful atmosphere of warmth and pleasant memories. Lucienne had married a Polish officer in the Royal Air Force in North Africa but had divorced him in 1963. At the time we met in Essert, a suburb of Belfort, in eastern France, in 1968, she was married to a D. Litt, headmaster of the most important school in Belfort. She had become very beautiful indeed, and seemed to be quite happy. Yet I had a distinct feeling that she still reproached me, unreasonably I thought, for there had never been anything but a warm friendship between teacher and pupil in Sidi-bel-Abbès.

Early in May 1941, together with about 250 Jewish and German fugitives from Nazism and a collaborationist Vichy government who were in no position to override any decisions taken by the Legion commandment, I was on my way by train from Sidi-bel-Abbès, via Oujda, to Casablanca. This began as a very boring trip in uncomfortable conditions. It was a slow train, with many stops where we were forbidden to alight, iron rations, for there was no buffet car or restaurant car, though civilian travellers were permitted to descend at certain stations to partake of refreshments. It seemed as if we were all going to die of boredom or starvation or thirst, but I had other ideas. I searched the first-class carriages for someone interesting to talk to, and was most fortunate to recognize the face of someone who did not really want to be recognized. Jean Pierre Aumont was at that time one of the most famous film stars in France and there he was with a female film star, whose name predictably escapes me. Excusing myself, I went into the reserved carriage and asked for an autograph on a postcard I had already written ready to post at Casablanca to my family in England. Jean Pierre noticed the address and immediately began to ask questions, introduced me to the girlfriend, and told me to sit down. I begged permission to inform my section sergeant of the situation, and as soon as I had done this, I went back and spent the rest of the trip in most pleasing circumstances. Since then, of course, I have seen my friend on numerous occasions, in films, and wonder if he ever recalls 'le petit anglais' of 1941.

Arriving in Casablanca, we were quartered in appalling conditions in the docks, waiting for the *Dupleix* to be ready for us. I was able to visit an ex-legionnaire friend in the centre of the city, a beautiful place of new white buildings. Borrowed mufti allowed me to go out to dinner with my friend, a master-printer with the local newspaper, and his wife, and I had a wonderful time. Much too soon, it was three o'clock in the morning and I had to don my uniform, now looking rather the worse for wear, and return to my quarters where I found everybody ready to go. No sooner had I managed to collect all my belongings than off we were marched to the quayside, where a narrow wooden companionway, with ropes on either side to assist one's ascent, stretched up, and up, at an angle of perhaps sixty degrees, towards a little hole in the hull of the 3000-ton cargo boat. We began to climb. In front of me was an old, pro-British, Belgian friend, named Merx. He was as drunk as a lord, which was his usual condition. I closed up on him, in view of his state, and it was just as well that I did, for when he was half-way up, he slipped and began to fall towards the dark and dirty waters of the Atlantic far below. As he passed me I made a grab and managed to catch hold of his equipment. I held on for grim death till our companions, above and below, lent their hands and we got him back to the ladder and safety.

Our commanding officer on the ship was an old friend (to whom I had given English lessons in Sidi-bel-Abbès), Captain Tokhadze, who was of White Russian origin. His deputy, Lieutenant Pepin-Lehalleur, had been at Saida during my instruction period, so I was sure that the trip to Indochina was going to be as pleasant as possible in the existing conditions, for under their command there were also 750 Indochinese soldiers returning from the late conflict in France.

I was put in charge of the library on board and spent most of the time organizing bridge and chess and *belote* (a French card game) competitions to distract the legionnaires and crew from the deplorably cramped conditions. Two and three-tier bunks had rapidly been constructed in the holds, and two huge water-containers erected for emergencies on the deck. This was a most fortunate idea, for when the captain found that the ship was listing to port when we were sailing well out in the South Atlantic to evade Allied traffic to the Cape, he instructed the chief engineer to transfer the fresh water from the port to the starboard side. The chief found that he had too much work to do coaxing the most out of his old engines so he told the third engineer to see to it (the second engineer was resting after his night watch). As the third engineer was carrying out some important repair work at the time, he ordered the fourth engineer to do the transfer. Now the fourth engineer who was, and still is, a friend of mine, knew nothing at all about engines, having been taken on only at the last minute to fill the vacant position. He wanted to go to Haiphong, in Indochina, to rejoin his father who was managing the French National Bank there. The ship was not carrying any real cargo but had tons of sea-water as ballast. Yes, my friend pushed the wrong button and the fresh water got mixed up with the salt water, and we were obliged to rely on the two tanks on the deck. No more fresh water showers or ablutions for anybody, an armed guard had to be placed on the now locked tanks, and the water was very strictly and severely rationed till we reached Madagascar.

By the time we arrived we had been some four hundred miles south of the Cape of Good Hope, for the German *Tirpitz* was creating havoc near the Cape at the time, and also we did not want to run the risk of meeting up with the British or Allied men o' war, for our destination was Indochina, and the Captain wanted to get there. I don't think I ever saw the Captain of the *Dupleix*, but I was often in contact with our own Captain Tokhadze who was pro-British, but pro-Legion before anything else as I was to discover later.

One of the NCOs had been seasick on a previous trip to Tonkin, but as Indochina was considered to be the 'Eden' of Legion life, he was prepared to suffer again. But this was to be a much longer voyage, and the bush telegraph had informed us that the Allies were going to allow free passage to the *Dupleix*, because she was carrying no war material, as far as Saigon. With the co-operation of one of the crew, the NCO worked out the centre of gravity of the ship and lay down on a mattress as near as he could to the exact spot, prepared to spend as much time as possible there. I never found out if it worked or not.

It had been interesting to stop in Dakar where the *Richelieu*, refusing to come over to the Allied cause, had been immobilized by an attack in the middle of the night by Royal Navy personnel. The great hole in her bows was sufficient evidence of their success. At Tamatave, in Madagascar, we found that a previous detachment of the Legion had resulted in a riot and now we had to suffer by being refused permission to land. I suddenly developed a very violent attack of toothache, necessitating, with Captain Tokhadze's blessing, a visit to the hospital dentist. The visit lasted all day during which time I went to the Catholic Church and made the acquaintance of a lovely Madagascan girl who proved that not only Metropolitan France looked after legionnaires with or without toothache. I managed to obtain a bottle of whisky to take back for the Captain.

We then went to Diego Suarez in the north of the island and for days the air was filled with coal-dust as we took on coal before beginning the long trip across the Indian Ocean. We had many games of bridge and chess on the trip across. My particular partner, most of the time, was one Corporal Ernst Frey, later to end his time with the Legion in Indochina, leaving to join the Vietcong who were destined to chase the French from the Far East. He became a full colonel and adviser to the famous General Giap who commanded the whole of the Communist Revolutionary Army. Afterwards Frey returned to his native Vienna to become a pillar of the Catholic Church and society there. I myself, besides being mentioned on occasions in Frey's own memoirs, *The Remarkable Monsieur Frey*, actually translated the book into English.

Another of our companions at that time, and during the years we were in Indochina, was Borchers, a most intelligent character who always kept to himself. He was at one time a teacher in Germany and a full member, it was later revealed, of the Communist Party. He was to become the head of East German Radio when he returned there from Indochina.

After my visit to the dentist, I saw that there was an American ship in port and sent a message by one of the boats that kept circling the *Dupleix* trying to sell bananas to say that I was English and did they have any reading matter for a poor legionnaire. The boat came back shortly afterwards with a load of paperbacks and an invitation for me to take a couple of my friends to dinner that evening. I took some of the books to Captain Tokhadze and asked for permission to take two of my friends to the American ship. Trusting me, he gave me the permission and off went three of us. On board we had a fine time and two master cooks gave us a splendid dinner. I tried to persuade them to hide us and take us off to join the British forces, but there was nothing they could do. If we stayed aboard, the French would just come looking for us the next day and there would be trouble. We rejoined the *Dupleix* at about ten o'clock, taking back a few bottles of booze. At midnight, I heard the siren of the American ship and a lot of commotion. When I went on deck, it was just in time to catch a glimpse of her as she slid out of port.

While on the American vessel, I had asked to see maps of the Indian Ocean and our probable route to Haiphong via Saigon. I noticed that the closest we would be to land was when we went through the Sunda Strait between Java and Sumatra. There were a number of islands in the vicinity, still under Dutch protection, and the Dutch were allies of the British. I might be able to do something there. A few nights before arriving at the Strait, I had it all arranged. One of the rowing-boats was loaded with all the supplies necessary for several days afloat if the boat was sunk. (I suppose all the other lifeboats were similarly supplied, but I was only interested in the one closest to the stern of the ship.) Only five more legionnaires were aware of my plans; they included Frey, a German-Canadian who spoke good English, a fair-haired Scandinavian called Nillsen, and two others who spoke English and appeared to be favourably disposed towards the British. On the night I had chosen for the attempt, the Captain issued orders for all the lifeboats to be guarded by Indochinese soldiers. The following day I was called in to the Captain who reminded me that I had signed a contract for five years, and as the French authorities had kept to their side of the bargain by feeding me and paying me, I should do the same and finish my contract.

A few days later we were through the Strait and in Dutch waters. I waited for night by an open port-hole below. With a torch I kept flashing an SOS I AM BRITISH signal into the dark, praying for it to be seen by Dutch or British ships. The next morning, about ten o'clock, a Dutch patrol boat suddenly appeared from behind an island and signalled for the *Dupleix* to heave to. The ship stopped and shortly afterwards a dinghy came over and a couple of Dutch officers and three sailors, all heavily armed, climbed aboard to be met by the Captain of the *Dupleix* and our own Tokhadze. I do not remember how it happened, but I found myself escorting them below decks. As we walked through the ship I told them it was their duty to take me with them, but they said that they had no instructions about how to deal with Englishmen in the French forces. They would not take me. I asked them what they would do if suddenly three or four of us threw ourselves in the water. They would return us to the French ship, they said.

I suppose that we could have jumped overboard during the night, but that was a risky thing to do, and we were not really too unhappy to be going towards the legionnaires' 'Eden', as it had been described by the seasick NCO.

When we arrived at Saigon, after exactly a hundred days aboard since Casablanca, we were confined to a barracks in the city while the ship was cleaned up and re-stocked for the next part of the voyage. I bribed the sergeant of the guard to let me out for a few hours and went to see the British Consul-General, Mr Henderson. He told me that he could do nothing about getting me to British forces as the whole of the city, and particularly the dockside area, was patrolled by the Japanese who had been given permission to do so by Vichy-France. Every possible means of getting out of Saigon was being very closely watched by the Nips. It was quite evident that there was no way out. So I had dinner and drinks at the Consulate and enjoyed playing bridge for several hours before going back to the barracks. Mr Henderson kindly sent a letter to my parents to let them know that I was in good fettle. I still have the letter.

Shortly afterwards we were on our way up through the South China Sea towards Haiphong. The approach to the port is a most remarkable scene with dozens of small islands, covered with trees. This is the Bay of Along and is probably the most beautiful piece of sea that I have ever seen, or could wish to see.

In Haiphong there were once more thousands of the little yellow men. Vichy had allowed them to remain there in order to prevent the Chinese taking Northern Indochina, or Tonkin as we called it. In reality they were there to prevent war supplies being landed by the Allies and sent by rail to China and Chiang Kai-shek. We then entrained for Vietri, the headquarters of the 5th Regiment of the French Foreign Legion where I was immediately given a job in the Bureau de Matériel – the Ordnance Office. The war in Europe seemed very far away at that time and I began to find pupils, mainly among the Chinese merchants who wanted to learn English as quickly as possible.

In 1943, the crack military academies of France – St Cyr, St Maixent, Poitiers and the Aviation School, were transferred, without the blessing of the Vichy Government, to San Toy, some twelve miles away, near the town of Tong where the 2nd Battalion of the Regiment was stationed. From what I could understand, St Cyr was for young non-military people who wanted to become officers in the infantry or cavalry; St Maixent was for promising NCOs who wanted to become officers in the artillery. St Cyr was actually destroyed by the Germans during the Second World War, but has now been re-established in the north of France, I believe.

One fine day I was called in to see Colonel Alessandri who commanded the regiment and informed me that I had been nominated as Professeur d'Anglais at the Military School of Tong and should leave forthwith. He told me that I must still carry out most of the normal duties of a legionnaire and he hoped that I would go in for promotion. I packed my belongings and departed for Tong where I was assigned to the 2nd Battalion's Headquarters Section in the CA2 which was the Support Company with heavy machine-guns, mortars of 60mm and 81mm calibre, and an Oerlikon 25mm anti-tank cannon. The company commander was a pro-Vichy, anti-English Captain Guillaume and the battalion commander was Major de Cockborne, later to become General and Military Attaché for France in Korea, before retiring to his ancestral home with his wife who had suffered great privations under the Japanese in Indochina. (French married officers were invariably accompanied by their wives and children). Their huge manor house stands in a large estate in the small village of Villeneuve au Chemin, near Troyes, in the Champagne country of France. It just happens to be exactly, to the mile, half-way between Le Havre and Lucerne in Switzerland, so when my wife and I go to visit her mother and friends in Lucerne, the General and his lovely wife insist we stop overnight, or for as long as we like, at their home.

I had only been at the school for a few days when Major de Cockborne called me into his office. 'Should one word of what I am about to tell you be told to anyone else in the world' – and he put his right hand on to the butt of his revolver – 'I personally will shoot you like a dog.' He then told me of the Resistance Movement he was about to form to combat the Japanese by subversive means and assist the Allies as far as was humanly possible. I soon discovered that the real head of the movement was none other than the Major Carbonnel who was the commanding officer of the Military School at Son Tay. For many months afterwards, until we began the famous retreat to China in March 1945, unknown to but a very small number of my colleagues, night sorties were made to collect arms, ammunition and medical supplies flown from Calcutta in RAF planes with Free French pilots, and dropped at pre-arranged points around the area, very often in sticky rice-fields.

With, or without, permission, we had to get out of the barracks and make our way to parked lorries that would wait, sometimes for hours, until the sound of the planes would be heard when we would light flares to disclose the area to the pilots. The huge canisters would be dropped and, we hoped, collected, carried to the lorries, and then taken to Hanoi for storage at the Citadel in Hanoi. This was rather an unfortunate choice of hiding-place because when the Japanese attacked in March 1945, one of the first places they stormed was the Citadel. My company commander, Captain Guillaume, was not in the movement and Pyl, Marciniak and I had to be very careful indeed to be either absent officially or present for the roll-call at 2200 and 0600 hours. Life was terribly exciting in those days, but I still gave English lessons, mainly to Chinese merchants, but also to a few wealthy locals and a few officers and their families, including Colonel Alessandri's daughter, who was to remember me much later on in my life, when we were in the south of France.

Like many of the *lin-tai* (French soldiers) in Tonkin, I had found myself a *co* (concubine) who looked after a small *ca-nha* (cottage in bamboo and grass, the usual habitation of the natives) that I rented in the village where I could relax from the hard work of barrack life, and from the long marches across rice paddies and down hot dusty roads in the scorching sun or torrential downpours. There was always warmth and humour from Nguyen Thi Sec, my concubine, who was a wonderful cook and demonstrated to me very often the use one could make of the simple green stuff to be found in the country. I paid her a monthly amount for her services, for which she was supposed to remain faithful, do my washing and ironing, cook my meals when I was at the *ca-nha* and bring me food and drink when I was on guard duties at the barracks. I would see her haggling for hours in the market over fish or meat or salads and I never had any complaints about her cooking. Quite an important part of the money I gave her was sent back to her father in Soc Trang, in Cambodia.

Accompanied by a German Jew legionnaire, I decided one day to go into the mountains and off we went with bread, cold meat and a bottle of wine each. After a couple of hours we arrived at a small village set in the middle of dense jungle, half-way up the mountain, and we were invited by the head of the village into his residence. His house was a very long bamboo building on wooden pillars raised about five or six feet above the ground, and it housed all the members of his family numbering, I suppose, about twenty or thirty people. They were self-supporting, more or less, and knew nothing about the war in Europe, nor about the presence of Japanese troops in their country. One or two of them spoke a little French and I was able to carry on quite a reasonable conversation with signs and pidgin French plus the many words and phrases in Annamese that I had learned from my concubine and the people to whom I taught English. I had also picked up quite a lot of Chinese words and phrases from Chinese merchants, and this was to prove very useful indeed later on when we were in China after our retreat before the Japanese.

The cattle, pigs and hens were in stalls beneath the house and the farmyard atmosphere in the heat of the jungle was rather overpowering. After sharing a communal lunch, we left them some piastres and began the return journey. As we hurried back through the jungle, I was leading. Just as I was about to place my hand upon a huge fallen tree trunk to vault over it, I suddenly saw a beautiful, vivid, almost fluorescent green patch and hesitated, my hand still raised. With a quick gasp, I jumped back, upsetting my companion who was close on my heels. It might be beautiful, but it was also one of the most dangerous snakes in Asia, the dreaded banana snake, and I think I was very lucky not to have been colour blind.

We eventually got back to barracks and stripped off our uniforms. My friend had been dressed in light khaki drill, complete with heavy army boots and riding breeches. He wore puttees from the top of his boots to his knees and heavy socks. When he took them all off, he found that his legs and feet were covered with leeches and he was bleeding profusely. With the lighted end of a cigarette which he jabbed on the waving ends of the horrible beasts, he quickly dispatched them and then washed and disinfected his legs and feet. I myself had been dressed in light summer wear with short-sleeved, open-neck shirt, shorts and sandals. I found two leeches on my bare feet and only a spot of blood. Throughout my whole life, I have always been fond of salt on my food and have never been troubled by insects as much as some other people and I wonder if the salt was the reason for my good fortune.

One of the most important jobs of the Resistance out there was rather more impressive than carrying the huge canisters from the parachute drops. The Americans were of course interested in the presence of the Japanese troops in Northern Indochina and made frequent bombing raids in the Hanoi area. There were numerous anti-aircraft positions, both French – for after all they did not like being bombed either – and Japanese, and occasionally the Americans were shot down and the pilot sometimes was able to use his parachute. Our own informants were scattered over a large area and whenever it was not too far away that a pilot had been seen to come down, we were alerted and teams sent out to find the American. This happened on several occasions and the pilot was invariably brought to the Legion to be locked up for safety and to wait until the Japanese hue and cry had died down. Then the American would suddenly disappear from his cell, for the Resistance, despite the secrecy covering its actions, had power. Our teams would move in and carry him to a distant point where he would be handed over to another team, often by roads and paths very close to the Nippon forces, and eventually across the border into China and safety. The American forces in China would be alerted as to the place and time of arrival, but I was never there at the final handover.

My job as English teacher at the Military School carried on meanwhile and I was kept very busy. Obeying the suggestion of Colonel Alessandri, I went in for promotion and became an NCO, a rank bearing quite a lot of responsibility, but a lot of power as well. We had 'boys' to do the chores in the barracks, clean our shoes and rooms, do the washing of uniforms and keep our packs straight for inspections. The Mess was a separate organization from that of the men. We did have to pay, but the food was excellent. A special gâteau was always made by the cook for the Feast of the Three Kings (Epiphany) and hidden in the cake were two small wooden effigies, one representing the King and the other the Queen of the Festival. On this one occasion each year, officers served the NCOs at table in the early evening. The elected King, at the end of the repast, had to make a speech, when he was allowed to make certain recommendations to the commanding officer of the battalion which were usually favourably viewed.

On 6 January 1944 the usual cake was prepared and cut. An officer passed the bits of cake round and I received the effigy of the King. Senior NCO (Adjutant Chef) Korst got the Queen, but immediately refused to accept the honour of being my escort. I was not surprised. He was a plump Jewish NCO who was actually the treasurer of the battalion and never participated in any fun. My friend George Rest (or was his name Pyl, or even Eberhardt – for I've known him under three names) – came to the rescue and offered his services. He was probably the most popular NCO in the regiment and was also a member of the Resistance. After the meal I stood up and announced an amnesty for all those in prison for fourteen days or less, and a holiday the next day for the battalion. The Commander, Major de Cockborne, of course, agreed. So I can call myself the last King of the Legion of Tong.

Other regiments at Tong at the time also nominated their own royalty, and after the meal I contacted the 'King' of the Artillery and that of the RIC, the Colonial Regiment and suggested a 'pousse' (ginrickshaw) race from Tong to Kim Dai, three or four miles up the road towards the Bavi Mountain. About a dozen of us dashed out of the barracks to collar any *pousse* in the vicinity – there were usually half a dozen or so waiting for customers outside the gates – and we were lucky to find enough for all of us. Then off we sped around the corner to the gates of the RIC to wait for the Colonial Infantry and the Artillery who did not keep us waiting long and off went the rickshaws towards the airfield at Kim Dai. Who worries who won the contest? All I can remember is that we all had a wonderful time and nobody died.

Another eventful thing happened to me at Tong – I caught jaundice and had to go into hospital to recover. I do not like hospitals, but on this occasion I really had to go for I felt just awful and the doctor, Major Baille, insisted that I must be taken away from all the temptations of the barracks and kept to a very strict diet. It also meant that I owed him something and he was rather keen on my giving lessons to his wife and son. I was in hospital four days only and then got back to work and the lessons with Madame Baille and the boy. They had a rather lovely visitor at the time who spoke excellent English. She was the wife of the general manager of the coal-mines at Moncay in the north of the country, and also the daughter of Général le Gentilhomme who was later, on 8 January 1943, to be given the responsibility of Madagascar's administration by Lieutenant-General Sir William Platt who commanded the British troops. Général le Gentilhomme was, of course, fighting for the Free French under General de Gaulle. I thoroughly enjoyed my evenings with the Bailles, but time was getting short. The enemy was massing, the parachute drops increasing.

4

CHRISTMAS IN THE LEGION

CHRISTMAS IN THE LEGION is the time when Germans, Swiss, Belgians, French, English, Hungarians, Austrians and all the other nations represented in that army of *hommes sans noms* become nostalgic and prone to the *cafard* (really a beetle, but also the name given to the very deep fits of depression that can drive even the bravest to stupid acts). There are no big parades at Christmas; the VIPs have other commitments to their families, but so have the legionnaires, for 'Legio Patrie Nostra' – the Legion is our Motherland – as their device says.

So no visits and no parades, but extra victuals, extra wine, and songs. The singing is supplied by the men, the wine and victuals by the 'ordinaire', that section of the regiment or battalion detailed for a period to look after the inner man of the soldier, the period being determined by whether or not the job is well done. When the men are happy with the food, there are no complaints, no sickness, no loss of manpower, then that section will remain responsible for the welfare of the men for a long period. When the food is bad, then there is trouble and the best way out is to put another section in charge. So when the NCO in charge of the section dealing with food 'shops around' and makes the most economical arrangements with suppliers without making too many deals on the side to line his own pocket, and keeps a watchful eye on the kitchen staff to see that the food is not diverted, there is a substantial credit balance between the amount of money received 'per capita' and the amount actually paid for the food and wine. This balance was put away to provide extra provender on festival days, for example the 14 July to celebrate the taking of the Bastille in 1789; 30 April to fête the most famous of the Legion's battles in Mexico, in 1863, when sixty men of the Third Company of the First Battalion of the Legion faced a Mexican army.

[37]

As the inscription on a monument raised by public subscription in their honour states, 'Life, rather than courage, deserted these brave soldiers of France'; and of course Christmas.

A few weeks before Christmas Day, volunteers were called for the usual music-hall show which would be held in the *Foyer du Légionnaire* (NAAFI) and they would be relieved of patrols and guard duties. There were Russians and Hungarians, pseudo-Russians and pseudo-Hungarians, similar Austrians, Germans, Italians and even one Englishman.

The Foyer at Vietri sat about 200 people. It was just outside the barracks so that civilians could be invited without the obvious complications of having to allow them past the gatehouse and into the vast unilluminated spaces of the actual barracks. Behind the Foyer was a large carp-filled lake which was dragged with nets at six-monthly intervals. The resultant mud-tasting catch was passed to the 'ordinaire' to supplement the rations.

Looking back, it seems to me that the various rehearsals of the different acts went on without outward commotion and life carried on as usual.

The first night of the show came – the dress rehearsal really – which was for the ordinary rank and file, not only of the Legion, but of the other regiments in the vicinity, and the police and prison services, with wives and girlfriends and children. The second night was mainly for NCOs and civilians holding minor positions in local government or business. The final night, on Christmas Eve, was attended by officers, official guests of the regiment and senior local officials or big businessmen with wives and relations.

This particular Christmas show began as usual with a fifteen-minute display of rifle drill followed by a display of gymnastics, led by my Tyrolean friend, George Rest, or Peps Pyl as he was then. Then were a number of Schubert songs sung by the talented Chief Corporal Bruckner, with resounding success, for they were the forte of this Viennese soldier. He had a fine tenor voice used mainly when he was out drinking with his pro-Axis friends. The beauty of a Legion show is that you always knew whether or not they liked what you were offering them. If they didn't like it, then you might as well give up, but if they did like it, then you could carry on till they tired of it.

After Schubert came my own humble sleight-of-hand act and a few card tricks. For this part I was billed as 'YARRUM' (Murray spelled backwards) *Prestidigitateur*. The tricks I had learned served a useful purpose much later when I was travelling on the same aeroplane as Prince Rainier's children between Nice and London, and the journey passed much more quickly for the children when I made my thumb disappear and pulled coins from their ears. I told a few stories of the kind to amuse soldiers, and then produced my astounding mind-reading act. This was so successful that it astonished me as well.

Hubner, a German who had spent most of his adult life in Paris, spoke excellent French and quite a lot of English, but what was much more important, he could dress according to the fashion of the 'twenties and really look the part. With a black lace dress complete with ostrich feathers, silk stockings, a corset, high-heeled shoes, a fantastic Parisian hat and with his face made up, Hubner was transformed into the most attractive piece of femininity that any of us had seen for months. He was a riot. He or she wore a bandeau over the eyes (it had previously been passed among the members of the audience to check that there were no holes) and it was tied firmly behind his head.

I then strolled among the guests and they all wished to know where I had found such a ravishingly beautiful assistant. Touching a popular muleteer on the head with my magical wand, I asked my assistant loudly to tell me who the person was. 'Madame Yvette', as I had named Hubner, responded in the most dramatic, husky voice, saying that she could detect the smell of animals and then began to sing a very spicy song of a soldier who joined the Mounted Regiment of the Legion. The audience collapsed with joy.

The question and answer game was repeated for numerous people in the auditorium, including the Adjutant, Major Corse. 'Madame' thought that this person was having a love affair with a *vrai vache* (right cow). Practically everyone present knew that the Major kept a cow called Clementine and the fact that he preferred a glass of milk to one of Pernod or any other strong drink made him somewhat ridiculous in the eyes of the Legion. Then on I marched to the main guest of the evening; I intoned 'Who is this person?' After laudatory remarks about the flash of well-polished metal lighting up the darkness behind the mask, and the smell of fresh oak leaves and acorns (on the *képi* of the French General), 'Madame Yvette' continued, 'I feel that this person came to us too late and left us too soon.' The crowd knew that it was our late commanding officer of the regiment, newly promoted brigadier-general.

During the act there was a call of 'Murray, Murray', just as I had expected, from the Senior NCO Driesch, who was to be a German teacher at the Military School. He wanted to be touched by the wand and to the delight of the Legion men present, I did this. He pronounced himself amazed when he heard how much the 'French lady' as he called my assistant, knew about him, even though she was wearing a mask and had not heard him speak. He had then been in the Legion for about seventeen years, had been living with the same *congai* for some time and had adopted, much to the disgust of most of the Colonials, a lot of Indochinese habits. This was just not done – the British not being the only nation to ostracize those who 'go native'. However, I felt also that there was much to be said for some of the local ways of living, and Driesch and I got on very well together. He had a great facility for foreign languages and spoke fluent German (he had been educated at Heidelberg as a trainee priest at one time), English, French, Hungarian, Spanish and Arabic.

Driesch was floored, which was something that rarely happened to him. The crowd loved it. On one occasion, Driesch the tartar was on duty doing the rounds of the sentries at Vietri when he was stopped at the usual distance from the powder-house by one of the sentries calling out 'Halt! Who goes there?'

'It is I,' responded Driesch. When he was asked for the password he bawled out, 'You know who I am, you idiot'. The sentry chased him back to the guard-house with his bayonet very close to that part of the anatomy where he would have felt it most.

When we were attacked by the Japanese in March 1945, Driesch and Captain van Weyenberg, Professor of Mathematics at the Academy, were instructed by Major Marcelin, in command of all personnel, civil and military remaining in the open city of Tong-Sontay, to bury all the arms and ammunition left at the Academy. An informer revealed the position of the cache to the Japanese commander, who forced Driesch and Captain van Weyenberg, neither of whom was in good health, to unearth the material. They were obliged to kneel at the edge of the hole they had dug, then the Japanese officer chopped off their heads and had them pushed into the hole and covered.

Major Marcelin was also murdered by Japanese, and another NCO, Warrant Officer Hardouvalis was forced to dig a hole just deep enough to permit his head to protrude when he was standing in it. They they bashed his head in and left him.

Next came the Hungarian dancers, dressed in their national costumes with beautiful white blouses, red velvet waistcoats, voluminous white trousers tied at the ankles, white socks and pointed slippers. The Hungarians of the 5th Regiment were like those I had met elsewhere, keeping very much to themselves and doing everything as a group. As always they provided their own musical instruments and musicians, their own wearing apparel and props – and even their own alcohol to warm themselves up before the show, to keep themselves bouncing during their dancing, and to celebrate afterwards. Where are they now – Szekelska, Szekeres, Maracek, Svoboda and the others? Not one of them taller than 5ft 8ins, but giants in valour, energy and stamina. Svoboda one day swore to me that he would never be taken alive by the Japanese. Later he was surprised with a small group by the enemy on a narrow mountain path on our retreat to China. They defended themselves as best they could, killing several attackers, but the latter were too numerous and the legionnaires were all left for dead by the side of the path, riddled with bullets. Yet, I was able to visit Svoboda six months later in the French Hospital at Chandernagore – then a French possession in India, just west of Calcutta. Swathed in bandages, he was quite undaunted, and couldn't wait to be up and about in uniform again, and though by that time the war was over, he still returned to Indochina to fight with the Legion in its violent battle against the Viets.

At the Christmas show, the Hungarians danced like the Tziganes they really were, up and down, round and round, leaping, swirling, sweating, while the fiddles and accordion raced along in rhythm, the pipes bubbled over with enthusiasm, the tambourines thumped as the czardas went from slow, to fast and faster to a final sudden, stamping stop, to the tumultuous applause from the packed audience.

After the first interval the Russian choir gave a grand performance of Volga laments and folk-songs while Lieutenant Elyseev, forty-five years old, and Private Popov, just as old (I remember I was twenty-eight at the time) gave a superb exhibition of Cossack dances. Elyseev, who was later to be wounded and captured at the Col-des-Meos, had been the colonel in command of the famous Cossack Riding School in the Ukraine until the Bolsheviks forced him to flee to France. His French was not very good when he joined the Legion and the 2nd Battalion in Indochina, and his English was not much better. However, we had long talks together when he asked me to translate his Russian Army records of service for the Legion authorities. He had a young son then but I cannot remember any wife. Later, when I was with Sir Winston Churchill, immediately after he handed the Premiership over to Anthony Eden, Mrs Clare Booth Luce (US Ambassador to Italy at the time) visited the Villa Politi Hotel in Sicily where the Old Gentleman was on holiday, accompanied by her Air Aide. He was most interested when I told him about Elyseev and his son and that I had heard that they were living in the United States where his son was in the US Air Force. (I got this information from my Legion friend in Paris, Jean Stokman.) He promised to put a note in the official US Air Force journal and I eventually heard from the son who told me that his father was dead, but not before he had put down on paper his own recollections of that famous retreat, and disclosed my own participation in a very tragic event which has been distorted by quite a number of French historians. I make no apologies for including the following, my own translation of Elyseev's words:

Having placed my own section in position as ordered, I saw that Boukaloff, a senior NCO, was already protecting the left flank of the 6th Company, but even while I was watching, he and his unit were recalled to his Company. In front, our forward posts were already engaged with the enemy. Shortly afterwards I saw a native soldier racing back and I knew that he was bringing bad news. Behind him a legionnaire approached rapidly, on Captain de Cockborne's strawberry-grey horse, Estafette [Dispatch Rider]. He was calling out that Captain Basset was seriously injured and transport was required. Then I saw a very solemn procession coming down the trail . . . a horseman, slumped forward on to the neck of his horse . . . he was not moving.

Two Sergeants of the Battalion HQ, Monch and Murray, were supporting him on either side and a third soldier was leading the horse by the reins. The 'injured' man's shirt, covered with blood, was drawn up over his head. His back was a bloody mess. The man was Captain Komaroff.

This was the first time my involvement had been mentioned by any person and even Elyseev had not seen the real event but only what had happened afterwards.

I was with the 7th Company at the time and had been having a very exciting life as occasionally, very occasionally, American 'Black Widow' light bombers came over to bomb the Japanese. These were difficult to find, of course, and so when we found evidence of troop concentrations, or obtained information from friendly natives of enemy ammunition dumps, my job was to wait until all the French troops had passed and then lay down the *panneaux de signalisation* (white linen sheets placed on the ground in certain prearranged patterns to indicate position, distance and direction etc. of objectives of interest) to direct the bombing. Much havoc was caused to the enemy and it is to be supposed that had we been able to do more, the whole situation might have changed.

Laden with my white sheets, rifle, grenades and ammunition I was looking for flat terrain for my signals for the Americans, should they appear, when Captain Komaroff rode up to offer me cigarettes. They had been dropped earlier by parachute with other material to General Alessandri some distance ahead. Captain Komaroff had been one of my 'pupils' in Sidi-bel-Abbès and he thought that I might like something to smoke. I told him that I could put the tobacco from the fags in my pipe, for I never did like cigarettes, and I placed them in my haversack. He was just about to ride off when a strange, awful look of surprise came over his face as a horrible red hole appeared in his forehead. He slumped forward in the saddle, quite dead. I called for assistance and Sergeant Monch dashed across. Holding the Captain in the saddle we led the horse quickly forward towards Battalion HQ. During the hours that followed, most of the 2nd Battalion marched past the body of Captain Komaroff to salute a well-loved leader and friend before he was taken ahead to Dien-bien-Phu for burial. The general impression was that he was killed by a piece of shrapnel from a Japanese mortar bomb – but I was with him at the time and I feel sure that the hole in his forehead came from the bullet of a Japanese sniper hidden some distance away on the side of a hill to the north-east. It was 1 April 1945.

The Russians in the Legion were a fine crowd, friends to everybody, terrific drinkers, grand soldiers when drunk or sober, always ready for an adventure, the more dangerous the better. It was Elyseev who taught me how not to get blisters on route marches. Instead of socks, general issue, he told me to place my foot in the middle of a clean piece of cotton shirt, preferably white, and to fold it around the foot before placing it in the army boot. The system was known as *chaussettes Russes*. I had seen soldiers do this before but thought it was just an economy measure, but once I was converted, it was for ever – well, for as long as I stayed in the Legion.

The Russian choir of the Legion was always a great success and annually toured the whole of Indochina giving concerts for Legion and other charities.

After the Russian choir came a short play, *Le Commissaire est bon enfant* (The Superintendent of Police is not a bad guy after all) with Driesch playing the Commissaire who was a bit mad. It was a short two-act farce but I cannot recall much about the plot except that I was the first person to come on stage to face the Commissaire at his desk.

'Well, Monsieur,' he shouted, 'what the hell do you want?'

I replied that I needed a permit to carry a gun as I was running a business where I often had to carry large sums of money at night. I was actually running a brothel. I do sometimes wonder why I was given that part, as an Englishman, when I'm quite sure it is more the role of a Frenchman, or an Italian.

Then came the second break. It was very important to have these breaks for the weather was very warm, and singing and talking and even listening and laughing, was very thirsty work. At last came Murray and his Boys – Bertoletti, an Italian who sang well, played the guitar; Hubner, who had assisted me in my magic act, also sang well; and Rudolf Schroeder, the son of a very rich banker from Cologne, who had emigrated to France in 1933, as soon as Hitler came to power. Having begun his studies in Germany he continued them at the Sorbonne, Paris, and passed his examinations with flying colours, staying on as Reader in German until the declaration of war. He was then twenty-eight years old, tall and thin, lazy-looking. Hidden underneath, though, was the resistance and stamina of a long-distance runner. He played the piano well, was a good chess player and a superb drinking companion and we had many very interesting evenings together. But he was a poor soldier, being rather slap-happy as far as military matters were concerned, so he was frequently in trouble. He had arrived in Indochina with the famous 'Phantom Detachment' in November 1941 after a most remarkable journey, the story of which has been told by Pierre Sergent in *Les Maréchaux de la Légion* (Fayard, Paris, 1977).

As Murray and his Boys we dressed as cowboys and the four of us came on to the stage from different directions, singing in French,

German, Italian and English, 'Goodbye Hawaii', looking at each other as if mystified and gesticulating to indicate that we could not understand one other. Then the Legion flag suddenly appeared and the song was sung again, in French, by all of us to show that we had been united by the Foreign Legion. We then sang a Legion marching song, followed by 'South of the Border, down Mexico way' with Bertoletti really coming into his own with his own arrangement on the guitar. It was a resounding success and we sang it at least three times. This song echoed through the barracks the next morning and become a favourite of the football and rugby teams of which I was second-row forward, and was to be heard in fact all over Tonkin for many months afterwards – Top of the Pops really. As a finale we gave them the ever popular 'Chant d'Adieu' in French and I sang the original version 'Auld Lang Syne' in English. It was a most appropriate farewell for there were no more similar festivals and the 5th Regiment of the Legion was to be disbanded before the Christmas of 1946, though it was once more re-formed to fight the Vietcong in 1949.

That Christmas Eve, as always with the Legion, we had to finish with the 'Boudin', the Legion song. *Boudin* is actually black pudding – part of the staple diet of legionnaires, wherever they are. When the Legion decides to stay a while anywhere, gardeners and pigmen are the first to be designated. Pigs mean pork and black puddings (the mere mention of which makes me feel hungry). Even when building roads – and the finest roads in Algeria, Morocco, Syria, Madagascar, Indochina and Tahiti are monuments to the Legion – on marches or on manoeuvres, there is always a *schleuh* (a peasant in North Africa) or a *nha-kwe* (a peasant in Indochina) who follows the troop with his donkey laden with beer, lemonade, chocolate, toffees, sandwiches etc, and *le boudin*. Though the food was rather good in the Legion, hard work always gives one a big appetite. So it was natural for the famous *boudin* to be immortalized in the marching hymn of the French Foreign Legion. 'Tiens, voilà du boudin, voilà du boudin . . . pour les Alsaciens, les Suisses, et les Lorrains . . . pour les Belges, il n'y en a plus . . .' I shall not proceed further out of respect for my Belgian friends, and delicate ears, but that is the Legion song, and that evening it was very well sung.

By the time the show was over and we had been congratulated very heartily by General Alessandri, it was just time for midnight Mass at the Catholic Church where soldiers were always welcome, whether of the faith or not. I was always surprised at the number of men who went regularly to church.

midnight Mass at the Catholic Church where soldiers were always welcome, whether of the faith or not. I was always surprised at the number of men who went regularly to church.

There were all-night parties at the NCOs' and officers' messes, and I was very lucky to be invited to the officers' mess with my team and the Legion Jazz Band, a special section of the usual Musique Militaire that played on these occasions, for extra money of course, from mess funds. I remember, during the course of the evening, noticing that the daughter of the Major-Doctor of the Regiment, one Major Tonnaire (pronounced like the French word for 'thunder', which suited his temperament) was giving me rather inviting looks (we were still dressed as cowboys). I decided to ask the Doctor if he would mind if I danced with his lovely daughter for the next waltz. He said that he saw no objection, but he did not think that she would accept. I plucked up my courage and asked her. She was delighted, but I just could not get the step right – the French waltz is quite different to the old-fashioned waltz my mother had taught me in Tantobia's Conservative Party Hut, so many years before. Nevertheless she seemed to think that the company was most enjoyable.

The evening meal at 5.30 pm consisted of soup, cold meat and salad, fruit, and again two glasses of wine. Rather a humble meal for the Eve of Christmas Day, but it was a day of rest for everyone and there were plenty of places in the village to obtain food, where there would be plenty to drink and make merry. For it is well known that men join the Foreign Legion to forget, and drink could possibly help to obliterate what one had joined the Legion to forget. The next day, our Boxing Day (apart from those in the defaulters' parade, or in the sick parade – heaven help them) things would be back to normal, or as normal as they could be in that remarkable army of *les hommes sans noms*.

5

THE GREAT RETREAT

THE TRAGIC CONDITIONS UNDER which the campaign in Tonkin was carried out in 1945 by the three battalions of the 5th Regiment of the Foreign Legion against the Japanese constituted what was probably a unique exploit in the annals of French colonial military history. No one could possibly proclaim well enough the merit of all these valiant legionnaires or evoke the great and terrible physical and moral sufferings they endured. Nor can anyone render sufficient homage to their virtue as soldiers. It must be made known that these men, wearied by a long sojourn in the Colony, weakened by illness and an unhealthy climate, fatigued by many days of marching and continuous battles, poorly fed, barefoot in some cases, in rags and without medical supplies, yet filled, despite the circumstances, with superb spirit and sense of sacrifice, did carry out during fifty-two days a magnificent resistance in spite of the massive superiority of the enemy in numbers and material, and sustained heavy losses. All this from the heart of the Tonkin delta to the frontiers of China, over more than five hundred miles.

The legionnaires only crossed the Chinese frontier when they were obliged to do so because of the complete exhaustion of their means of fighting. They had all sworn never to fail: their sacred device was HONOUR AND FIDELITY. They did not fail and the citation to the Order of the Army contains the highest praise they could ever receive: 'They have written a new page of glory in the golden book of the Legion', Signed: Alessandri, General, Ex-Colonel Commanding the 5th Regiment of the Foreign Legion.

I shall leave the description of the units involved, the privations they suffered, the battles they lost and those they won, of the roads they travelled, the paths they made, of the jungles that hid them and the enemy as well, of empty villages where inhabitants had fled

[47]

taking with them everything edible, to the writers of history. What I can say is that I saw deeds done by legionnaires, and French airmen, Colonial infrantrymen, and men of the Artillery that would make their mothers and their fathers, brothers, sisters and girlfriends very, very proud of them. I too did things I previously thought I might be able to do, but had never been called upon to carry out, thanks to the inspiration and example of my friends and colleagues. How proud I am, and always will be, that I was there.

On 9 March 1945, four of us were playing bridge in the sergeants' mess – Senior NCO Korst, Sergeant Garcia, myself and one other. I was well ahead and Korst owed me quite an amount. Shortly after 21.15 hours the sound of a bugle shrilled through the night air. I alone listened, for the sound of a bugle was very common, but this call I knew: I had heard it long ago in Sidi-bel-Abbès when war had been declared. It was 'la Générale'. I immediately jumped up and called on everyone to go to their rooms to prepare for immediate departure. I also went to change as quickly as possible into battle-dress, then to the arms room to collect my rifle and ammunition. I rushed out into the courtyard to organize my group and wait for orders. At 22.45 the 1st and 2nd Battalions of the 5th Regiment left the Mehl Barracks, Captain Gaucher, mounted, at the head of the First and Major de Cockborne, on Estafette, very skittish, happy to be off for a promenade, leading the Second. I began to sing 'Il y a des cailloux sur toutes les routes' (There are stones on every road) and soon two hundred voices hurled their defiance to the night air. Action at last. The Japs had attacked.

Massacre at Ha-giang

Meanwhile, at Ha-giang, the main Legion prison, a sudden attack by the Japanese in force, found the Legion not totally unprepared. At the first sound of fire they organized the defence of their quarters, using whatever material came to hand – mattresses, tables and cup-boards were used to the best effect, and during the whole of the night from 9 to 10 March, the small amount of ammunition they had was used effectively, each shot being made to count. Their leaders, NCOs Sury and Jost, inspired the men as they dashed round the rooms calling on the legionnaires to be watchful and careful.

Just when they came to the end of their ammunition, they

received a visit from the officer in charge of the village defence who called upon them to surrender their arms to prevent the total massacre of the native population, who had no means of defence. The legionnaires fixed bayonets to charge, but a final, pleading request from the officer, made them regretfully obey. They went to the assembly point indicated by the Japanese, leaving their weapons behind. No sooner were they assembled than with incalculable fury and bestiality they were massacred by the Japanese with bayonets, swords and even picks. Only a few of the detachment who were on outside work were spared to bury their comrades.

The Tragedy at Langson

At Langson the sad story of the heroic action of the small Motorized Group of the Legion has had to be put together gradually, for there were no survivors. The Group was under the orders of Lieutenant Duronsoy, who had been one of my pupils at the Military School at Son Tay. He had come out top in the final examinations and a fine future was predicted for him in the Legion, in a regiment of his choice. After a running battle with the Japanese, he and the remaining members of his group attained the Brière-de-l'Isle Fort to continue the fight. (Brière-de-l'Isle was a descendant of Rouget de Lisle, composer of the French National Anthem, 'La Marseillaise'.)

Duronsoy and nearly all his men were wounded during the defence of the fort which lasted for twenty-one hours till they at last ran out of ammunition and were obliged to surrender. They were lined up just outside the walls of the fort. Japanese machine-guns threatened them as they awaited the decision of the victors. Dispatch of the wounded and the slaughter of prisoners-of-war did not seem possible. It was so contrary to the rules of civilized nations. Yet it did appear to be distinctly probable from the actions of their captors. Duronsoy took a step forward and in a firm voice said, 'I am the leader of these brave soldiers and alone responsible. Kill me but spare them.' The Japanese officer in charge shook his head. Gathering all his energy, the young French officer, in the finest spirit of the Legion and France, holding his head high, began to sing that most inspiring of anthems, 'La Marseillaise' 'Allons enfants de la Patrie, le jour de gloire est arrivé . . .' As the words rang out echoing through the hills and down the valleys, in the accents of most of the countries of Europe, there came the chatter of machine-guns as the officer lowered his sabre, and the song ended.

Tong – open city . . . of death

The area Tong-Son Tay was declared an open city on 10 March 1945 to try to preserve the lives of the civilian population after the departure the night before of the 1st and 2nd Battalions of the Legion. Lt Col. Marcelin, an ancient of the Legion, was left in command of the town to deal with the questions that would inevitably arise in the new situation, to see to the women and children, the sick and the injured. He took his place in the Town Office and assembled his secretaries and messengers . . . and waited.

At about 6.30 in the morning, a group of Japanese burst into the military bakery and slaughtered everyone there. Another group flung itself towards the administrative offices and massacred all within by hurling grenades through the windows. A further group of ten Japanese dashed into the office of Lt Col. Marcelin, firing indiscriminately, killing two officers on the first floor and very seriously wounding the Colonel himself. They then speared him with bayonets and left him to die several hours later in the afternoon.

Hanoi – Present Arms

While Lieutenant Duronsoy had remained at Langson, where he and his friends of one group of the Motorized Section of the Legion had been massacred, the rest of the section had made their way to Hanoi, en route for Tuyen Quang where they were to meet up with the rest of the Regiment, as per orders received. Among them were two of my rugby-playing friends, CSM Lecroix, one-time member of the French national rugby team and a very popular captain of the 5th Regimental team for which I played, and Sergeant Rivera, another of our players. There was also one of my very best friends with whom I had shared rooms, drinks, marches and stories during those hard weeks at the Corporals' Training Course, Chief-Corporal Olszensky, of Polish origin. They were not only friends of the rugby field and bars, but they had also been members of the Resistance and had participated mainly in covering our routes to and from the dropping-zones to fight off any Japanese interruption.

The group were quartered in the Citadel on Friday 9 March and due to leave for Tong that evening at 21.50, en route for Tuyen Quang, their final destination. Captain Fenautrigues, in command, went to see his fiancée, for they were to be married shortly. He left RSM Roman in command. The Captain was still absent when, at 20.10, explosions began to rend the air and someone shouted that the Japs were on their way. Roman immediately blew his whistle and his men appeared. Three of the armoured cars they had brought with them from Langson were placed opposite the main gate to the Citadel, facing south, and the other driven to guard the north gate.

Captain Fenautrigues, on hearing the explosions, left the restaurant where he was having dinner before going to see his girlfriend and, summoning two NCOs who were also from the Citadel, he began to make his way to rejoin his men. Half-way there they met a group of Japanese soldiers who immediately opened fire, felling the Captain.

By 21.30 the Citadel was surrounded by the Japanese, but Roman soon discovered that at least two generals, Massimi, who commanded the Citadel troops, and Mordant, until recently the officer in command of all the troops in Indochina, and leader of our Resistance movement, did not think that the attack of the Japs was to be taken seriously. Roman knew otherwise, especially as hand-grenades began to explode in the courtyard where Roman, his men and vehicles, including ammunition lorries, sought the protection of the surrounding walls. Soon Roman was wounded in the eye and in his left leg, Kornmann was seriously hit and Rivera tried to help him, despite his own severe bleeding. One of their Indochinese soldiers lay dead. The more seriously wounded were taken to shelter in downstairs rooms, but Roman and Rivera remained at their posts. The armoured cars under Sergeants Klug, Kohz and Chief-Corporal Olszensky opened fire on the enemy as they breached the south wall and tried to come through the main gate, while the other armoured car, a Panhard-Levassor with its special gears and controls which allowed it to move forwards and backwards so that the two machine-guns, fore and aft, could fire without any interruption, changed its position according to the greatest threat. CSM Demont occupied this one, while a similar vehicle was occupied by Captain Omess, of the Colonial Regiment. Kohz's car was hit by a bomb. Janata, one of the drivers, had a leg blown off and Klanaec, a gunner, was badly wounded, but kept control of his gun. Another bomb struck the car and Kohz was obliged to drag his men out of the blazing vehicle. He then threw each of his remaining hand-grenades in the direction of the enemy before finally retreating. Suddenly, just as Roman was about to utilize some of the contents, one of the ammunition lorries was hit and went up in flames, the fire rapidly spreading to the other lorries, illuminating the whole courtyard. Still the battle, led by Roman and Demont, carried on. A number of Colonial soldiers joined the legionnaires, while many more just stood and watched. Roman was seriously wounded in the spine and in several other places and was carried into a room and laid on a table by Corporal Giorsetti. Only a few of the Motorized Detachment survived. Herlet, Frank, and my friend Olszensky were dead, their rifles still hot in their hands. Roman, with the help of half a dozen Indochinese soldiers, four of whom were shot down as they carried Roman to the First Aid Post, finally got there. But there was no one capable of helping him.

At 1700 on 10 March, the bugle sounded the 'Cease Fire' and all resistance stopped. At 1800 the Japanese allowed the medical staff from the Lanessan Hospital to succour the wounded. As Roman was carried on a stretcher through the main gate that he had helped to defend so valiantly the Japanese guard presented arms.

Meanwhile Alessandri's column, composed of three battalions of the Legion, several battalions of native troops, an artillery group and diverse other groups, were messed around Tong to await the order to advance through the Japanese belt surrounding them. But during the action, which succeeded in getting the column to the other side of the Black River, much material had to be destroyed, and the native troops sent home, for the General realized that they were entering into guerrilla warfare and it would be very difficult to provide food for his main force, let alone the native troops as well.

Alessandri was left with the depleted three battalions of the Legion, the French officers and NCOs of the native troops, the artillery battery, a section of airmen from Kim Dai and a few soldiers and others who happened to decide to join us. The retreat towards China, via Tho Son, Thanh Son, Thu Guc, Tule, Son La, where a particularly intensive battle took place, Col des Meos, where I won the Croix de Guerre with palm, Tuan Giao, Dien Bien Phu, Kuong Khouo, Pak Ban, Phong Saly to Ma Li Tao where our final, and most bloody, encounter occurred, was executed with great dignity and courage. There were many battles and many fine officers and men found unmarked graves. We encountered an enemy prepared to descend to the greatest possible depths of bestiality. The Legion lived up to its renown . . . and I was there.

We crossed the Chinese frontier after Ma Li Tao on 30 April 1945 and when we came to the plain of Yunnan, I and my group were sent on ahead to make contact with the Chinese forces. It is probable that I was chosen to lead because I was English and it was thought that this would be to our advantage.

After a few miles we met a mounted Major of the Chinese Army, with a mounted batman. With the little Chinese I spoke, and in pidgin English, I managed to explain the situation. I was delighted that the Major spoke a little English. He escorted us to his General at his headquarters and there I asked for permission for the column to proceed through his area. He had received instructions as to what was to happen to the French troops arriving from Indochina. All arms and military material were to be deposited there and we were to follow his directions towards Tze Mao Ting and thence to Mong Tseu and Tsao Pa.

Through my friend the Major, I pleaded with the General to permit us to retain our weapons, for the Legion intended only to rest for a while in China before returning to fight the Japanese invader of Indochina as soon as possible. After much discussion we were allowed to keep our arms.

During the next few days – or was it weeks – the Chinese Major marched by my side as we made our way towards Sze Mao Ting. As I mentioned before, he was on horseback, and he offered me his batman's horse to ride with him. My own men were on foot so I regretfully declined. The Major insisted on walking as well. Each day when we were a few miles from the village where we were to stay the night, as per the orders of the General, Major Wu would mount his horse and gallop off to arrange things. I always found that a small hut had been reserved for me, and as he knew how much I liked sweet things, there was also a saucer-shaped block of sugar, a very rare commodity, to thank me, as he said, for the English lessons I gave him. Once we were out of the area of command of his General, however, he had to say goodbye. I was sorry to see him go. Later I wrote to him from Calcutta on two occasions and received replies. When I returned to Britain the correspondence stopped.

*　　*　　*

Just before Sze Mao Ting, I came to the end of my engagement. It was 12 May 1945. I remembered the last General Orders concerning the release of legionnaires at the end of contract in the Far East — they said FAR EAST, not Indochina. Provided the representative of the country of origin of a legionnaire who wished to be released agreed, then the soldier would be allowed to go. How could the British Council in Kunming refuse, I said to General Alessandri, at the reunion of officers called to study my demand for release? Despite opposition from a number of officers there, who suggested that I was much too good a soldier to let go, and it could cause a precedent inviting others to follow me, General Alessandri decided in my favour. I shook hands with most of my friends, then as the regiment marched through the village the next morning, en route for Mong Tseu and a well-earned rest before the return to Indochina after the fall of Japan to face the rebel Vietcong, I stood on a wall and saluted my brave comrades in arms as they went by. I was a civilian once more and I did not know whether to be pleased or not. All I knew was that the Legion were out of the fighting for some time to come and I had to get back to the nearest British organization to carry on the fight against the yellow peril.

Near Puer-fu, there was an American meterological station with an airfield, and I went there where I was very well received. A few days later, groups of military personnel arrived from Indochina, on their way further north to Kunming or east to Mong Tseu. Air transport was very limited. In fact the US lieutenant in charge of the station said that he was forbidden to allow anyone but American personnel to use the plane. Seeing the state of some of the French soldiers, he called me in to decide, or help him decide, on those who should be evacuated by plane to Kunming. At least two of my friends who had been wounded and had malaria rather badly were permitted to leave, and a few others who seemed to be in a parlous state, while a number of others, mainly officers of the higher ranks, were politely sent on their way.

The few days I spent as a guest of the 14th US Air Force were very pleasant with fantastic food after what I had been eating for the past couple of months, film shows and pleasant company, and I owe a debt of gratitude to the airmen there. Then came the day when I said goodbye to my new friends and flew to Kunming to begin a new life.

6

WHOOPIES AND RUPEES

ON ARRIVING AT KUNMING I immediately went to the British Military Mission, up the back stairs, and was met by the captain in charge. On seeing the state of my clothing and the really tired appearance, he immediately pressed a buzzer and a beautiful blonde girl came into the little room. The captain asked her to get me a cup of tea and biscuits and shortly afterwards I was partaking of typical British hospitality for which I was extremely grateful. I was then asked if I would prefer to wait some weeks for a commission in the armed forces or be signed on immediately as a civilian officer — both would be with a clandestine intelligence organization. I accepted the latter proposal and was taken outside the city and introduced to the personnel of the China station. After a week or two of serious training, I was told to go to a certain address in Calcutta. There would be a plane waiting for me at Kunming Airport, but as I had no identity papers, I would have to get through the Airport Control, British and American, by any unofficial means I could devise.

There was only one other passenger on the plane and he was sitting in one of the numerous bucket-seats of uncushioned metal when I got in and sat down. He was Captain Drake, in uniform. He was not very communicative at all. We took off. Shortly afterwards we crossed the Himalayas and it was very, very cold indeed. We wrapped as many blankets around us as we could find, but the plane was just a DC3, an all-metal, twin-engined monoplane that had seen quite a number of years' service, and it was very dangerous to move out of the mini-seat. I do not know at what height we were flying but I do know that we were both very happy, and the view through the windows as we crossed those fabulous mountains was unforgettable. The sun was shining brightly making the cotton-wool clouds too white to look at, and below there stretched the remarkable ever-changing folds, the grand snow-covered mountains.

Once over the mountains we landed to refuel and then went on to land at Dum Dum Airport, close to Calcutta. I was dressed no longer in Legion uniform, but in American GI shirt, cap, trousers and boots but without any badges or markings, for I was a civilian. I went up to the American sergeant at the gate marked 'US Personnel' and told him that I was British. 'Well get the hell out o'here,' he shouted, 'there's a British Control over there where it's marked BRITISH personnel. Are you blind?'

The British gate was just a hundred yards away and the sergeant must have heard the altercation because when I got to him, he asked me if I was in trouble. Putting on my very best American–French accent, I tried to explain, rather incoherently, that I was shell-shocked and on my way to the French Hospital in Chandernagore, then a French possession not too far away from the capital. The US sergeant was in a bad temper and did not want to know any French bastards, so I came to the British who looked more friendly, I told him hesitantly. The sergeant asked me if I had any papers and I told him they had been sent to the hospital because the French military authorities in China thought that I would lose them. By this time the sergeant was really confused and gave up, telling me to hurry away and get lost. I did so and went to look for transport which I knew would be there. I did not have to look for long because a few minutes later, Captain X came up to me and suggested that I might be looking for him and would I get in the car and stop looking so lost. We drove along the dusty road to Calcutta where I was introduced to the colonel who was to be my boss for quite a while. For a few days I stayed at the officers' mess in Ballygunge, to the south of the famous *maidan*, some 1,283 acres in area, and had a good rest before being sent, by train, to the Puri area on the Bay of Bengal, about 320 miles from Calcutta. The old name of the city was Purushhottam Puri, the city of the greatest being, and was the seat of the shrine of Jagganath, which is the form under which the Hindu god Vishnu is worshipped there. The word means 'lord of the world'. Buddhist influence has been detected in the most important of the numerous yearly festivals, the Rathayatra, which takes place in June or July. The rough-hewn wooden image of the god is placed in a car so heavy that the efforts of hundreds of devotees are required to move it, dragging it through deep sand to the country house of the god. The journey takes several days and thousands of pilgrims participate. We derive our own word 'juggernaut' from this ceremony.

On a beautiful beach site, in pleasant bungalows, I replaced Major R. as Officer in Command of a training camp for agents who were to be dropped, for the main part, behind enemy lines in Burma and Malaya. The job fitted me like a glove. On the first night, Major R. said that we should celebrate, for the very first message from HQ, that I decoded, indicated important victories against the Japanese. Would I take the 15cwt and find some company for a buffet-dance? 'There's a hotel a few miles down the road towards Puri, where you will find a few ladies of impeccable character. Then Mrs Wood's place is also down the road in the other direction. She runs the guest-house and I have heard that there is a honeymoon couple there. Do your best to get them here and they will have a lovely evening, I promise you.' So off I went in the truck – with a driver of course.

When I arrived at this hotel, I asked for the manager and we had a drink together. At the bar were three very beautiful ladies and the manager introduced me to them. I had a drink with them and invited them to the party. They accepted and got into the truck – there were seats in the back and it was quite clean and comfortable. When I arrived at the bungalow, now my bungalow, for R. was leaving by train early the next morning, I deposited the girls on a settee and set off for Mrs Wood's place.

I found that the guest-house was a typical bamboo-type bungalow, much larger than usual, and with a ground floor and an upper floor. I went in and introduced myself to Mrs Wood, a very charming Indian lady. She looked rather astounded when I told her that I had come to ask the 'honeymoon' couple to attend our party to celebrate my taking over from Major R. There was no 'honeymoon' couple, she said. Sitting at a table, in the distance, I saw a couple sitting with drinks and suggested to Mrs Wood that I might be permitted to invite them to the party, so off I marched. To see me then, of course, no one could possibly suspect that a few weeks previously I had been in the French Foreign Legion, fighting tooth and nail with the Japanese, for now I was dressed in smart white drill that suited me well. I introduced myself to the couple, not disclosing that I was a member of an intelligence organization of course, and bought them a drink. Then I invited them along to the party for the departure of a colleague and they happily accepted as there was not really much to do in that part of the world and they were a little bit bored. While Mr D. left to shave, I bought another drink for the smartly dressed lady and then asked, 'Are you on honeymoon?' She denied it. Unthinkingly I plodded on and on while she continued to deny that they were a honeymoon couple and she did not know of any honeymoon couple there. Still I carried on, getting deeper and deeper into the mire. At last, just before the gentleman returned, she said, in despair, 'Oh dear, Mr Murray, as I can see that you are determined to carry on all night asking the same question, I feel that I must tell you. Actually we are both married, but you see we are not husband and wife.' I collapsed in shame but they were not at all embarrassed. The man was divorced, and the lady about to be divorced. They just had to wait a bit, that was all. In fact, later that year, when I was back in Calcutta, I attended their wedding, by invitation, and had a wonderful time.

At the party I deposited the young couple on a sofa, found them drinks and began to circulate. We were about twenty people by then and the drinks were flowing freely as the record-player played sweet music in the background. Some of the more venturesome danced on the quickly waxed wooden floor disclosed by the removal of several grass mats. The three young ladies I had brought from the hotel were still on the settee and I talked to them. They were employed by a firm in Calcutta and were allowed to have their holiday at the fine hotel at the expense of their firm when prices dropped in the off-season. That was how they came to be there. Their names were Mary, Joan and Helga. When I heard the name Helga, I immediately said that this was a name I would never forget, it was the name of the lovely blonde girl who had given me that famous cup of tea in Kunming, in China. I reminisced a little and came back to earth. The pretty brunette smiled coyly, while her friends laughed outright as she said, 'I have dyed my hair and changed my hairstyle, Mr Murray'. The three girls were employed by the same organization as myself. So we had a grand party and R. left the next day with a headache. The next time I saw Major R. he was in civvies, walking down a side road from his house where he lived with his mother, in Golders Green. I was then in the uniform of a police constable stationed at Golders Green.

Towards the end of the war, just a few short weeks later, I had to send the remaining agents back to Calcutta for they were no longer required to work behind the Japanese lines. There were practically no Japanese lines left. I followed them shortly afterwards. The colonel in command told me that I was being sent to another training camp far away in the north and that I would be leaving early the following day, by train from Howrah station. The next morning I presented myself at a certain office and was given a pouch for the Training Station. I had to lock it by a chain to my left wrist and was instructed not to remove it until I arrived at my destination. I jumped into the truck that was waiting for me – another 15cwt – and the Indian military driver put my case in the back. I got up in front beside the driver and away we went. It was not too far to the station but I had time to chat to the driver on the way. He spoke very good English. At the station we drove almost on to the platform. I jumped out and nearly hanged myself on the pouch attached by its chain to my wrist. The driver came round to the back and got my case out to put it on the ground. I quickly separated the pouch and its chain from my wrist, completely forgetting my instructions about not taking it off, and handed it to the driver assuring him that I would only be a couple of minutes. I dashed to the ticket office with my warrant and rushed back. My bag was there but no driver. Swearing a little, I grabbed my bag and hurried on to the train, already waiting and raring to go. I was terribly excited at this new form of transport and the fact that I was on my way to a new assignment that was reputed to be one of the best.

I took my seat in the first-class compartment with no other company but myself, and as the train moved off, I watched with interest the passing scene. Then I must have dozed off. My first thought when I awoke was, where is the blooming pouch? Very quickly the awful thing that had happened dawned on me and I hurried out to discover from the guard where we were and what could be done. Just nothing, but wait until we reached the next stop, which happened to be the stop that was my destination – five hundred miles from Calcutta.

On arrival there, the officer I should have replaced was waiting on the platform. We had breakfast together, then in execution of the instructions from Colonel T., telephoned through, I took the next train back to Calcutta. That had probably been the most important mistake I ever made. But if I had taken command of the camp there and then, I would probably not have been asked to go to Japan, would not have refused to go, would not have returned to England

when I did and would probably not have taken the job of first courier which was to lead to my winter job with the *News of the World*
which in turn led to my meeting the finest and most loyal lady
anyone could ever meet– my dear wife.

On arrival back at Calcutta, I put forward a host of arguments
about the whole business, but, in my heart of hearts, I knew I had
been wrong. It was just a moment of thoughtlessness which caused
no harm to anyone except that the personal mail of the staff of that
camp was delayed by at least forty-eight hours.

I then took over the running of the officers' mess of that clandestine organization and the food supplied there in Ballygunge was
recommended as the best in India. Most of the officers, both regular
and civilian, were involved in stupendous acts of bravery. Many did
not return from their incursions into enemy territory, and their
exploits must for ever remain secret. Should any of them read my
story, I should like them to know that their colleagues appreciate
what a debt is owed to them.

A short distance away in Ballygunge, there was a residence for
young ladies of the services who were also doing very important
work in the intelligence groups, and to sort of keep it in the family,
when we wished for some relaxation or company to go with us to
the cinema, theatre or restaurants, they were usually permitted to
do so by the ATS Senior Commander in charge of the residence. She
was a bit of a tartar, but she probably had a very difficult job. Lots of
the women, all officers, had very impressive backgrounds and they
were a wonderful lot. I was particularly interested in a Miss E. first,
then a Miss Irene D. I remember taking Irene out one day. I'd just
returned from a mission and as we walked towards Chowringhee on
this lovely afternoon, Irene turned suddenly towards me and asked
me if I had a safety pin. I was rather surprised, but answered, after
searching through my pockets, that I did not. She told me not to
worry. Her elastic had snapped so she just stopped walking, wriggled
a little, sedately stepped out of her knickers and stuffed them into
her handbag. The next time I met Irene was on the underground
station platform at Golders Green.

Shortly after my arrival in Calcutta, in the early evening, I was
strolling down Chowringhee, on the *maidan* side, when suddenly
shouts came from the other side, in French. There was a group of my
ex-colleagues of the Legion, accompanied by a young lady in the
uniform of the French equivalent of the ATS or FANYs.

I was in officer's uniform, myself, as I was proceeding to a meeting where it was more convenient to be so dressed, and I crossed the wide road to greet my friends and be introduced to the young lady. She did not appear to be very interested in me till she found out that I knew her fiancé much better than she herself knew him. He had been serving under the name of Silva and had apparently been sent on a mission by the Communists to Lao Kay, but I do not think that this was true. I heard, however, that he and another legionnaire, also reported by Frey to be a Communist, had tried to swim across the Red River. He had succeeded, but his companion had been drowned in the fast-flowing torrent. The next time I saw 'Silva' was in Marrakesh when I was there with Sir Winston Churchill. His fiancée, Janine, was very attractive and we formed an attachment for the rest of the time I was in Calcutta. She had a French friend from Binic, Brittany, who was engaged to a major in the French Air Force and we had some very interesting weekends at a Dak bungalow at Fulta, on the Hooghli River not too far from the city. On that very first time that we met, with my friends from the Legion I invited them to dinner at a small restaurant I used, and afterwards went to a large dance-hall in Chowringhee, on the first floor. A very large table was arranged for us and bottles of wine produced, naturally. We proceeded to continue to enjoy ourselves, drinking, talking and dancing. There were a number of hostesses available for my friends while Janine and I paired off for the evening.

There were a lot of American soldiers in the restaurant as usual, drinking very heavily and one of them who had had a drop too much asked my companion to dance. She declined in French and I translated.

The American returned a couple of times and met with the same reasons on each occasion, but the third time he grabbed the young lady by the arm. I stood up to restrain him and he took a swing at me. Wham! went my right fist and he sailed in a most undignified fashion, on his behind, right across the polished dance-floor, landing among the feet of his American friends on the far side. The manager disappeared immediately to fetch the MPs. Meanwhile the grey-dressed Americans grouped together and made their way across the room. 'La Légion . . . à moi', I called, and the response was immediate. We advanced on the Americans and by the time the US MPs arrived their compatriots were in no fit condition to resist authority. The dance was then able to continue without further trouble.

A few days later I went to the French authorities at Chanderna-gore, which was still a French possession, to receive my back pay and discharge papers and while there I visited some of my former colleagues in hospital.

7

THE WAR ENDS AND I TRAVEL ABROAD

BACK IN CALCUTTA, THE war came to an end and it was suggested that I go to Japan. I asked for a fortnight's leave in England before going there, but it was refused and I handed my papers in. My French girlfriend, her friend and the major all came to Howrah to see me off on the train to Bombay where I was booked to leave on the SS *Strathmore*. I had thought that I should be very lonely and bored as a first-class passenger on a troopship, for I was not cut out to spend days and days listening to oft-repeated tales of derring-do told by high-ranking officers and civil servants and their wives and families, while the real men were segregated and kept off the first-class deck and amenities, such as they were. That was what I thought it was going to be like. How wrong I was.

I made the acquaintance of Jimmy Horrocks who was to remain a firm friend ever afterwards, even though he was a member of the Press. He had been a war correspondent out there and we hit it off right away. Later, after he had married Margot, a lovely lady with a delightful daughter, we used to meet frequently at the Savoy Hotel, when Jimmy was with the Hickey column of the *Express*. After Sir Winston's funeral we retired to the Savoy for lunch and rather a hectic wake. On the *Strathmore* Jimmy and I made friends with Margaret Burton who had just made her stage debut in Calcutta in an ENSA show and was returning to England. Margaret had her real beginning in showbiz when she sang as a girl soprano on the BBC in 1939; then followed oratorio solos in Haydn's *Creation* and *Elijah*, and Handel's *Messiah*, *Samson*, and *Judas Maccabaeus*. She was married to David Nixon in 1947 but they were divorced in 1950. Her début in London was as principal boy in 1954 at the Palladium and her long legs and powerful voice made her a leading principal boy for a decade. She also starred in a number of West End musicals, having the title role in Offenbach's *La Belle Hélène* at Sadler's Wells in 1963. She played a blowsy barmaid in Kenneth More's 1963 film, *The Comedy Man* and the title role in *Annie*. Her last appearance in 1983 was as a Hollywood columnist, Louella Parsons, in the musical *Marilyn*. Margaret Burton died in the early 1980s at the age of sixty. Jimmy Horrocks and I had a very interesting and exciting trip home, thanks mainly to Margaret and a senior fire officer, J. Spellman, who was returning to his native Ilford, in Essex. I still have a Chinese ten-yuan banknote with our signatures as a souvenir.

The ship was dry and as I had several bottles of Scotch and gin in my suitcases and tin trunk, I found that I was very popular indeed. We had good fun throughout the trip that took us through the Suez Canal, an experience I had long looked forward to savouring. A case of smallpox on board meant that we had to divert to Malta, the George Cross Island, which was again very interesting, and we arrived back in Southampton late in January 1946.

I was in my cabin packing the last articles. There was no hurry as the case of smallpox had been notified to the health people and everyone on board had to go through a thorough examination. The dock workers refused to handle the luggage and that meant that everyone had to spend the night on board and relief workers would take care of the luggage the next day. I left my cabin, noticing a man I had not seen before on the ship, lounging beside the wall of the corridor. He was dressed in a dark suit and was smoking a pipe. I knew that he had not travelled with us on the voyage, so I felt that he must be something to do with immigration or customs. I walked past him, and from behind me came the authoritative voice, 'Are you Mr Murray?' I stopped and turned towards the stranger. 'I am Inspector Brown of Scotland Yard.'

Immediately, like a man plunging to his death is reputed to do, the whole of my past life began to race through my mind – to stop at the fact that I had left England almost ten years ago, without a passport and on a return ticket of which I had only used one part. He stuck out his and hand said, 'I am very glad to meet you, Mr Murray. Your brother is on the quayside and wonders if it would be OK to come aboard.' I shook hands warmly, with relief, and assured him that I would be delighted to see my brother.

Tom came to my cabin and explained that he had received the Marconigram I had sent him at the police station in Islington and had made inquiries as to when the *Strathmore* would dock. He had spent the night at the Southampton Docks police station awaiting the arrival and had made himself known to Inspector Brown, who was in charge, as it happened, of the Special Branch team on duty there in those days. The telegram read, 'Prepare fatted calf, Love, Eddie'. He had told my mother and the rest of the family that I was on my way home without further details, except the day of arrival. Despite the ban on the removal of luggage until the next day, Tom was able to organize things, and suddenly my luggage was out of the cabin, I had said my adieux to my friends, a dock policeman loaded the luggage on to a trolley and off we went to the taxi rank. We caught the first train to London, and almost before I knew it we were at Waterloo. We managed to carry two or three suitcases, but left the cabin trunk in the left luggage office to be collected the next day. We got on to the escalator to go up to street level, and there, on the way down, was my mother. She had to go down to the bottom then return on the up escalator before we could meet to clasp each other tightly. On the way to her home in Acton, she explained that although Tom had only told her that I was arriving that day without further details, she had looked in the *Daily Telegraph*'s Shipping Movements and found that the only ship arriving back from India was the *Strathmore*. She rang Waterloo and found that the boat train from Southampton was due to arrive in London at a certain time, and so she came a bit early to be sure of meeting me. She knew nothing at all of the smallpox, the strike or the delays and the fact that we had not returned on the boat train from Southampton Docks Station, but on an earlier train from Southampton Main Station. It was just one of those marvellous coincidences that happen but rarely.

A few days later Tom again came to my rescue by introducing me to one of his friends, Bela Ullman, who was the deputy manager of a very well-known hotel in Half Moon Street, Fleming's Hotel. He was going to start a travel agency and would I be his first courier. I jumped at the opportunity and shortly afterwards, Fourways Travel Bureau opened in the basement of Marshall and Snelgrove's in Oxford Street, London. For the first few months while tours were being organized I worked in the office, dealing mainly with passports and visas, and gradually I began to know my way round all the embassies in the metropolis. The biggest visa job was when one of the top directors of Gestetners wanted to visit all the countries in North and South America. Visas were required for every last one of them and he wanted it done in a hurry. Towards the end I had to get him an additional passport to affix to the previous one as there was not enough room in one for all the visas required. Gestetner is still a very big firm so I suppose their business trip was not a failure. Lady Campbell, the wife of Sir Malcolm, was another lovely person whose passport and visas I obtained.

The business flourished and soon I was one of several couriers taking tours by coach, via Dover, to France, Belgium, Luxembourg, Switzerland and Italy. Really, the Continent, just recovering from the force of the Nazi jackboot, was not ready for tourists. In many hotels, the rooms, though very clean, did require refurnishing and toilet facilities awaited modernization. Mr Ullman himself frequently travelled abroad visiting the hotels he was booking for his tours and his instructions to his couriers were to ensure the maximum comfort possible for the clients. Many were the letters he received from satisfied customers. A number of these, in my favour, were printed on the back of the brochure sent out. It was very hard work, but that was something I was accustomed to, and I have always discovered that one gets out of a job satisfaction equal to the amount of dedication one puts into it.

Fourways Tours were well organized and, except for the occasional hiccup, the majority of holidays went off without a hitch. One of these occasions was when we were within sight of the Swiss frontier, near St Louis, Basle. I was checking the passports of the travellers and discovered that one of them did not have a Swiss Visa. I had to return, with the coach and thirty-five passengers, to Mulhouse in order to find the nearest Swiss Consul. He lived just outside the city, and it was after office hours. We went to his private address and parked the coach outside. Ringing the bell was something I don't ever want to do again, for the visas should have been checked before leaving London. I suddenly remembered that the client in question had joined the tour at Ostend where the coaches provided by the Belgian firm of Hoyez always began. The first and last part of the tours were by the Golden Arrow, and Victoria Station. I waited in trepidation until a servant came and departed with my message for the Consul, and came back to invite me into the Consul's bureau. The Consul listened politely to my story and supplied me with the necessary document. He also gave me a cup of coffee.

On another occasion there was a man for whom nothing was right. The reserved seat on the Golden Arrow was facing the engine and he always liked to face the rear; he wanted a cabin on the boat so that he could rest; when we got into the coach at Ostend he grumbled at the seat he was given. He was most objectionable and by the time we got to Besançon everybody was fed up with him. At the railway station, I stopped the coach and asked for a show of hands. Did they think I was justified in expelling him from the tour, or not? They were unanimous. They were sick and tired of him. I heaved his luggage into the railway station, bought his ticket back to London and left him there. Every passenger on the coach sent a letter to Fourways Travel stating how impressed they had been with my conduct of the affair.

One of the most memorable incidents happened towards the end of the summer of 1946. There were thirty-two people on the coach and we had stayed the night in Brussels. We then travelled via Namur and the Ardennes to Bastogne for lunch, passing on the way several derelict tanks, for it was here that the momentous stand took place of the American 101st Airborne Division, reinforced by part of the 4th US Armoured Division, against the mighty Fifth and Sixth German Panzer Armies.

After lunch, which was always extremely good at the family-run Hotel Lebrun, we drove towards Luxembourg and stopped in the centre of the city for a brief visit. On the main square, I was astounded to recognize a well-dressed man as one of my erstwhile colleagues of the Legion in Sidi-bel-Abbès. He unfortunately had a very urgent business appointment, and I had a coachload of tourists, so Koehner and I could do no more than slap each other on the back and hope for a longer meeting some time in the future.

Then as we drove through the city, we were stopped several times by the police and told to get off the main road and stay there for a couple of hours. Winston Churchill was arriving at the frontier with France and the road was to be kept free. I did stop the coach and found a Union Jack somewhere which I managed to fix to the windscreen without impeding the view of the driver. With one of the ladies' lipsticks, I also made a huge 'V' sign on the windscreen and we went on our way. Each time we were stopped by police, I informed them that we were an official reception party for the frontier meeting with Churchill, and we managed to get to within perhaps one hundred yards from the actual post, before the final policeman forbade our proceeding further. Luckily there was a side street on the left and we parked the coach just a few yards off the main road and hurried off to the frontier barrier. Minutes afterwards the official convoy arrived and Churchill got out of one of the cars, walked through the gates and was in Luxembourg. He took off his grey Homburg and waved it to the crowd, while we sang 'For he's a jolly good fellow' after he had saluted the guard of honour and the flag. He got back into the car which drove off, while I and my tourists hurried back to the coach to drive on, trying to make up lost time and reach Nancy where we were due to stay the night. My thoughts at the time were that at long last I had seen the famous Mr Churchill. Little did I know then that I was to see much more of him in the not-too-distant future.

The lipstick and the flag remained on the front of the coach and were there when we moved to spend a few days at a four-star hotel. I, of course was sitting in the front seat, on the right-hand side, watching the street as we went on our way. Just a few yards before we were due to turn left to reach the hotel, I called out to the Belgian driver to stop, for there on the pavement, looking me straight in the eyes was Loerscher, one of my late colleagues of the Legion. Because he had very severe malaria on arrival at the American Air Base where I was helping to check and authorize air transport, I had been able to find room for him on the plane. I found out later that he had actually had a story of the event published locally, in Montreux where he lived and worked, in which he had stated that I had saved his life. We made hurried arrangements to meet afterwards, when I had settled my people in the hotel, and I jumped back into the coach. We arrived at the hotel just minutes later and the clients and their luggage were dealt with. Informing the passengers that I would be available for the next hour, I ordered a drink and sat down in the lounge. Before I could finish my drink, one of the clients came to me, furious. She had been insulted in the lift by one of the hotel staff, and she demanded instant apologies. She told me the story and I called for the manager, who found the alleged culprit. He told a different tale, but I honestly believed my client. As no apology was forthcoming from either the man or the manager, I called for the luggage to be brought down at once. After I had consulted other passengers, and phoned a better hotel – the Suisse et Majestic, just a short distance away, in a better position, practically on the edge of the lake – I had the driver bring the coach round, and we all went to the new hotel where we received a very warm welcome. I phoned Ullman in London and was assured of his whole-hearted co-operation. It was perhaps easier than it sounds for every hotel in Europe was looking for regular customers.

Later I met with my friend and a big reception was arranged for the next day at the Château de Chillon, a few miles away. The clients had a free evening so they did not suffer. Loerscher picked me up in his car and drove to the Château. Actually the reunion did not take place in the castle where François de Bonivard, a Swiss liberator who inspired Byron's *The Prisoner of Chillon* was imprisoned, but in the restaurant of the same name, just opposite. My friend had assembled at least twenty of his cronies there and *la fondue*, the famous Swiss melted cheese dish, was on the menu. They told me that I had created a new way of dealing with penalties incurred when a piece of the bread used on the end of a long fork fell into the hot cheese: instead of wine, I insisted on Scotch whisky, which was more expensive. They did not mind, for this was a celebration, and I had saved Loerscher's life.

The best part of a courier's revenue in those days came from tips from satisfied clients who usually handed over what remained of their foreign currency just before we got back to Calais or Ostend. A hint was usually given to one of the male passengers, discreetly of course so as not to offend, and he went round with a hat while the bus was still travelling. The resulting collection was then handed to me, which I shared with the driver who could be very, very useful indeed on a trip – or a very big nuisance if he wished, and it all depended on whether the courier was known to be generous or otherwise. On this particular occasion the routine had been followed, and we arrived at Dover. I usually had with me just a small travelling case and an attaché case for travel documents, so I was quickly through Customs and Immigration, and on to the train to reserve as many seats as possible for the clients. Though it was usual for these to be reserved in advance by Fourways often enough other users would park themselves in reserved seats. When the time for departure was very close, I noticed that the young Chinese lady who was part of our group was not on the train. She was a charming person who spoke very good English and was attending Edinburgh University. Inquiries of the others made me realize that she was still with the Customs people. I hurried back to the shed, and there she was, weeping profusely. Making myself known to the officer concerned, I found out that she had not declared several items that had been found in her luggage and she did not have, or so she said, enough money to pay the charges.

I asked the officer what had not been declared, and he pointed to the articles, including perfume and a watch. I persuaded the Customs Officer that the watch could be imitation gold, and the perfume not worth the advertised price. In those days quite a lot of the Customs people were used to me passing through the crowds of tourists and very often they were most helpful. The final amount of duty charged was in the region of eight or nine pounds, and as the young lady had said that she had no money, I forked out and she promised to send the money to Fourways as soon as possible. She picked up the articles in question, stuffed them into her handbag and accompanied me to the train, which left immediately. She took her seat and I circulated with the clients as I passed along the corridors. When I came to young Miss Wong she said that she would now pay me, opened her purse, took out a roll of pound notes – there must have been at least a couple of hundred – and paid me handsomely for my trouble. She then gave me a visiting card of her uncle and invited me to ring up soon and have dinner with them. I did so shortly afterwards and he just happened to be the Chinese Consul-General and lived in Golders Green. They had gone to a lot of trouble to make the evening a memorable one, for Miss Wong was a great favourite and the meal was one such as I had not enjoyed since the King's birthday dinner at the British Consulate, somewhere in China, just after the end of the war in the Far East. I do hope that Miss Wong was not smuggling drugs, or that I had unwittingly participated.

Because of the difficulties of heating hotels and ensuring continual hot water in those days immediately after the war, there were no coach tours organized in winter, so I was now out of a job and stayed with my mother in Acton, West London. This was going to be a welcome rest – or so I thought. Then just before Christmas 1946, the telephone rang. It was Reginald Bezzant, production manager of the *News of the World*, who had travelled with his charming wife on one of my early tours. He wanted to know if I would consider going to the capitals of Europe for the *News of the World* to see if anything could be done to get the paper to European cities faster than other newspapers, and to arrange other points of sale.

I quickly planned it all and quoted my price for the two-month trip, taking note of the fact that I should not only get a reduction off my bills because I was on the newspaper staff, but also a travel agent into the bargain. The *News of the World* was very generous and I hope that the information I supplied later, and all the little metal plates I nailed on to lamp-posts all over Europe, paid them for their generosity. But the tour to Paris, Lyon, Marseilles, Cannes, Nice, Milan, Rome, Geneva, Lausanne, Montreux, Berne, Zurich and Lucerne was probably to be more important to me than to them. At the time of departure I was more or less engaged, by proxy, as I have previously mentioned, and I asked my fiancée to meet me in Marseilles. She never turned up and I have not heard from her since.

During my tours with Fourways, we nearly always had lunch at the Hotel Lebrun at Bastogne, on our way between Brussels and Switzerland, where I admired the younger daughter of the house, Annie. She had been decorated by the Americans for her courage during the Bastogne Pocket affair, and she served us at table. During the *News of the World* trip, we had spent some good hours together in Paris where she was staying with an aunt. But we finally decided that there was no future in the courtship for she was a very devout Catholic as were all the members of her family and she could never consider a future with anyone but a staunch Catholic. This I certainly wasn't and had no intention of ever being so, so we had kissed and said goodbye.

Between Lausanne and Interlaken lies the town of Château d'Oex and I had often been there with my tours and formed a friendship with the Director of Entertainments of the town, Roy Juvet. As I was approaching Château d'Oex in the train, I suddenly decided that I would stop off there for about half an hour, just to have a quick drink with Roy. I got off the train with my luggage, made inquiries and found that the next train was in half an hour. I entrusted my bags to the station-master who knew my friend, and went to the hotel he usually frequented. He was not there, but the manager phoned the ski-station where he was and passed the phone to me. Roy suggested I spend a few days there, but I said I was catching the next train and had left my luggage there for that purpose. OK, he said, I'll be with you in a few minutes.

I had a drink with the manager while I waited. The minutes passed and still Roy was not there. The time was up and I told the manager to give my regards to Roy and apologize for me. He said that it was useless for me to go, for my luggage was no longer with the station-master and Roy had instructed him not to disclose where it now was. The result was that I had to stay, at Roy's expense, at a fine hotel and he supplied all that I required for skiing. I decided that this was true friendship and so I accepted it all with a laugh. On the third day I nearly broke my neck on the ski slopes, but the damage turned out to be only a strained knee, necessitating a tight bandage and a stick. On the tenth day a reception was organized – actually not to receive me but to say goodbye, for I had made many more friends there. I threw away the bandage and the stick and danced for the best part of the night with the Mayor's daughters. Then I set off to Interlaken with my whole schedule now upset. Instead of staying there for three days, I spent only a few hours, and then quickly visited Berne and Basle, arriving in Lucerne almost back on schedule. With the tours, I had always stayed at the Gotthard-Terminus, right opposite the station (it is now a restaurant and offices). On this occasion I did the same for I was known there and always welcome and perhaps a bit spoiled.

Then I went round the corner to the Flora Garten where, with clients, I had spent many happy evenings. In fact, wherever we spent the evening, I used to go out with the travellers to taverns or restaurants where local colour could be seen, and in most cases I used to entertain them myself by singing songs they knew and some they did not know. Among my favourite orchestras, with whom I had sung in many Swiss towns, was that of Georg Wigner with his pianist/accordionist Marcel Keller, singer Charles Eschman, bass Olav Ledingruber and especially the Hungarian violinist Nora Barabàs who could make her instrument talk to us. There they were now, playing for a *thé-dansant* at the Flora. Immediately Georg suggested I come along to the Flora that evening, for it was Fastnacht. Fastnacht in Lucerne, and Basle particularly, is the time when the ladies are permitted practically anything. They dress up in strange clothes, and masks, which they usually take off at midnight, and go out to enjoy themselves. During that evening, I danced and danced to Georg and his orchestra and then at midnight, Georg invited me to go up on the platform to sing a few songs. Delighted, I agreed, and sang songs in French, German, Italian and English, finishing with 'Sheikh of Araby', before I felt that it was time to go. To loud applause I went down the steps from the platform to the floor and had one foot on the last step and one foot on the dance floor, when a charming young lady stepped towards me, dressed in old black lace from head to toe, with a funny wee old-fashioned lace cap on her head and carrying a black mask, just removed, in her hand. In perfect English she asked if she could please have the next dance.

How could I refuse such a charming request? I knew that my bachelor days were now almost over for before the end of that waltz, I had told her that she was the only girl in the whole world for me – would she be my wife? She thought I was mad at the time. Nevertheless Beryl Mary Häfliger and I were married before the end of the year, on 26 December 1947, and have lived happily ever since. When her mother was eventually told about me and my proposal, she was apparently quite happy for she herself was English and had been brought up in Exeter. But her father was of a very old distinguished Lucerne family whose name, Häfliger, can still be seen on many fine buildings there, and he was definitely against the union. He disapproved of the fact that I was a courier travelling widely in my job with much temptation elsewhere and would never be at home. However, when my papers of acceptance into the Metropolitan Police Force came through, he gave his accord immediately for he thought that our London policemen were wonderful. He had been in London from 1912–22 and had visited Kew Gardens one day. It was Sunday and he had a very important appointment early on the Monday. A thick, green fog came down and all transport was stopped. He began to walk back towards Islington, in North London, during that late afternoon, and became of course hopelessly lost. Then out of the thick fog there appeared the huge figure of a policeman who asked him what he was doing out in such a pea-souper. In his halting English he explained the situation. The policeman took him to the end of his beat and waited until his colleague on the next beat came along and passed him over into his care. This second policeman took him to the end of his beat and handed him over to the next colleague and at long last, in the early hours of Monday morning, Mr Häfliger was back in Islington. Hence his very high regard for London policemen.

I was attached to Golders Green police station when we got married in Switzerland. Because of all the post-war restrictions, it had been decided that we should have a ceremony, or really two because the legal union of two people in Switzerland takes place at the City Hall in a civic ceremony and the church wedding is more or less incidental. One was to take place in Switzerland, to be organized by Beryl, and then another, after our honeymoon in Engelberg, in the Golders Green area for the sake of my own family. I phoned the

Bishop of London and asked for advice on how to become Church of England rather than Catholic. He suggested I should go and see Edward Yorke, the vicar of St Luke's, Hampstead, and very soon I was singing in the choir there and had also made arrangements for our wedding to take place in January 1948.

Then came Beryl's invitations, for form only, for my family and friends, to the Swiss ceremony at St Luke's Church in Lucerne on 27 December 1947. Both weddings taking place in St Luke's was rather a coincidence and augured well for our future. A friend of Beryl's sang a beautiful 'Ave Maria' while Nora Barabàs, the Hungarian violinist, played Handel's 'Largo'.

After we were married in Lucerne, there was a reception at The Du Lac – Flora Garden with mountains of food shared by numerous members of my new family and lots of Beryl's friends. Beryl's brother Raymond rose to read messages and telegrams. 'There are here two telegrams,' he said. 'Both of them wish the newly married couple much health, happiness and children. The first one is signed SHERLOCK HOLMES of Scotland Yard, London, and the other one comes from WINSTON CHURCHILL of No 10 Downing Street.' Both were made up by the MC, Heiri Schurman, but within the next two years or so I was not only at Scotland Yard, but was also on protection of Winston Churchill. How strange is fate.

We went to Engelberg for our honeymoon – to ski, we had hoped, but it rained the whole time we were there – until we were coming back down the mountain by rail, when it snowed beautiful snow, transforming everything within minutes into a lovely white wonderland, ideal for skiing. But it was a grand holiday at a lovely hotel with nice clients, and plenty of dancing and we enjoyed it very much.

The journey back to England by train was really awful, for the whole of north-eastern France was under water and the train could only travel very slowly. There was no restaurant or buffet and we soon got through the food and drink we had brought with us. I decided that I would get out at the next station and buy something to eat and drink. The station arrived and the station-master said that there would be plenty of time so I dashed for the buffet. Suddenly I heard the horn blow and looked round to see the train pulling away from the station. I hurried out, waited for some of the coaches to pass and then, considering that our coach should be just about to pass I jumped on. I found myself in a third-class compartment full of local people with their dogs, cats, pigs and chickens. I struggled through them to the end door where I found a guard. The door was locked and he informed me that because of the lack of engines, a couple of local coaches had been hitched to the rear of the express Basle–Calais.

I waited patiently for the next stop, got out and rejoined the front portion of the train and walked into my original compartment to find everybody staring at me, wondering where I had come from. They had searched every coach on the forward part of the train, from locked end door to locked end door, not knowing, as I had not known, that two local coaches had been added. They had come to the awful conclusion that I had been left in the station buffet miles away. There was a happy reunion and I told them that the train had been moving so slowly that I had decided to run behind to get some fresh air. I told the truth later, of course. When we eventually arrived at Calais, it was to find that the boat-train had left hours before and we were being shunted to Boulogne for the ferry there. At Boulogne we had several hours to wait, but a meal had been laid on for the train passengers, which was composed of the fattest, oiliest steak and chips the world has ever seen – and this before the coming crossing of the English Channel, in a violent storm with waves of tremendous proportions. But we were all hungry and most of us did try to consume some of the repast though most of the passengers later lost it overboard. Beryl and I eventually arrived at Hendon, where my sister had a nice cup of tea and sandwiches ready. We were twenty-six hours late.

Shortly after our wedding in Hampstead, the vicar, Mr Yorke, invited us to dinner and during the fireside chat afterwards, I told him the story of the Catholic girl, Annie Lebrun, and how we had liked each other, but that her religious views and mine did not coincide and that we had had to say goodbye. Mr Yorke listened very carefully to all I said and at the end he quietly asked me, 'Would you like to have her address now?' Beryl and I were absolutely dumbfounded, but he explained that for many, many years he had spent his holidays at the Hotel Lebrun in Bastogne and knew the family extremely well. Annie had married an American and was living happily in the United States.

8

A COPPER IN UNIFORM

MY SERVICE IN THE UNIFORMED branch of the Metropolitan Police Force was quite undistinguished. I considered myself a good policeman and could take care of any situation that cropped up on the beat, but nothing extraordinary seemed to occur in my neck of the woods, and in those days if you had any information concerning real crime it had to be passed to the Criminal Investigation Department. Later on, the uniformed branch were allowed to continue investigating crimes that they had uncovered, but always with CID advice. Though it might not have been terribly exciting, one felt that one was doing a service and there was satisfaction in knowing that the job was a permanent one, for England will always require a police force. There was no shortage of foreigners in the area and it was very interesting to be able to converse in different languages with them. There were also times when, even though I was used to the sight of blood after eight years in the Legion, I was shocked. The worst occasion was when a poor man threw himself into the path of an underground train at Golders Green Station. It served no purpose to ask people to keep away from a certain area of the platform because there had been a horrible accident – they wanted to see the awful truth. They then blamed the staff and police force when, having seen the blood and guts lying about, they were violently ill. Thank heavens it does not often happen.

Millionaires' Row was also on our manor and several times I discovered that some fine houses had been broken into and I was obliged to call the Station for CID officers to attend. Nothing could be touched until the fingerprint men had done their work, but the horrifying things that human beings can do to the rooms and walls of houses, and the personal belongings of fellow-citizens, have to be seen to be believed.

One Sunday I was on duty in Hyde Park, near the Serpentine Bridge. There were hundreds of police on the roads in the Park for motorists were demonstrating against the rationing of petrol. I was, like the others, carrying my rolled oilskin cape, now discontinued but in those days a very useful instrument of dissuasion in delicate situations. It began to rain and I started to unroll my cape. Suddenly from the direction of Alexandra Gate loud screams were heard, then came the menacing trample of a rapidly approaching horse and there it was, having passed dozens of police officers in uniform lining both sides of the road, coming towards me. Clinging wildly to the horse's neck, with reins trailing dangerously almost to the ground, a young woman was shrieking for help which till then had not been forthcoming. When I saw the animal charging towards me on the other side of the road, I dashed across and waited, my cape at the ready. I ran alongside the horse, threw my cape over its head and grabbed the reins, succeeding in bringing the scared animal to a halt a few yards further on.

The young woman descended, took the reins rather shame-facedly, said a very brief 'Thank you' and turned to make her way back to the mews near Albert Hall, I suppose. Part of the stirrup had made a small rent in my trousers, on the thigh. It was not visible because it was hidden by my cape which I wore for the rest of the afternoon to protect me from the rain. But it was my Sunday uniform and the next day I reported to the stores to change them. A report of the details was submitted, I was charged three shillings and sixpence, and nothing further was ever heard about my having saved the rider from probable serious injury.

One day after some eighteen months' service, although I knew that two years was the usual period required on the beat before assignment to plain-clothes work, I submitted a report to the Superintendent, pointing out that I had really taken the job not to try shop doors for ever and ever, but in the hope that my knowledge of foreign people and their languages might be put to good use. Could I please be considered for the Special Branch? Within a very short time I went for an interview at Scotland Yard and then it appeared in Police Orders that I had been accepted and should report to the Chief Superintendent of the Special Branch on a certain date. I was a Detective-Constable at Scotland Yard at last. The work of Special Branch at one time was never disclosed to the public. Today more and more criticism is levelled at them in this new England of ours where to use a riot shield to protect oneself against the darts and stones of illegal pickets, is a sin; where shouts and calls for help when being attacked by a crowd of hooligans land on deaf ears; where senior civil servants can disclose confidential information to newspapers because they do not agree with the purport of it, and be acquitted in court. The militant trouble-makers and their supporters wish to emasculate not only the Special Branch, but the Police Force as a whole.

In those days, and I am sure it is still done in the interests of justice and the security of our land, a close check was kept on everything subversive and the ports and airports were watched to keep wanted men in and unwanted men out. I enjoyed the work very much and did not mind all the typewriting of reports, even though there were times when those reports came back from one's chief to be corrected and retyped. Very often I had coded messages from Interpol to translate which was interesting work, but they always seemed to come in the middle of the night when I was on Reserve Duty with the phone going every five minutes, and involved searches in the Criminal Records Office or our own records which were right at the top of the building in very dusty premises. I suppose that I complained as much as any of the others, but I did find the work rewarding.

Listening to speakers at Communist or Fascist meetings was a bore though, for they were always saying the same things. If the meeting was in a hall, then it was not too bad, because there was always the possibility of the chairman asking the stewards to check on the party membership of the audience, and if one was slung out, then that made the report that one had to complete so much shorter. In fact, some of the older officers who had been in the Special Branch for ages, told me that it had been common practice in the old days to wear big boots, smoke a pipe and look as much like a policeman as possible just to be thrown out.

The interviewing of applicants for naturalization could be very pleasant for they nearly always supplied a cup of tea or coffee and biscuits. But if they offered to buy you dinner, or lunch, then the papers they produced, and the stories they told, were always suspect and great care had to be exercised to make sure that undesirables were not proposed for naturalization.

In 1949 I spent six months in Newcastle on port surveillance working alongside the Immigration Authorities. I had to visit ships coming in and out of Tyne, checking on personal identities. I was also doing the same job at Newcastle's Cremlington Airport which was not very busy in those days. I enjoyed it very much for I thought it was a job well worth while, even though it did keep me separated from my wife. She was able to visit me pretty often though, because I was staying with an aunt and Beryl was always welcome.

Back in London one evening, on my birthday, I invited Beryl and two friends, Stephen Jay and his wife-to-be Angelina, to the Savoy for dinner. Stephen Jay ran a language school in Hendon Central, and Beryl gave German lessons there. During the course of the evening, Stephen disappeared for a while. Then came the announcement by Freddie Ballerini, one of the two orchestras at the Savoy at that time, that they were going to play 'Anita', a waltz composed by Edmund Murray. Stephen, in the background, had been given permission to record the song on tape, and though it is not very good, I still have it and it makes a lovely souvenir of that memorable evening. Beryl and I went often to the Savoy where we were treated as royalty every time and, in fact, were usually given the table where Princess Margaret was wont to be seated when she went to the restaurant. On each occasion thereafter, my waltz was played and people danced to it not knowing that the composer was in their midst.

Life at the Yard had not really changed very much by 1950. Through being on reserve during the night, I was slightly involved in a couple of very interesting spy cases which hit the headlines, but for the most part I was dealing with reports on subversive activities. On one occasion a famous star of the screen and television from outside Britain was the subject of my investigation. The person is now dead but I must say that, though there had been some connection with a subversive organization abroad, there was absolutely no evidence against him when the person became famous and spent most of the time in England. A Labour government was in power and there was not much unrest really, for after all, they printed a lot of paper money and borrowed a lot of foreign money so that they could keep the workers, who voted them in, as happy as possible.

Scotland Yard was a hot and airless place that torrid August in 1950. When I say Scotland Yard, I mean the old headquarters of the Metropolitan Police Force on the Embankment, just a stone's throw from the Cenotaph in Whitehall, and from the Houses of Parliament, not the modern building down in Petty France. With as much enthusiasm as I could muster in such weather, I waded through a pile of routine documents in the Special Branch office. I had just spent six months on port work at Newcastle upon Tyne, checking on people entering and leaving the country in ships, and also on planes using Newcastle Airport. I was now back at the Yard, spending a lot of time on Reserve or on the usual duties of the Branch like interrogation of aliens who had applied for naturalization, inquiries into the conduct of those suspected of subversive activities (in those days there were a number of Jewish terrorist organizations around). There were also Fascists, Communists and Anarchists so, though lots of the work was routine, it was not dull.

Time was sometimes wasted, as when, with another officer, I occupied a room in a Territorial Army Depot for a whole week, watching the HQ of the Anarchist Society. They had been printing pamphlets which did not really harm anybody, but had omitted the name of the printer on the pamphlets which was contrary to the law. At last, on a Friday afternoon, a taxi drew up at the door opposite our window, and we knew that our vigil was at an end – for out of it stepped a known anarchist, carrying boxes of pamphlets. We dashed down into the street and stopped the taxi as he prepared to drive off. He said he was not available as he was going to lunch, but when we produced our cards he changed his mind and asked how he could help. My colleague, Inspector Bill Jones, told him to drive us to the place where he had collected his last fare. After some argument about the ethics of it all, the cabbie finally took us to a West End location. It was the printer's, and down in the basement the printer himself denied that he had printed any pamphlets without his name and address. Bill then told him to pack up and come with us to the Yard for further investigation and he then owned up and promised that he would never do it again. We knew that it would be very difficult to make up a case against him but, in any case, Bill, who was more involved than I in the Anarchist movement, knew what he was about. He insisted that the man should carry on printing the pamphlets, but six copies of each one printed were to be sent to Inspector Jones at Scotland Yard in order for him to be kept up-to-date with the Anarchists' news.

When I had been in Special Branch but a short while, I had to go to the East End of London to interview an applicant for naturalization.

There were various exits from Scotland Yard in those days and I left my office on the third floor, traversed the bridge between the Old and New Building and started down the stone staircase leading to the Back Hall where most visitors had to report before being escorted to their destination. As I approached the half-glazed swing door at the bottom I heard raised voices and through the glass I saw a man with his right arm raised, his hand clutching a long butcher's knife. He seemed to be about to bring it down on the head or shoulders of the uniformed police constable sitting there at the table. Straight through the door I threw myself and smashed the would-be assailant to the floor, wrenching the knife from his grasp. Assisted by another constable who arrived at that moment on the scene, I took the man to Cannon Row Police Station, in the precincts of the Yard, and he was charged with attempted assault with a deadly weapon. I signed the charge sheet and the man was incarcerated. I returned to my room to type out a very short report of the event. 'At 11 am on . . ., the . . .th day of . . ., while passing through Back Hall, I heard . . . and then assisted by PC . . . I took the man to Cannon Row Police Station where he was charged.' I signed the report and placed it on my Squad Chief's desk (Chief Inspector Wilkinson) and off I went to my interrogation of the applicant.

Returning to my office at about 3 pm I was surprised to see my short report on my desk. Written in red pencil across it by the Chief Superintendent at that time, Frankie Bridges, was, 'You have not explained what you were doing in Back Hall at 11 am in the morning'. I retyped the short report, adding that I was on my way to catch a bus, and placed it on the absent Chief Superintendent's desk. That was the last I heard of the affair. Oh well! Another life saved, another commendation not made.

I was in the Reserve Room not many days later, hot and bored, when the buzzer sounded summoning me to the Chief Superintendent. 'Haven't you got a decent suit, Murray?' he said, frowning at the lightweight jacket I was wearing as relief from the heatwave.

'Yes sir,' I said crossly, 'I have several good suits, since you ask.'

'Don't use that tone of voice,' he grated. I told him that I was just answering his question.

'Well,' he said, 'you are going to need a suit for the job I have in mind for you. How would you like to go on protection?' Suddenly a memory flashed into my mind of the past New Year's Eve when I had been sent along to Carlton House to spend the night protecting

[81]

the Foreign Secretary, Ernest Bevin. Somebody had suggested the issue of an automatic pistol for the job, but the Superintendent spluttered, 'Not bloody likely. His truncheon will do.' I don't really know how he meant that. Wasn't Mr Bevin important enough? Or couldn't he trust me with a gun?

'It depends very much on the person I should have to protect,' I answered.

'So you are a policeman with prejudices are you? Well, I don't imagine you can have any reservations about the man I am assigning you to . . . it's Winston Churchill.'

Of course there were no objections. Some politicians I might have jibbed at, but if I had been invited to choose a man to act as bodyguard to, it would certainly have been Mr Churchill. Not once during the nearly fifteen years that followed did I really have any cause to regret my sentiment.

The assignment was the third memorable event of that August of 1950. The first was the birth of my son, William Anthony Lawrence a couple of weeks previously, and the second was the present my wife gave me to celebrate this birth – a set of oil paints.

9

I Become Churchill's Bodyguard

A WEEK LATER, HAVING DISPOSED of all my outstanding reports to the satisfaction of Frankie Bridges, on 4 September 1950 a police car shrilled its way out of Scotland Yard and across Westminster Bridge. I sat beside the driver, Bert Pringle, from the police car pool at Lambeth, a newly issued Webley Scott pistol tucked awkwardly into my jacket pocket (I was later issued with a shoulder holster) as we threaded our way through the London traffic. Our destination was Chartwell, near Westerham in Kent, the home of the Churchills since 1922, when he had bought it out of the twenty thousand pounds from the sale of *The World Crisis*, six volumes of a war history.

On the way to Chartwell, as we rolled through Streatham, Crystal Palace, Penge, Biggin Hill and Westerham, I pondered on this fascinating assignment. I had hardly seen Mr Churchill, let alone met him, and in his finest hours his name had come to me – thousands of miles away in a foreign army – as little more than an echo. But I knew that we had one thing in common: as young men we had both led highly adventurous lives. Curiosity, tinged with awe, mounted as the miles ticked away on the speedometer of the police car.

At length the car swung off the road, through a pair of high double gates, and into a short, semi-circular drive. It pulled to a halt in front of a largish, pleasant-looking manor house – Chartwell.

As an active politician, and Leader of the Opposition Party at the time (although other men in similar positions in the past had not had protection except on rare occasions), it was considered by the Home Office that there were sufficient reasons for Mr Churchill to have two Special Branch officers to protect him. As might be expected in Britain, their duties in peace-time consisted of dealing with minor nuisances, occasional threatening letters, bomb hoaxes and over-enthusiastic well-wishers, rather than any serious attempt on his life or on those of his family. But there was always a state of alert for one could never be certain. It was to replace one of the bodyguards, a sergeant who had been transferred to the Malayan Police Force, that I had arrived at Chartwell.

Sergeant Williams, who was to be my colleague until Sir Winston's retirement from the office of Prime Minister on 5 April 1955 – when I took over the job single-handed – came out of the house as the car drove up to the door. I was taken into the hall at Chartwell.

On a red leather-covered bench just inside the door sat Winston Churchill. The inevitable cigar was wedged firmly in his right hand, his head was tilted forward, his eyes closed. He seemed totally immersed in thought. Had I been asked to guess how he would have been dressed when I first encountered him, I might have cast my mind's eye over the thousands of newspaper photographs I had seen of him and might have found the right answer. He wore that highly individual outfit which had so often delighted the hearts of Press photographers. A beige Stetson sat squarely on his broad head, and he was clothed in that celebrated wartime garb he claimed to have invented, the siren suit; on his feet were black zip-up shoes. Sergeant Williams coughed discreetly, drawing Mr Churchill away from his deep concentration. He opened his eyes, inclined his head to an angle of about 45 degrees, and regarded us appraisingly. 'This is Murray, sir,' said Williams. Mr Churchill moved his cigar to his left hand. I took his extended right lightly in mine, taking care, as I had been warned, to avoid clasping it too firmly. It was a warning I was to give in future years to hundreds of people, distinguished and humble alike. The great man shook my hand, inspected me carefully . . . and belched.

As I struggled to keep surprise from my face, a smile, an immensely friendly smile, suffused his cherubic pink and white features. 'So you are Sergeant Murray. I trust that we shall get on well together for I have heard much about you. You have had a most interesting life . . . and I hear you even paint in oils.'

After our introduction had been completed, Mr Churchill left the house with a decided air – to impress me of course – and climbed slowly into the estate car which was waiting at the front door. Sergeant Williams took the driving seat and I climbed into the back beside the young valet, Norman McGowan. Before we set out I watched the valet place a flask in the back of the car. It contained ice and whisky and soda but we called it lemonade. He also loaded in a basketwork chair and table. The Master of Chartwell was off on his afternoon's overseeing.

We drove about a mile to a meadow on Bardogs Farm, owned by Mr Churchill and adjoining the Chartwell estate. There a group of farm workers, including three German ex-POWs, were levelling the land for pasture.

The table and chair were set up, another cigar selected from the leather case, a glass of the 'lemonade' was poured, and Mr C. settled down to direct operations for the next few hours.

The war memoirs of some of his colleagues, soldiers and politicians, tell how he loved to have a finger in every pie, often to the consternation of the pie-maker. Watching him that first afternoon, I realized something of the trials and tribulations which he must have constituted for them, when he would lend great enthusiasm to some project for a short while, only to change his mind completely some time later, usually to the advantage of the original project.

I describe that first afternoon not in any vein of carping criticism, but out of sheer amusement, because it was thoroughly amusing to me, although doubtless exasperating to the men on the job, to see the way he would decide on one piece of work one moment, like the levelling of a particular area, the sawing down of a particular tree or the removal of a certain boulder, only to stop everything and switch to something quite different after a quarter of an hour or so. But the main thing that was quite certain in all this, was that he thoroughly enjoyed himself on these occasions when he could find time to escape the rigorous calls to official duties. One of the first lessons I learned was the amount of subterfuge required, usually quite wasted, in the process of getting him to the meal table on time. The procedure on my second day was typical.

'Lunch is at 1.15 but do try and get him back by one o'clock,' Mrs Churchill whispered to me as we prepared another trip to Bardogs Farm. Then she said to her husband, 'Lunch at one o'clock darling, do not be late.'

The morning passed in much the same way as the previous afternoon, and as one o'clock approached I looked at my watch.

'It's one o'clock, sir,' I said, 'time for lunch.'

With great deliberation he pulled out his pocket watch and consulted it. 'No,' he said at last. 'It's only five to one. Why do you wish to rob me of five minutes of my life?'

'Sorry sir. My watch must be fast . . . but lunch is at one.'

He steadfastly sat at his open-air table, continuing to direct his workers, with no intention of returning for lunch. Twice more I mentioned the time, but it was nearly 1.30 before he finally returned to Chartwell.

That was a comparatively minor skirmish. On occasions, when he was completely absorbed in painting – and I do understand the feeling – I have watched a whole procession of his family, headed by Mrs Churchill, troop out to warn him of the passage of time and, often, of the fact that guests were waiting. The biggest explosion I ever heard from Mr Churchill, I think, was when he was painting either in Venice or Marrakesh. After repeated efforts by members of the family to get the Old Man to the luncheon table, Mrs Churchill sent one of the secretaries to tell him the time. It fell to the lot of young Jane Portal, niece of the famous Lord Portal of Hungerford, Air Marshal and Chief of Air Staff during World War Two. Jane waltzed down, just as she seemed to waltz blithely, charmingly, and sometimes solidly through life, to break into Winston's deep concentration on the painting he was doing. She began, 'Mr Churchill . . .' but that was as far as she got. I had warned her to cough, or scrape her shoes, or make her presence known.

'Goddam and blast it. Willyoubloodywellgoaway!'

I quickly stepped in and risked the blast falling on my shoulders. 'Sir, it is getting very late . . .' He got up and came, and I know that he was rather ashamed of his outburst, but he also knew that Miss Portal should have been more thoughtful. She was in his pay, and he could expect consideration so it was not really his fault. That I am sure, is why he never shouted at me – or was it perhaps that I always considered him first before I undertook anything in which he was involved?

Looking back, and fresh from a little reunion of the Churchill International Society when his nephew John Churchill, well-known artist, deposited a wreath on the Churchill grave at Bladon on the twentieth anniversary of his death, I realize that, with the exception of Grace Hamblin, Lady Churchill's housekeeper for so many years, and Jo Sturdee who was to become Lady Onslow, the other secretary-cum-typists were scared stiff of Mr Churchill. This led to quite a number of silly mistakes that had to be paid for.

One of the most important day-to-day chores of the bodyguard was to ensure that the cigar case carried by the detective was always full and available. Mr Churchill could never carry it himself for it was much too bulky and disfigured his form and destroyed his pockets.

Some people seem to believe that the cigar was nothing but a recognition symbol, a gimmick like Chamberlain's umbrella or Mr Baldwin's pipe, and that in private life Mr Churchill was far less addicted to cigars. But nothing was less true. Not only did he smoke them constantly during his waking hours (I only once saw him smoking a cigarette, at Nice airport, when he threw more than half of it away), but he even retained, with great care, all his part-smoked cigars. If we arrived at the House of Commons, for example, with the cigar half-finished, it was my task to extinguish it, roll it carefully in a tissue, to dry it, and place it in the ashtray in the back of the car. He insisted on this procedure and none of his cigar butts was left lying around. All unwanted butts were sent to Chartwell and given to one of the gardeners, Mr Kern, who dried them properly, crushed them, then used them in his pipe. It may well have been that the Old Man, as he was affectionately known, was determined to avoid repetition of the incident in America where someone did obtain one of the partly smoked cigars, and promptly auctioned it.

My role as honorary protector of the cigars did not begin auspiciously though. Mr Churchill's attitude towards his protectors was partly one of amusement. He could never quite agree with Scotland Yard that he needed to be protected, and he jokingly counselled me on arrival, 'You may have a gun, Sergeant Murray, but my cigars are more important to me than your gun.'

One wet afternoon, soon after I had taken up my new job, we left Chartwell to visit his pigs at Bardogs Farm. He was accompanied by his son-in-law, his daughter Mary's husband, Capt. Christopher Soames, who then managed his farm. He was fresh from the lunch table and was 'wearing' a brand new cigar in his mouth which should have lasted about an hour and a half. He dropped it as he got out of the car, in a deep puddle of water and mud. It was then I suddenly realized that I had left the cigar case on my table downstairs at Chartwell. Catastrophe.

'I'm sorry, sir,' I had to announce awkwardly to his request for another cigar. 'I have my gun but no cigars.'

'Oh dear, I am so unhappy without a cigar.'

Christopher offered him a cigarette, but he didn't want any of those 'atrocious things'. I offered to go back in the car to Chartwell, but he said that would be depriving my gun of the opportunity of

[87]

protecting him. During the next hour he must have repeated his desolation at least a dozen times, and he even refused to visit the market garden where he was expected, because he was without the cigar. I never ever repeated the mistake. Henceforth, cigars and gun were with me whatever the circumstances.

During those early days when he used to visit Bardogs to supervise the remodelling of the landscape, we gradually grew to know each other. To his evident approval I would lend the labourers a hand from time to time, shifting a boulder perhaps, or sawing a tree, and sometimes he would suggest that I would perhaps like to help move a rock to the bottom of the hill, and I would comply. However, I felt that I must let him know that protection, not destruction of the landscape, was my job, and we would join in battle. I would tell him that the boulder was too big and I couldn't manage it.

'I'm sure you can move it if you try,' he would say.

But knowing already what had happened to the last protection officer who had strained his back before he was chosen for the Malayan Police Force, which was one of the reasons that I was actually there, I would say, 'Sorry, Mr Churchill, but my principal aim in life at the present moment is the protection of your life, not to prejudice my own.' And he appeared to accept that doctrine without demur, knowing full well that I was right. He was just testing, seeing how far I could be pushed, and whether I could stand up for myself. This was a method he employed for all members of the staff before he was prepared to accept them.

One month after joining the Churchill entourage we were off to Denmark. It was the first of dozens of foreign journeys I was to make with him during the next fifteen years.

Mr Churchill was due to receive a number of awards in Denmark, including the much-prized Order of the Elephant, the Danes' highest decoration and one seldom given to commoners. He was also to be awarded the Danish Resistance Medal. When we arrived at Copenhagen I realized for the first time just how immense was the esteem in which he was held abroad. A crowd of about one hundred thousand had turned out to greet him on his drive from Kastrup Airport to the City Hall.

But a tiny handful of the crowd – Communists – found the visit anything but welcome and they paraded banners bearing the unequivocal demand that 'Churchill go home', as we made our way in a convoy of cars through packed streets. It was from this group that I received the one uneasy moment of the trip. The car in which I was travelling with two Danish security men was an exact duplicate of the one in which Mr Churchill was riding. Our car led the way, a device designed for trouble-makers. Suddenly a small object with sparks shooting from it flew in a lazy arc above the heads of the crowd to land immediately beneath our car. There was an instant of icy uncertainty, then a loud explosion came from beneath the car . . . and nothing else except volumes of evil-smelling smoke. It was only a firework thrown by one of the Commies.

We left it to the crowd to show their disapproval of the unfriendly gesture. They were doing this most vigorously, by tearing up the Communist banners and wading into the trouble-makers as we drove on down the street towards the City Hall. There Mr Churchill spoke from the small balcony to a vast sea of faces thronging the square below. Wearing on his left arm the insignia of the Danish Resistance, he declared, 'I am no enemy of any race or country, but it is the duty of every man and woman to resist tyranny from whatever quarter it comes, whatever language it speaks, whatever uniform it wears.' He received tumultuous applause.

We stayed at the Royal Palace as guests of the delightfully informal Danish Royal Family. King Frederick IV used in those days to shop regularly for his Queen, making his forays to the shops on a bicycle.

Several times while wandering round the Palace I met him. 'Hallo,' he would inquire briskly, 'how are they treating you? Do enjoy yourself while you are here.' He would then pass on, rather in the manner of a headmaster greeting a member of his sixth form.

Two incidents demonstrated King Frederick's thoroughly informal nature to me.

Norman McGowan, the valet, had served during the war in the Royal Navy and had acquired a number of tattoos on his arms. In his shirt-sleeves he was pressing a pair of Mr Churchill's trousers in an ante-room of the Palace when the King walked by. He stopped and they began to chat about the sea while I, in an adjacent room, could not help but hear what they said. 'Those are very interesting tattoos you have there. Would you like to see mine?' said the King, and when I looked into the ante-room, there he was rolling up his sleeves to show his marks to Norman, revealing some fine designs of birds and dragons on both arms. 'And I have more on my chest,' the King remarked as he went on his way. I later discovered that he was indeed a Navy man, having worked his way up from the lower deck in the Danish Navy which he had joined when he was a boy of seventeen.

In the second incident, the valet and I had gone out together for the evening, and we were sitting in a café in the famous Tivoli Amusement Gardens when a Palace servant rushed up in great consternation. (I always made a point of leaving details of my whereabouts with some responsible member of the staff when I went out.) The servant announced breathlessly that Norman had forgotten to prepare Mr Churchill's soup and the whole Palace was in turmoil as the VIP was complaining loudly. Every evening the Old Man would take a few spoons of jellied cold consommé, just before going to sleep, a ritual of many years' standing. On this particular evening, under the spell of the cabaret in the Gardens, Norman had completely forgotten.

We dashed out of the café and back to the Palace as fast as we could get through the busy streets. But when we arrived close to Mr Churchill's rooms, we found that all was calm. There were certainly no signs of commotion. King Frederick, hearing of the contretemps, had gone to the kitchen himself and prepared the consommé, then had placed it in a silver bowl and served it to the Old Man himself. The valet spent a rather anxious night, visualizing a severe reprimand the next day. But in the morning Mr Churchill said to him, with an amused glint in his eye, 'Norman, I don't at all mind you not finding time to do your valeting – so long as you always find a king to do it for you.'

We returned to London after three days, and twenty minutes after landing, Mr Churchill was airborne again, this time heading for the Newmarket races, where his horse Colonist II was running. His schedule was a remarkable one for a man of seventy-five years, for here he was after a most strenuous three days in Denmark, able to find time to attend the races at Newmarket before flying on to the Conservative Party Conference at Blackpool, which he was to address the following day.

I, too, was going to Blackpool, with some of Mr Churchill's luggage which he had not been able to find room for in the small plane, but my journey was by car. Hendon was more or less on the route between the airport and Blackpool, so I had just time to drop off to see my family and pick up some clean clothes, before setting off once again.

Now Blackpool was a long, traffic-crowded journey from London, for there were no motorways in those days, and to add to our troubles, we had a puncture near Derby. It was close on 11 pm when we finally reached Blackpool and the hotel at Lytham St Annes where the party were staying. On entering the hotel it seemed as if everyone there had been waiting on tenterhooks for our arrival, but it was not until I saw Norman that I found out what it was all about. Mr Churchill's bedroom slippers were in one of the cases we had brought from the airport, and Mr Churchill had been shouting for them all evening. I hurried up to his room with the case and found him sitting up in bed. Two secretaries were perched beside the bed and another was typing away furiously in an adjoining room – Mr Churchill had decided to redraft his conference speech. On such occasions there was always frantic activity. I have even seen a secretary sitting in the back of his car, a typewriter balanced precariously on her knees while Mr Churchill made last-minute alterations to a speech en route to Parliament or an important meeting. He looked up as I entered the room. 'Good morning, sir,' I said, 'I hear you wish to see me.'

'Oh! there you are,' he roared irascibly, but seeming to sense that he really ought to wait a little for an explanation of our late arrival, he continued on a calmer note, 'I say, did you get lost? Do you have my slippers?'

'If your slippers are in this case, then I have them,' I said.

'Thank you very much, but you have been a very long time you know. I have been here for hours.'

'Yes, sir,' I replied, 'but you came by aeroplane and I by car. What's more we had a puncture at Derby.'

'Ah!' he said, and he glanced down at his papers for a moment. Then he looked up at me over the top of his reading spectacles and with that warm, indescribably puckish, wonderful expression that could occasionally transform his stern features, he added, 'I do remember so well when I was young, we always managed to break down, and it was always in a big town.'

He chuckled momentarily at this recollection of his youth, then turning to the waiting secretary, he said, 'I do beg your pardon, that was very important. Where were we? For many years now the Socialists have been . . .' I left the room to look for my own luggage.

The politeness he had shown to his secretaries on that occasion was entirely customary. His code of courtesy with its strong

Victorian-cum-Edwardian undertones, was deeply ingrained. One rather charming vignette, an incident at Chartwell, illustrates this.

As a man always surrounded by aides of one sort or another, it was perhaps not surprising that he had no real idea of handling the London telephone, with its outwardly forbidding dial of letters and numbers. One afternoon we were sitting in his studio when he looked at the telephone then said to Miss Sturdee, the secretary of the moment, 'Well, I suppose I shall have to learn to use one of these new-fangled contraptions some day.'

'It's really quite simple,' said Miss Sturdee. 'All you do is dial the first three letters of the exchange you wish to call, and then the number you require. For example,' she continued, 'if you wish to speak to Sergeant Murray at home, you just dial SUN, for Sunnyhill which is Hendon, then 2705 which is the number. But there are also special numbers, for instance, if you want to know the time you just dial TIM.'

'Really? Then I must try that now,' and he lifted up the receiver and carefully dialled TIM. After a moment a woman's voice was heard to announce with precise enunciation, 'At the third stroke it will be three twenty-five and twenty seconds.'

'Thank you very much,' said Mr Churchill, checking the time with his own pocket watch. He was about to replace the receiver when the precise voice went on.

'At the third stroke it will be three twenty-five and thirty seconds.'

'Thank you very much,' said Mr Churchill, quite overwhelmed by the persistently efficient female at the other end of the line. Before he could get the receiver back on the cradle, there she was again.

'At the third stroke . . .' and there was a grave look of puzzlement on his face. He was about to express his thanks again when Jo enlightened him by telling him that it was just a recording and if he did not put back the receiver the voice would go on all night. 'Well, you might have told me earlier,' was his rather shamefaced comment.

One of the most fascinating aspects of my work was to see the galaxy of famous people attracted to the Churchill residence at Chartwell, the London house at 28, Hyde Park Gate in Kensington and, in the periods of Premiership, to Downing Street and Chequers.

In those early months as bodyguard to Mr Churchill, three special visitors come particularly to mind: the Queen, who was then Princess Elizabeth, Field Marshal Smuts and Margaret Truman, daughter of the then President of the United States. There was always plenty for visitors to see at Chartwell. They admired the fine gardens, the pools, the golden orfe of which Mr Churchill was very proud, and the famous black swans, a post-war gift of Western Australia. He would invariably show his visitors around the estate, and normally the tour would include a few minutes feeding the fish from a special supply of gentles or maggots as they were commonly called, sent regularly express by train from Mexborough, in Yorkshire. Those maggots were certainly of a vintage variety and I can remember Mr Churchill telling all his guests, including the three I have just mentioned, and others like Vivien Leigh, Laurence Olivier, Margot Fonteyn, Lord 'Pug' Ismay and Princess Margaret, to mention a few, that each one had a pedigree and they should really consider feeding them themselves from the tin lid he always offered them. During the rail strike of 1955 the supply of maggots was cut off so I had the idea of producing my own, in an outhouse at Chartwell, but the resultant stench was so awful that Mrs Churchill persuaded me to abandon the project, even though it was proving successful. Luckily the strike did not last long so the fish did not really suffer.

Although always scrupulously attentive, Mr Churchill seldom seemed to make conversation with his guests on these tours of inspection, particularly if within general earshot. On the visit of Princess Elizabeth and her sister, for instance, it was Mrs Churchill who made practically all the conversation, and it was much the same with Field Marshal Smuts' visit. When they walked together and other people were within range, the conversation was of the most banal variety, but I noticed that when they were able to wander away from the rest of the party, they became deeply engrossed. It wasn't surprising that these two great statesmen always got on harmoniously for I think that the Old Man had greater respect and admiration for the Field Marshal than for any other man living at that time.

In public I frequently noticed that Mr Churchill became very bored. On visits to places of interest, for example, he was seldom roused unless there were strong historical associations, especially with naval history. For this subject he nurtured a deep and lasting passion. It was partly because of the accurate historical allusions they always contained that he would devour each of C. S. Forester's Captain Hornblower stories as soon as he laid hands on it. He was such a devotee of the celebrated Captain, in fact, that Forester would send him, from his home in America, an autographed copy of each new work. When the author came to visit England he was invited to Chartwell for lunch.

10

MARRAKESH AGAIN

In DECEMBER 1950 CAME MY second visit to Marrakesh in Morocco. I had known Marrakesh from my days in the Foreign Legion, and Mr Churchill was no stranger to the town either, having spent some time there with President Roosevelt after the Casablanca Conference and then again when he was convalescing after a bout of flu picked up in the Middle East. He became very friendly with the Pasha who died in 1956.

On this trip I found myself plunged almost at once into one of the most intriguing encounters of my career. Hardly had the party, comprising Mrs Churchill, Lord Cherwell ('The Prof'), General Sir Henry Pownall, two secretaries, Sergeant Williams and myself, settled in when I was informed by the French police that a certain retired colonel of the French Army had disclosed his intention in Casablanca to visit Mr Churchill. Now this man, whose sanity was very suspect, was known to the police of the area because on a previous occasion he had succeeded in getting an interview with Mr Churchill, due to a misunderstanding by a member of the staff. That was before I joined the household. He had apparently arrived just at the time someone else had been expected, and had been admitted to Mr Churchill's presence. The mistake was only discovered a few minutes later when the correct visitor turned up.

This time I was determined that no such mistake was going to happen and so I suggested to the manager of the Hotel Mamounia that when the colonel tried to book his room, as it was felt he would, he should be informed that the hotel was full. A French police inspector and I fell in behind the lean, tanned figure of the colonel when he got off the train and we were happy when, following him to the Mamounia, we saw him accept with resignation the news that the hotel was full. Off he went to another, smaller hotel some 500 metres away, where he took a room but informed the receptionist that he would be taking his food at the Mamounia. This we could not reasonably ask the manager to object to. My French colleague and I entered the colonel's hotel room with the manager as soon as possible and made a quick search of his baggage. Only one object interested us – a loaded 9mm revolver which was immediately confiscated, even though, as a retired officer, he probably had permission to carry it with him.

Back at the Mamounia I arranged for the allocation of a table in the restaurant for myself and an adjoining table for the colonel as far away as possible from the Churchill table in the corner. All other tables were to be marked 'Reserved'.

At lunch the first day, everything went according to plan. I had been seated for just a few moments when the colonel arrived, to be shepherded to the next table as arranged. He began his meal, but after only a few minutes he brought out some papers which he placed on the tablecloth. 'Waiter,' he called, 'is there a mathematician in the house?'

The waiter began to say that he did not know, when he caught my eye and said, '. . . unless Monsieur knows anything about figures.'

'Why as a matter of fact,' said I in my almost perfect French, 'I know about some kinds of figures, but I am certainly not a mathematician, ha! ha!'

He took the bait and the conversation started. After about ten minutes we had joined our tables and he was telling me that Mr Churchill was staying at the hotel, that he knew him and intended having a long conversation with him. He also had something for him (this last was stated with some apparent menace, and I did not like it).

All this time, from the other side of the restaurant, Mr Churchill kept throwing glances in my direction, obviously wondering how on earth I could protect him from the other side of the room. The colonel put quite a different interpretation on these glances, and his interpretation was strengthened when Mr Churchill and his party made to leave at the end of the meal. As they moved towards the exit, the Old Man looked towards me and bowed in recognition. The colonel was delighted. 'See,' he said, 'he remembers me.' He rose quickly from his seat and took a pace forward, but I rapidly put a restraining hand on his arm and said, 'Take care, sir. Do you see that heavily built, moustached man behind Mr Churchill?' (It was Sergeant Williams.) 'That is the bodyguard and I've heard he can be very rough with anybody who tries to approach the Old Man.'

He hesitated for a moment then took my advice and returned to his seat. As we continued our meal he told me, with a strange fanatical look in his eye, that his real name was Count Jean Georges Boudila de Villecomtel and that he was a descendant of St Louis of France through his aunt, the Marquise de Villecomtel, and of Henry IV of France through his father, Count de Par-le-Bosc. After retiring from the Army where he had been the Colonel Commanding the Setif Region in Algeria, he had become a lecturer in politics and had suggested a Western bloc against Russia to be composed of France, Britain, Italy, Holland, Belgium, Spain, Switzerland and Portugal. For four days the Colonel and I ate together at the hotel, and in fact, I only left his side when he returned to his own hotel to sleep, or when Mr Churchill left for his painting expeditions and I was able to join the entourage without the colonel's knowledge. He thought that I was there on business and had to go visiting in the district. The main reason he had to see my protégé, he unveiled to me at last, was because he had devised a mathematical formula for ensuring world peace. I had no doubt at all that he was mentally unbalanced, so potentially dangerous. I stuck, leech-like, to him and throughout that period he never once suspected that I was anything but a business traveller, with a taste for enjoying my travels. My Legion-acquired French passed a very severe test with flying colours on that occasion.

The subject of the missing revolver never arose between us, although he had missed it at once and reported it to the police. It was eventually returned to him in Casablanca.

On the fourth day of our strange liaison, there was a *thé dansant* in the ballroom of the hotel, which the colonel and I attended. Mr Churchill was not going out; he was resting, as he was receiving guests that evening. I was dancing with the French wife (though they were, I think, separated) of a Nottinghamshire man. She was very friendly with the French Consul, if I remember rightly, a very pleasant lady, and we had met at a Foreign Legion reunion in my honour, and her friend was dancing with the colonel. Now she knew that I was with Mr Churchill, but she did not know why I was associating with the colonel, of course. They had been dancing for a few minutes, when he suddenly stopped in the middle of the dance floor, looked hard at me, and walked straight out of the hotel.

Back at his own hotel he packed his bags, settled his bill, and went to the railway station where he caught the first train back to Casablanca. His companion, completely taken aback at his impoliteness in leaving her so abruptly, explained to me that all she had said was, 'How long have you known Mr Churchill's bodyguard?'

Of course I could then tell the whole story to Mr Churchill who was most amused and glad that he had not spoilt my fun by coming to speak with me in the restaurant, and he congratulated me for having his safety so much at heart.

The day-to-day routine of the protection officer is frequently leavened by minor alarms and excursions, not long-drawn-out intrigues such as the affair of the colonel, but sudden upheavals. I vividly recall two such incidents on that visit to Marrakesh.

On the first occasion Sergeant Williams and I were standing outside Mr Churchill's suite in the hotel when an almighty roar emanated from inside. We moved very quickly towards the door when it opened suddenly and Norman, the valet, emerged, grinning broadly. All was well, he assured us, and explained that his boss had been taking his bath and as usual, had turned over on to his hands and knees preparatory to bringing one leg at a time over the edge. As he did so his behind had come into contact with the hot water tap – hence the roar.

The second incident also involved Norman. He had been sent up to Mr Churchill's room to get some eye-drops for him. Mr Churchill was sitting in the lounge at the time reading a dispatch he had just received. Norman returned with an eye-bath full of the lotion and placed it in Mr Churchill's hand. Without looking up from his papers, feeling a glass in his hand, he did what he usually did, rather absent-mindedly on this occasion; he took a drink from it – and in an instant the lounge was in an uproar. When he saw Norman struggling unsuccessfully to contain his laughter, he began to storm once more, but very suddenly his rage subsided and he smiled and said grudgingly, 'Well, I am sure that I would have laughed as well, had I been in your place.'

This fundamental tolerance towards members of his staff was a factor I came to notice increasingly as time went on and a very good example occurred at Chartwell a few months afterwards, when once more the valet was involved.

It was late at night and the old manor house was silent save for the sound of a gramophone in Mr Churchill's study. Through the half-open door came a selection of old-fashioned nostalgic songs. 'Tipperary', 'Keep the Home Fires Burning', 'Soldiers of the Queen', Peeping into the room at the top of the stairs I could see the Old Man deep in his favourite armchair, his chin resting on his chest, his eyes closed in reverie. The brave, sad songs came rather scratchily from the well-worn records, while he constantly twisted the gold ring on his right hand, pausing occasionally to wipe away a tear from his eye. Suddenly the blare of jazz blazed forth from the machine, but he was so deep in the past that for several seconds there was no reaction, then suddenly, 'What the hell is this then, Norman?'

With a grin Norman said, 'I thought we should have a change from all those old records.'

Mr Churchill appeared to be quite displeased for a moment, then relented and said, rather wryly, 'Well I don't think much of your choice. Mine was much better.'

It was in Marrakesh where I was first assigned a role I was to fulfil throughout the many years of service as bodyguard to Mr Churchill – official photographer to Churchill the artist.

His Leica camera was placed round my neck, on its strap, one morning when we were out painting the Ourika Valley view towards the Atlas Mountains, by Mr Churchill's great friend 'The Prof', Lord Cherwell, the Oxford scientist. I was then instructed by him in its use. The idea was to take photographs of the scene that Mr Churchill was painting so that should he leave the scene because of inclement weather, meals or recall to London, he would be able to complete the painting in the studio or in a hotel room. By the use of sticky tape, scissors and a lot of ingenuity I proved myself equal to the task and quite a number of the Churchill masterpieces remain as proof.

This practice was excellent experience though, because combined with my own knowledge as a painter it enabled me to choose scenes that I knew the Old Man would like to paint when he asked me to go out and select sites for him, as he frequently did, to save time.

As an amateur painter he showed great talent, there is no doubt of it, but he often maintained that my work was better than his. I had tried and failed several times to have a painting accepted in the Summer Exhibition of the Royal Academy, an exhibition at which several of his works were on view, he being an Academician Extraordinary. On one occasion I had my paintings in the back of my car which was parked opposite his house in Hyde Park Gate, Kensington. While we were chatting in the lounge, there being some time to spare before he went to Question Time at the House of Commons, the subject of painting came up as it often did – it makes such a nice change from politics he once told me. I mentioned the fact that my three pictures had been rejected, as usual. He said that he would like to see them, so I brought them in and leant them against three chairs in the room.

He looked at the first. 'Very good.' He looked at the second. 'Very, very good.' He looked at the third. 'Excellent. You know, they are much better than mine' – then he sort of giggled with his eyes squeezed up and shining impishly – 'but yours are judged on their merit . . .'

During those painting forays at Marrakesh in the Valley of the Ourika River with the Atlas Mountains so tempting in their icy glory, Mr Churchill became friendly with a gregarious young goat – a black, skinny, one-eyed creature which Arab children used to bring each day to the spot where he was at work on his picture. The goat allowed itself to be patted and would willingly accept food from the picnic table. But after a week I noticed that when the children came, the goat was not with them. They said that it had been sold in the market place. Mr Churchill, unaware of the tragedy, for tragedy it was for us, started to inquire about the goat, so I asked the young people to fetch us another one, to placate the Old Gentleman. The second goat was almost identical to the first one, he was black and very skinny, but there the resemblance ceased, for it was fractious and, what was more apparent, it had both eyes. After a short, very suspicious inspection by Mr Churchill, during which it was held very firmly by one of the children, the goat fought its way to freedom and resisted all attempts at blandishment, and the deception, already a fiasco, was condemned to complete and utter failure when the Old Man suddenly realised that it had both its eyes. He was disappointed in us quite a bit, and I saw tears in his eyes when I said to him, 'We are in Morocco, Mr Churchill, and everything is "Inchallah" – by the will of God.'

One of the great attractions of Marrakesh for Mr Churchill was the man I have already mentioned, Haj Thami el-Mezueri el-Glaoui, the Pasha of Marrakesh, a figure as fabulous as Kublai Khan. For fifty years, until he died a broken man in 1956, El Glaoui lived the life of a great potentate from A Thousand and One Nights, absolute ruler of some three million Berber tribesmen. At the time of his death he must have been one of the richest men in the world, his fortune built from the tithes he wrested from all the almond, saffron and olive harvests in his vast domain, and from his substantial interests in French-run mines and factories in North Africa.

The Moroccan Nationalist Movement first made its appearance in 1934, and Sultan Mohammed V Ben Yussef acted as the acknowledged leader. When he refused to sign agreements with the French and get rid of the Astiqlal members of his entourage, they enlisted the help of the Pasha to induce the Sultan to come round to the French way of thinking – or almost. On 3 August 1953, pushed again by the French, about 350 pashas and *caïds* with some two thousand notables grouped round the Glaoui and declared their intention of deposing the Sultan. He would not abdicate, but agreed to go abroad to Ajaccio, Corsica, and then later he was taken to Madagascar. On 4 November 1955, the French again changed their policy and ben Yussuf returned to France. Four days later, France declared that he was the legitimate Sultan of Morocco and on 8 November, at St Germain-en-Laye, the Black Panther kneeled at the feet of the Sultan and begged forgiveness. The following year he died, humiliated.

The Sultan had pardoned the Pasha, but thenceforth he had been obliged to travel in a bullet-proof Rolls-Royce, surrounded by bodyguards and with a sub-machine gun on his lap. In 1950, at the time of our visit, he was practically omnipotent, running his own army and police, with his own courts to punish enemies and rivals. The banquets we attended at the palace had a splendour straight from the Arabian Nights. I did not dine in the main banqueting hall, of course, for I had to make frequent patrols outside to check on the security and gain face in the eyes of the Moroccan detectives by proving that protecting Mr Churchill was a very important job. With a number of the high officials of the palace, we ate in an adjoining room with one or other of the Pasha's numerous sons presiding.

There were no knives and forks at these functions, of course, as it was expected that one should eat with the fingers. In so doing one paid them a considerable compliment and guaranteed their respect and friendship. The ritual was always the same. Soup came first, then an immense silver bowl, nearly a yard across, would be placed on a low table round which we all sat cross-legged. In the bowl would be pieces of meat, nearly always lamb, never pork, the mere mention of which would have caused outrage. The lamb was liberally coated with fat sauce, and rice or cous-cous (ground semolina). Into this we would dig the thumb and first two fingers of the right hand, then work the meat and grain into a sticky ball with the fat, and pop it into the mouth.

After so filling a dinner it was never difficult to produce the polite Arabic response to a good meal – a belch. Whenever I did this, (something my colleague Williams refused to emulate, and he was so 'I'm-never-coming-down-to-your-level'-minded that he used a knife and fork and looked forward to when he could return to the hotel and a sandwich), one of the servants would immediately bring along a new bottle of champagne, for although nobody at the palace drank intoxicating liquor (in front of witnesses or the Pasha) there was always plenty for the guests. I got on very well with the Black Panther and his sons and my Arabic expressions, picked up in the Foreign Legion, seemed to amuse them immensely.

I last saw El Glaoui, not in his own domain, but in London, where he was the guest of Mr Churchill, or Sir Winston as he had by then become as a Knight of the Order of the Garter, at the Coronation of HM Queen Elizabeth II, in 1953. The incidents of the visit I recall are the delight with which both men watched the fireworks display from the top floor of the Air Ministry building, off Whitehall, and the absolutely fantastic crowd that waited for them when they returned to the street level once more. It was after midnight and Collins, the No 10 chauffeur from the Ministry of Works in those days, and I had great difficulty getting the two of them, Sir Winston in dinner jacket and El Glaoui in full Arab ceremonial dress, across the pavement and into the car. The crowd was cheering like mad and singing 'For he's a jolly good fellow'.

At last we were in the car, but even then the crowd was so thick that after we had moved only a few yards, we found ourselves confronted by a big Post Office van which had been invisible because of the people sitting on the bonnet. We had to reverse very, very carefully before being able to continue on our way. Gradually the last remaining well-wisher jumped off the bonnet and we sped towards the Savoy Hotel, where the Pasha was staying. Sir Winston asked me to see him to his room, but it was not necessary as his own bodyguard was waiting for him. I never did find out why they had not been with us before.

I was very saddened to hear of El Glaoui's downfall and of the aura of disgrace which hung around him at the time of his demise. When I knew him, age had worn down his iron hand and he seemed to be nothing more than a benevolent old man.

When he left London, Sir Winston asked me to accompany him to Victoria Station in his own car, with Collins, the chauffeur. I made arrangements, in Sir Winston's name, for the car to be allowed right on to the platform, to the level of the Pasha's compartment. Just before he stepped on to the train, he turned and handed a fiver to Collins, and shook my hand warmly saying, 'Barak Allah fik,' (May Allah bless you) and I replied, as we both salaamed 'Wa alaikum salam sayyidi' (and on you be the peace of God) though it is generally supposed that the greeting is used only between Moslems and never to any infidel. Back in the car, Collins turned to me and said, 'Eddie, that was the whitest coloured man I ever met.'

The pitfalls which await the famous in their public appearances must be manifold, and once or twice Mr Churchill came near to grief when I was in attendance. The first occasion was in May 1951, a few months after our return from Marrakesh. He had gone to Glasgow to attend an important civic function at the City Hall and suddenly, when he was surrounded by a host of dignitaries, he called me across and explained, very briefly, that he had forgotten his false teeth at the hotel. 'I can talk all right without them, but I'm afraid I shall find it very difficult to eat without them. Would you be very kind and fetch them for me?'

I hurried back to the hotel, found the teeth, and returned with equal speed to the City Hall. Mr Churchill was just entering the lift as I entered the hall, accompanied by the Lord Provost and several other eminent citizens. I squeezed in with them. I had the teeth in a clean handkerchief and I said, in a conspiratorial fashion to him, 'I've got them, sir.'

'What have you got, Murray?' he replied, in the full hearing of the group of dignitaries, all very interested of course.

'Something you forgot at the hotel,' I whispered, not wishing to embarrass him.

But my secrecy, intriguing to the party in the lift, was having exactly the effect I was seeking to avoid. Mr Churchill was becoming increasingly hot under the collar.

'Well, do tell me what you have for me,' he blurted out.

By now the lift had reached the floor of the banqueting hall and there was a general movement towards the doors. 'Your false teeth, sir,' I said, quite at the end of my tether. 'Here are your false teeth . . . I hope you have a very good lunch,' and I thrust the handkerchief and contents into his hand.

'Thank you very much,' he said, and beamed at me.

A rather similar sort of incident occurred during the 1955 election, when the Old Man was speaking at Bedford on behalf of his son-in-law, Captain Christopher Soames, husband of Mary, and the MP for Bedford at the time.

On the way from London, with Sergeant Williams in the car with Mr Churchill and myself following in the police car, we pulled up when we had gone about half-way. Williams came across to me and said that the Old Man wanted to have a word with me. This was not unusual, because I was his paints man, his interpreter and his photographer all rolled up in one; he seemed to rely on me in any unusual circumstance, so I went across to the other car. 'My dear Murray, I have left my reading spectacles behind and I must have them for tonight. Can you retrieve them for me?'

'I'll certainly do my best,' I told him, intending to telephone Hyde Park Gate and have them sent on by some means yet to be devised. The two cars set off once more and as we drove I looked hopefully for a telephone box. But I might as well have been looking for champagne in the middle of the desert as to search for a telephone booth in the wilds of Bedfordshire. Mile after mile unfolded, and ne'er a glimpse of a telephone. Three times the Old Man stopped the cars to ask what I had done about his spectacles, and three times I assured him, with much more confidence than I actually felt, that he would have them in time for his speech at eight o'clock that evening.

Eventually we entered the outskirts of Bedford town and there was a car from the local police station to escort us. I stopped the procession and transferred myself to the police car escort and was whisked away to the police station. Everything came to a stop there when I explained the situation. Before long I was speaking with the secretary on duty at Hyde Park Gate. I told her to find the spectacles and I would contact a certain Government department and get them to send a dispatch rider to collect them.

Having arranged everything, I reported back to the Master and while he rested prior to the dinner, I changed into a dinner jacket and prepared to sweat it out until the motor-cyclist arrived. I knew, of course, that it was going to be a close thing, but then to complicate everything it began to rain heavily and there was quite a bit of fog about.

The time dragged on, with no sign of the DR, and eventually it was 7.45 pm and time for Mr Churchill and his party to leave for the meeting. We got to the hall and Mr Churchill wanted to know what was happening. Once more I found myself saying, 'Don't worry, sir. You will have them in time for the speech.'

What he did not know was that I was in constant touch with the Chief of Police by radio, and that the whole force had been alerted to watch out for the motor-cyclist and to escort him to the hall as quickly as possible.

The meeting began with a speech by the chairman, but I did not hear it for I stood haplessly outside in the rain, trying to compel the DR to arrive by mental persuasion, not daring to contemplate the consternation on the platform, and the wrath of Mr Churchill, if he were forced to admit that he could make no speech as he was without his reading spectacles.

The chairman's speech ended, and in the applause, Captain Soames rose to address the huge audience. On and on he talked, for he knew about the missing spectacles and was playing for time. Eventually he had to come to the end of his peroration. His last words had died away and the applause was swelling through the hall, when I heard the roar of a motor-cycle engine outside. I dashed to the rider, told him to wait for me, snatched a parcel from his hand and hurried along to the platform. There the Chairman was just announcing the *pièce de résistance* of the evening as I tore the brown paper cover from the packet. To my utter consternation, I discovered that the secretary had sent, not one pair of spectacles, but three. Which were his reading glasses? I stared at them blankly for a few moments, bewildered. Suddenly the answer dawned on me for I recalled that each pair had stars on the side to indicate what they were for. Quick as a flash I remembered that the reading glasses were five-star like a certain brandy he often drank. I passed them to the first person in the line of people stretching along the dais, then he passed them on to the next person, and to the next, and the next, and at the instant he was getting on to his feet to speak, they were placed in Mr Churchill's hands. Amidst the great explosion of applause which greeted him as he rose, I saw him look towards the side of the hall where I stood, and with a wave of the hand and spectacles, and a very warm smile, he acknowledged the safe delivery.

As the Churchill oratory began to roll through that hall, I departed to organize a welcome meal for the dispatch rider, and a substantial tip which I knew would be reimbursed later by Mr Churchill.

But between the incident of the teeth and that of the glasses lay four momentous and eventful years.

11

ON OUR TRAVELS AGAIN

IN THE SUMMER OF 1951 we were off on our travels again, to France, Switzerland and Italy this time. The first stop was Paris, where Mr and Mrs Churchill spent a few days before moving on to Annecy, and ultimately on to Venice.

In Paris the Old Man decided that to ease an annoying skin rash from which he was then suffering, he required a hip-bath.

Now such an item, to say the least, was a rarity in Paris and the hotel manager seemed to doubt my sanity when I asked if he had one. 'What is wrong with our beautiful white baths, Monsieur?' he asked. So I had to venture into the streets of Paris, for a dozen telephone calls had failed to find one. For hours and hours I visited hardware stores in the French capital, but I might have been asking for a piece of the moon to judge from the reaction of most shop assistants. At last (no one could ever accuse me of giving up on a job) in a remote *arrondissement* I found one, paid for it, then bore it back in a taxi to the hotel in triumph. As I carried the strange object through the foyer of the hotel, all eyes were turned in my direction, including those of the manager, who could not believe his eyes. But I was very proud of my success and Mr Churchill was most gratified to receive the bath. For about a week he used it regularly, till its efficiency fell into doubt and it was discarded, and sent back to England to be put into storage at Chartwell, where it might still remain.

From Paris, the entourage moved on to Annecy, by train, where during the seven days we were there, it poured with rain unceasingly, and as we took the train for Venice, it was still raining.

As we neared Venice Sir Winston stuck his head out of the carriage window to study the approaching city. I was at his right shoulder for we had been talking about his painting material. Lady Churchill was out of the compartment at the time, preparing for the reception committee that would inevitably be at the station to meet us. Suddenly I grabbed him by the shoulder and dragged him back from the window . . . as a pylon, only inches from the side of the train, flashed past. There was no comment . . . for none was needed. He remained seated for the rest of the journey.

Venice, on the other hand, was golden in the unbroken sunshine. A city packed with people, most of them there for the film festival, a busy, excited and very exciting city. We had passed the night in a train, at Lausanne, Switzerland, in a siding, so that the party could enjoy the rest of the journey in the daytime between the Alps to Brig and the Simplon Tunnel, then across the Lombardy Plain to the Adriatic.

In the City of the Doges, most of the eminent visitors seemed to have booked in at the Excelsior Palace, where the Churchills were staying. Orson Welles, for instance, was frequently to be seen, and from the way he seemed to sit and study Mr Churchill from a distance, strategically placed in the lounge, one formed the strong impression that he was contemplating a film about Churchill's life, with Welles in the leading role. The Old Man, if he was aware of his regular surveillance, raised no objection to it. Whenever he encountered Welles, he would incline his head courteously in recognition, for he was a film addict, and would receive a reciprocal greeting.

Another resident of the Excelsior, who did not receive the Old Man's acknowledgment, was Errol Flynn, who was frequently more or less on hand, as if hoping for an introduction, but throughout our stay he went unnoticed – or at least unhonoured.

Mr Churchill bathed in the sea every day accompanied by his wife, just as they had done during their honeymoon, in September 1908. On this occasion they had been allocated a small canvas cabin immediately at the foot of the steps leading from the hotel to the beach, and it was my job, along with my colleague Williams and half a dozen Italian detectives, to ensure that the couple were not disturbed and that their privacy was not intruded on. To this effect, the Old Man had given strict instructions that on no account were photographs to be allowed. There was not much one could do, of course, about the photographs taken of them from boats while they were swimming or by long-range cameras, but our job was to ensure that no close-range snoopers were permitted to approach.

On one of the early days on the beach, Mr Churchill was sitting just outside the cabin after his swim, with a towel draped around his waist, when suddenly I spotted a man with a huge 35mm cine-camera creeping round the side of the cabin. Having got himself into a good position, he began to film my protégé who was just gazing at the sand being slightly weary, I suppose, from his exertions in the sea. I dashed towards the rear of the cabin, but the man saw me coming and rapidly moved off in the direction of the hotel. I overtook him and placed myself stubbornly in his path.

'*Niente tirato*,' he said, 'I took nothing.'

'No,' I said, 'then just show me how to open this camera.'

'You press the button there,' he said pointing to the relevant button.'

'Then press it,' I told him.

He protested, but I told him that he had said that he had not taken any photos, so if on opening, all the film was on one reel, that would prove him right. Should there be some film on both sides, he had been telling lies. 'Now press that button.'

He understood that there was no escape and opened up the camera and proved me right. Almost half of the film had been used. The photos were of course ruined by the exposure to the light, and the man angrily pulled it out, strewing it all over the beach. Miles and miles of it there seemed to be, lying forlornly on the sand like some defunct serpent. He shut the camera and left, fuming. The incident was at an end, or so I thought, while an audience of Williams and the Italian police who had stood by doing nothing but watch and smile, broke up and dispersed to their positions.

Next morning I was in the hotel lift with Mr Churchill, en route for the beach once more, when he said 'The *Daily Herald* informs me that you have been executing my orders. I am most pleased.' He said no more so I remained in a state of mild curiosity until he had finished his morning bathe and I was able to dash off and look at the newspaper. Therein was a report that one of Mr Churchill's secretaries had taken an unauthorized film from an Italian cameraman.

That afternoon, on returning from the beach with Mr Churchill, I was approached in the foyer of the hotel by none other than the unfortunate photographer. As he came forward to speak to me, I looked straight through him and went on my way in the lift with the Old Man.

The next day the British Consul-General came to see me and announced that the Chief of the Venice Police wished to interview me about an incident reported to him by a photographer. A member of the Consular staff accompanied me to the police station where the Chief showed me the complaint filed against me by the cameraman. This alleged that I had damaged his camera beyond repair and added for good measure that I had beaten the man so severely that he had to spend a day in hospital and avail himself of the services of a specialist. He wanted some two hundred pounds in damages and a written apology signed by Mr Churchill.

I made a statement, giving the true account of the incident, and as I signed it I asked the Police Chief to let me have a copy of it for transmission to Scotland Yard. He wanted to know what Scotland Yard would want with a copy of my statement. 'Because I am a Scotland Yard officer,' I told him.

'But the newspapers said that it was one of Mr Churchill's secretaries who had committed the terrible act,' he stuttered.

'Surely, sir,' said I, 'you do not really believe all that you read in the newspapers, do you?'

Without a further word he took the statements and tore them into small pieces, rose and bade me goodbye.

Yet even that was not the end of the story. On our return to England, my colleague Williams, who was in fact my superior, put in a report to the Special Branch to the effect that I had overstepped my authority in tackling the photographer, and that I should have left it to the Italian police. I was rebuked by the Chief Superintendent, but remained on protection.

What would have been Mr Churchill's reaction, I wonder, and that of Scotland Yard for that matter, had the cameraman made his escape, as he surely would have done had I not intervened, and unflattering pictures of the Old Man in near-nudity had appeared all over the world?

There was another incident, which fortunately remained secret, that occurred during that holiday in Venice. It happened actually at Burano, an island to the north of the city where Mr Churchill had gone to paint. For a couple of hours he worked hard at the picture of a small bridge across the canal, with a row of pink and white houses in the background, and while he worked I took the usual photos of the scene to be used later in the studio, if necessary. He began to show signs of discomfort and after a while moved to discreet shelter beside a wall a few yards away at the end of a terrace of houses.

Toilets were impossible to find on Burano. He pulled up the zip of his trousers and made to return to his canvas, but before he had covered more than a couple of paces, an aged crone, all in black, came darting out of the house he had used, and began to berate him in a torrent of fiery Italian.

She knew who Mr Churchill was, of that I am sure, but she was trying her luck to see what she could get out of it. It was a cunning move, really, because he backed away from her like a bewildered bull, acutely embarrassed by the affair. As the tirade continued, he turned to me and said, 'You'll have to give her something to keep her quiet.' I went towards her with a thousand lire note in my hand, and as if I'd waved a magic wand, the tumult stopped. I'm sure that Mr Churchill had never been blackmailed like that before. But here again, it was very noticeable that both my colleague and the Italian policemen failed to step forward to intervene.

From time to time during that holiday in Venice the Churchills would be joined by a serious-looking young woman who, exactly a year later, was to spring into national prominence. She was Clarissa Spencer-Churchill, daughter of Mr Churchill's brother who died in 1947; the girl who was to become the second wife of Anthony Eden.

My early impression of her was of a most sober person, exceptionally so for her age. A young woman who dressed with almost nun-like severity either in black or white, who rarely smiled and who seemed to bear the entire troubles of the world upon her slim shoulders. It was very difficult to reconcile this picture with that of the gay young débutante-of-the-year, which she had been voted thirteen years earlier, in 1938.

The romance between her and Mr Eden, then Foreign Secretary, was an exceptionally well-kept secret. I remember them visiting Chartwell together one August Sunday in 1952. Until then there had been no whisper of their impending marriage. But that day I felt that there was something in the air, an aura of excitement that aroused my suspicions and so I was not really surprised when the newspapers the next day announced their engagement and I was able to congratulate them and wish them luck before they left.

Another, rather gayer acquaintance of the Churchills who joined them occasionally during that holiday was the British film actress, Anne Crawford, who unhappily died very young in 1956. It was a remark she made at a luncheon party in the 250-year-old palazzo of the Contessa Volpi di Misurate, a long-standing favourite of the

Churchills since their honeymoon stay in Venice, that started a series of events which proved how efficient and co-operative the Italian police could be on occasions.

Mr Churchill was always ready to try out old wives' remedies, and at this time, in addition to the skin rash which led to the purchase of the hip-bath, he was suffering from a series of painfully irritating boils. Anne mentioned a certain ointment and he decided he must try it. He would always listen attentively to a pretty girl. We were due to return to England soon after the luncheon, and about twenty minutes before the train was scheduled to leave, the Old Man handed me a slip of paper with the details of the ointment written on it. It was always I who got the most impossible tasks to perform. Normally it would have been a simple matter to obtain the ointment, but it was Sunday and chemists' shops were closed. By the time we arrived at the station, I could only think of one possible way to get the stuff. I handed the prescription to the Chief of the Venice Police, my old friend of the cameraman incident, who was with us to take part in the official farewells by local authorities, and asked him to telephone it through to the various cities we were due to stop at. Police in these places could possibly obtain it and let me have it en route. I had only a very faint hope of success.

Yet the arrangement worked perfectly and at the very first city, Verona, a police officer came aboard the train, asking for me. He handed me a box of ointment and would accept no payment, saying it was a gift from the Chief of Police of Venice. Mr Churchill was very impressed by the system I had devised to satisfy his wish.

Having got the ointment, however, he only used it once on the journey back to England, then appeared to forget all about it. But some two years later his valet told me one morning that Mr Churchill had just asked for the ointment Sergeant Murray had obtained for him in Venice. It was recovered from the depths of the medicine cupboard and used regularly for several months afterwards.

In Venice, there was another story in which Norman was involved and which discloses his sense of humour. During a previous luncheon, Miss Crawford and the Contessa thought that Mr Churchill's painting of the famous Rialto Bridge from a balcony of the Palazzo was finished, and that he should now go and see the beautiful Tintoretto painting *The Marriage at Cana* in the ante-sacristy of the church, Santa Maria della Salute, at the end of the Grand Canal, opposite St Mark's Square. No sooner said than done, so a motor-boat was called and Mr Churchill, Anne, Norman and I got into it. My colleague Williams had tummy-ache and had remained in the hotel.

In a few minutes we were at the side of the very fine church which had been built in 1632 by Baldassars Longhena as a votive offering to the Virgin for having stayed the plague which devastated the city in 1630. Considering the age in which it was erected, it is singularly pure, and well adapted to the site, showing its principal façade to the Grand Canal, while its two domes and two bell-towers group most pleasingly in every point of view from which Venice can be entered on that side.

The pillars of the church were brought from the noble amphi-theatre of Pola. Before the high altar is a grand bronze candelabrum by Andrea Bresciano, and the vault of the choir is by Titian. He was also responsible for the fine painting of St Mark in the sacristy. But the wonderful painting we had gone there to see was superb in its magnificence. It was immense, some twenty-five feet long by fifteen feet high and was one of the few that Tintoretto signed with his name, to demonstrate, I suppose, how much he favoured the paint-ing himself. The whole merit of the picture, in the eyes of the intelli-gent public, lies in the long table, one end of which looks farther off than the other. The table is set in a spacious chamber with windows at the end letting in the light from the horizon, and those in the side wall, the intense blue of an eastern sky. The spectator looks all along the table, at the far end of which sits Christ and the Madonna, the wedding guests on either side of it, men on one side and women on the other. It is a sober and majestic picture with masses of colour and both Mr Churchill and I were very impressed.

But I must say that we had had a certain amount of difficulty in getting into the church in the first place for it had taken Norman and me some effort, because the tide was very low, to get the Old Man out of the motor-boat, on to the fifty-yard long asphalt-covered approach to the back door. When I reached the door, where the opening times were displayed, I found that although our timing was good, a prolonged ringing of the bell failed to produce any result. Workmen on ladders at the side told me to insist, but after almost ten minutes, the Old Man, grumbling loudly, began to walk back towards the boat. Miss Crawford held his arm as he marched back and Norman and I followed a few steps behind. Norman giggled and took my arm. 'Eddie,' he said, 'I was just thinking. For the first time in twenty years he wanted to go to church without being obliged to go – and they locked the blooming doors on him.' Then suddenly there was a shout behind us and a priest came running after us, asking forgiveness for not answering the bell with his usual dispatch. He had been washing his hands. I explained the situation to Mr Churchill and he agreed to return to the church. He was not disappointed, as I have already intimated.

On one occasion when General Arnold, Commanding General of the US Army Air Forces, went to Chequers he told Mrs Churchill of a ride in an ox-cart he had had with his wife from the dock at Guam to the little town of Agana when they had landed there on their honeymoon. Mrs Churchill had said, 'Tell Mrs Arnold when Winston and I visited Venice on our honeymoon. I wanted to ride in a gondola, but he insisted on a motor-launch – he said it was far more healthy – the fumes killed the germs, and so on. So we rode in a gasoline launch.' Then she added, 'There is not much romance in Winston.'

12

THE HUSTINGS

THE EXAMPLE OF THE SERVICE rendered by the Italian police in the matter of the ointment was typical of the efforts people would make to be of assistance to Winston Churchill. Although he seldom made direct reference to this special help or kindness, I know that he was always deeply appreciative of it.

Gifts, mainly from very humble people, would pour in to him at all times. Cigars came in profusion, and there were flowers on many occasions. A very good example of the esteem in which ordinary men and women held him occurred when the 1951 General Election campaign began, not long after our return from the Continent.

Mr Churchill undertook a speaking tour of the north of England and Scotland. Huddersfield, Newcastle upon Tyne, Glasgow and Edinburgh were on the itinerary, and the journey was made entirely by rail, a special coach being supplied for the Old Man and his staff. In this everyone worked, ate and, on one or two occasions, slept. The visit to Huddersfield was a gesture typical of Mr Churchill, for he went there to speak not for his own party, but for a Liberal, Lady Violet Bonham–Carter. The issue there was a straight fight between Liberal and Labour, so Winston was able to speak on behalf of his friend of long standing.

Huddersfield was one of the places where we used the coach for sleeping purposes. It had been shunted into a quiet siding just outside the city for the night. The following morning I took an early stroll round the coach and I saw a very old lady making her way slowly down the track towards me. In her apron were six fresh eggs from a nearby farm – they were for Mr Churchill's breakfast.

To watch, from my vantage point, the building-up of that General Election campaign which was to sweep Mr Churchill and the Conservatives back into power, was a most fascinating experience.

From the moment that the polling date was announced, the house in Hyde Park Gate began to hum like a beehive. Information on home and foreign affairs poured in hour by hour, gathered by the Conservative Central Office and the Press. Secretaries pounded typewriters to produce copies of draft speeches, to amend versions of draft speeches and then to retype them. The Old Man revelled in it all and wrote, rehearsed and rewrote speech after speech. It all seemed so utterly incoherent, but gradually, as trips to the hustings approached, Mr Churchill settled down more and more to deal with No 1 speech, then No 2 speech and so on as the programme established itself and certain definite themes stood out. His constant touch with up-to-the-minute news was reflected in all his speeches. In Newcastle, for example (I was amazed and delighted at the fantastically warm welcome given by the people of my home area where the majority, mostly miners, voted Labour in my days) at St James' Park, the home of Newcastle United, 'The Magpies', he was able to refer to the assassination of the Pakistani Prime Minister, an event which was news to most of his audience.

It was intriguing to observe Mr Churchill, the unrivalled public speaker, preparing for a meeting. Days before the engagement activity among the secretaries would increase in pitch as the first outlines of a speech took shape. Frequently it would be composed in bed because, unless he had a morning engagement, the Old Man seldom got out of bed before 1 pm during this period. There he would carefully study the newspapers, even the *Daily Worker*, and discuss events with various aides. When a speech had been drafted, a copy would go to Mrs Churchill at once, and she would study it just as carefully as he had, then come to his bedroom to suggest options.

'Yes,' she would invariably say, 'I think it's very good, but . . .' and on most occasions he would accept the alterations.

Once as we made our way to Woodford where he was to address his constituents, Mrs Churchill took him up on one minor point in his speech. 'Don't you think you ought to say "should" instead of "might"?' she queried.

'No, my dear, I do not think so.'

'I think that you should consider it.'

A long discussion followed and eventually, Mr Churchill, wishing to get on with his revision, declared pacifically, 'Very well my darling, I will say "should".' The discussion lapsed, but his wife knew full well that her husband intended to say exactly what he wanted to once he was on the platform. Sure enough, he kept to the original script and said 'might'.

His speeches were always spaced out so that he knew precisely when to pause for greatest effect, though he did not really rely on the typescript when he was discoursing, for he was almost always word-perfect.

Every speech was polished with immense care. In the evenings he would rehearse the words, pacing his study at Chartwell in the presence, perhaps, of his son, Randolph, or Mrs Churchill, or a senior colleague, testing his sentences to discover the most telling way of delivering each line. And always, to uphold his reputation as a concise, pungent, plain-speaking orator, he would seek for simplicity of expression. Those speeches were always dictated in the first place to relays of secretaries for Mr Churchill had not used a dictaphone since the end of the war. The secretary/typist would be kept going until the very last moment.

Before setting off from Hyde Park Gate, or Chartwell, for the speech, a doctor would call to spray his throat with a special preparation, though sometimes the spray was taken along for the job to be done on the spot. At the meeting itself, although he always dominated the proceedings, Mr Churchill loved the true atmosphere of the hustings and would be most disappointed should there be no hecklers. The manner in which he quelled interruptions with just the right reply often made it seem as if the whole thing had been rehearsed.

I remember on one occasion when a particularly persistent heckler was making it very difficult for the Old Man to give his speech at all. The whole audience dissolved in laughter when Mr Churchill suddenly stopped in mid-sentence and said, 'You know, I rather think that they have come along to listen to me.' There were no more interruptions after that.

One of the places we visited during that campaign was Plymouth, where Randolph was to fight an unsuccessful battle against Michael Foot. He deserved a better fate for he had stood for adoption at a much safer seat, but had withdrawn as soon as he heard that Mr Macmillan was also in the running, saying that Mac had a better right to it than himself. The Old Man spoke to a huge audience on his son's behalf, wearing for the occasion his celebrated square bowler. It was a very fair fight with the antagonism confined to politics and not personalities, and I was most impressed by both contestants for a change. Once back in the special coach inevitably provided for him by the railway authorities, he called for his valet, demanding his normal Homburg. Off went Norman to the adjoining compartment, and reappeared moments later. By this time his boss was immersed in the pile of newspapers I had procured for him, as per usual custom, and just did not respond to the valet's 'Your hat, sir.'

The valet had a second try. Still there was no reaction, and the valet removed the square bowler and replaced it gently with the Homburg. He had just left the compartment, when a loud roar called him back: 'NORMAN!'

He hurried back, and Mr Churchill growled at him, 'I asked for my other hat. Why don't you bring it to me?'

'But you have it, Sir.'

'What do you mean I have it. Get my other hat at once.'

'It's on your head, sir.'

'Do not play the fool with me, Norman. On my head. On my head indeed.' He raised his hand and removed – the Homburg. 'Oh, it is there. Why did you not tell me?'

Without further word Norman turned and left the compartment. It was all part of the game when Mr Churchill became oblivious to the world outside while he was studying papers of any kind and it was not the first time Norman had received a rocket, of the nicer kind, and it would certainly not be the last.

A few minutes later, he heard once more, 'Norman', and he went in, this time bearing a whisky and soda to forestall the usual placating measure. Now everything was back to normal.

In his constituency of Woodford, most of the routine social work was done by Mrs Churchill, which appeared to be natural in view of her husband's vast commitments. But on polling-day he went through the procedure of attending the count and the announcement of the final result with all the solemnity and attention to traditional detail of a candidate contesting a seat for the very first time.

Back at Hyde Park Gate, where we would arrive after midnight, a score-board would register the state of the parties. A tape machine would have been installed to give up-to-the-minute results and a thermometer type of indicator, with a red column for Labour, a blue one for the Conservatives, and a yellow one for the Liberals, would be recording the exact number of seats held by each party.

There would be about thirty people in the house, members of the family and staff, and usually at about one o'clock, in 1951 at any rate, bottles of champagne were opened, glasses filled and handed round. The Conservatives were back in power; Churchill back in command. Turning to Rufus II, the dog, who had never actually been to Downing Street, he said, 'We'll be going back to No 10, Rufus,' and sure enough within a few days, Mr and Mrs Churchill, with the dog, were once more walking into the tiled hall of No 10 Downing Street with the staff lined up to greet them. It was very difficult to decide who was most touched, the Churchills or those who had known them in more momentous days.

Re-election as Prime Minister meant for Mr Churchill not only the tenancy of No 10 Downing Street, but the use of Chequers, the estate in Buckinghamshire presented to the nation in 1917 by Lord and Lady Lee of Fareham. This estate of Chequers Court, to give it its correct name, was first occupied by the Prime Minister of the day, David Lloyd George, in 1921. There are about 1,500 acres, near Wendover, some thirty miles to the west of London. The original draft indicated that the Prime Minister of the day could afford to live there even if he only had his official salary to rely on, and to tempt the Prime Minister to visit regularly, an endowment was made to cover the employment of a small domestic staff, the upkeep of the grounds and gardens, maintenance and other usual expenses. In fact these days, most of the kitchen and house staff are supplied in turn by the women's services. The draft required the unaltered preservation of the house and its contents, among which is a fine collection of Cromwellian portraits and relics, and a secret staircase.

I believe that there was an allowance, in those days, of fifteen pounds to the Prime Minister for every visitor to Chequers, but this was no inducement to Mr Churchill to neglect his beloved Chartwell, and so Chequers was used far less by the Churchills than by their predecessors, the Attlees. Even so, Mr Churchill had sufficient feeling for the estate, which was mentioned in the Domesday Book, to make a gift of beech trees in 1957, some two years after retiring as Prime Minister. These now form a fine avenue.

It was at Chequers that he came very close to losing his life on one occasion. Tropical fish were his passion at the time, and he had several tanks of these exotic specimens transferred from Chartwell to Chequers. He would spend as much as half an hour at a time, watching the fascinating multi-coloured fish, occasionally putting his hand into the water to drop in food. He had been warned that in one particular tank the wiring was faulty and it would be dangerous to touch it. But in true Churchillian fashion he ignored the warning, and he received an electric shock which threw him across the room. This engendered in him a distinct distaste for tropical fish for a long time afterwards. Eventually, when his interest finally waned, the tropical fish were presented to the London Zoo.

One of the features of Chequers I best remember was the scene each Christmas. For the Churchills, like most other families, it was an occasion when sons and daughters, and more particularly the grandchildren, assembled for a brief space of time. There would be a children's party with a puppet-show and the inevitable and much anticipated arrival of Father Christmas, a role usually played by the then son-in-law, Mr Duncan Sandys, now a peer of course. With his appearance there would be presents for everyone from the tree, all neatly wrapped by Mrs Hill, the Curator of Chequers, who had been one of Mr Churchill's personal secretaries during the war, and the WRAF or WREN girls who staffed the house in turn. They would also be there to receive some small present in accordance with the spirit of Christmas. The traditional gift for the detectives was a packet of cigarettes, but I always received a five-pound note with my Christmas card.

Mrs Churchill, with her passion for croquet, made an important change at Chequers when she had the tennis court converted into a croquet lawn and, as at Chartwell, I was always called in to provide opposition when no other players were on hand. The only alteration her husband made at Chequers was to take out his paints one day and touch up a picture of one of Aesop's Fables, the one about the lion and the mouse, which hung in the hall there.

It was at Chequers that I had what might have been described as an embarrassing experience. Walking through the grounds on my usual morning inspection at about 7 o'clock, I spotted an elderly man, in a rather scruffy raincoat, not to put too fine a point on it, small and slightly stooping, strolling across the field at the back of the house. Now Chequers is usually guarded by the local police, but it is not impossible for people to get to the house for there is a road past and footpaths abound. It was rather early for house guests to be taking the air so I decided that an investigation was necessary.

Approaching the man I politely inquired as to what could he be doing on private property so early in the morning.

'I have a reason for being here,' he replied, 'but do you have a reason for asking me?'

'Well yes, sir,' said I, 'I am from Scotland Yard and on protection duties with the Prime Minister. I am Detective-Sergeant Murray and this is my warrant card.'

'Then, Detective-Sergeant Murray,' said the man, 'I am very happy to see you carrying out your duties so conscientiously – I am Lord Goddard and one of the Prime Minister's guests for the weekend.' He was of course, the Lord Chief Justice at the time. Had he been wearing his judicial robes, I would probably have recognized him, but in a scruffy looking raincoat at 7 am . . . ?

I apologized and he said no apologies were necessary as I was only doing my job, and very correctly too. We continued our separate paths.

On another occasion an intruder did penetrate the police screen when an elderly lady cycled up to the back door. She had actually dismounted and was approaching Mr Churchill who was sitting in a chair on the lawn, when I intervened. She talked like a person somewhat deranged, so I led her gently but firmly away to hand her over to a uniformed constable, now watching the scene.

The Prime Minister had risen and entered the house before I caught up with him and explained. 'Do not hurt the poor woman. Give her a pound note and a slice of cake and let her go.' The old lady got her pound note, but not the slice of cake, and nothing further was done about it.

Although Mr Churchill's principal affection lay with Chartwell, his wife certainly had very strong feelings for Chequers, and that was scarcely surprising. It was a house full of historical undertones and though few events of any moment had taken place there, a sense of the past lay over it like a veil. For eight hundred years, from the beginning of the twelfth century until 1912, the Chequers estate never changed hands except by inheritance. Not until the last owner by inheritance died without issue in 1912 was it sold to Lord and Lady Lee of Fareham, who presented it to the nation some five years later.

There was one room in the house, however, which did have poignant historical associations. This was the small garret room known as the 'prison room' for it was there that Lady Mary Grey, sister of Lady Jane Grey, was held captive for two years on the orders of

Queen Elizabeth I. She was detained there not because she was considered dangerous, as an heir to the throne, but because she had married Sergeant Porter of Elizabeth's court without the knowledge or consent of the Queen.

William Hawtrey, then the owner of Chequers, had just completed the rebuilding of the house, and as documents show, he did not like the idea of being ordered to keep Lady Mary detained under lock and key.

In the 'prison room' were facsimiles of some of the touching letters she wrote to Sir William Cecil, later to become Lord Burghley, beseeching him to employ his influence with the Queen to secure her release.

13

CHURCHILL THE MAN

CHURCHILL THE STATESMAN, CHURCHILL the politician, Churchill the orator, are figures known to the world at large, in greater or lesser degree, through the media of the Press, the radio and the cinema, but what of Churchill the man, the real Churchill as seen by those in constant and close contact with him?

One of his most conspicuous traits was his great fondness for animals of many varieties. A real minor tragedy was the death in a road accident of Rufus I, the reddish-brown-haired French poodle to whom he was extremely attached. This happened at Brighton in 1947, and when I arrived in 1950, Rufus II, similar in appearance to the first, was on the scene. But he never forgot the original dog and when we walked round the garden, with Rufus II accompanying us for the first few hundred yards before he got bored, the Old Man would stop at the grave of Rufus I, and with his stick tap lightly on the gravestone, and say, 'There also, my dear Rufus, will you find a resting-place when you go to join your predecessor.'

The original Rufus was being taken for a walk in Brighton by one of the maids (it was during the Conservative Party Conference) when the maid saw the valet on the other side of the road. She let the dog off the lead and he dashed across, only to be hit by a lorry. Martha, the maid, had been instructed not to let the dog off the lead and so she was terrified of the consequences. It was generally agreed that the Old Man should not be told of Rufus' death until after the end of the Conference. He was extremely disturbed when he heard of it and although he did not reprimand the maid, he did not speak to her for months afterwards.

Rufus II was a very friendly creature and would sleep on his boss's bed and eat in the dining-room with the rest of the Churchill family. A plate of food would be brought in and set down beside Mr

Churchill's chair for the dog, and from time to time he would receive a titbit from his lord and master. Then Rufus II contracted tooth trouble so his breath did rather smell, and to cap it all, he began to have stomach trouble leading to more evil smells, so he was no longer allowed to come to the more confined, and indeed refined, abode at Hyde Park Gate and had to remain at Chartwell in the tender care of Miss Hamblin, Mrs Churchill's housekeeper-cum-companion.

Nevertheless, when he did pass on to the happy hunting-grounds of French poodles, as promised there was a resting-place and tombstone next to his predecessor, Rufus I, just around the corner from the front door of Chartwell, near the bottom of the steps leading to the croquet lawn. I always find it sad to remember animal friends who have left this world where they had no say in what happened to them yet always seemed to dance with joy and happiness, ever trying to bring pleasure into the lives of less happy creatures.

After the loss of the affection of Rufus, for gradually the dog transferred this to Miss Hamblin, to the evident disappointment of his master, there came a new interest in the shape of Toby, the budgerigar presented to the Old Man by his breeder, Lord Montgomery. I had one at home from the same source. At meal-times he would always be on hand, often flying round to perch on the heads or shoulders of guests, sometimes to their embarrassment. He was really a very handsome bird and he had a number of expressions, including, 'Who goes home', 'Good morning Winston', in English, and quite a few others in French and German acquired from foreign members of the staff who were forever being changed.

In the latter years Toby travelled with us to the Continent, but it was not a simple matter in the beginning. Through diplomatic channels, talks over many weeks ensured that the bird could go to join Sir Winston at Cap d'Ail or Monte Carlo, first by Air France both ways, and always accompanied by a secretary. Then one way via Air France and one way by British European Airways, still with a secretary. Then at last both ways with Sir Winston in a British aircraft. But there was always a proviso – Toby must never be allowed to fraternize with local budgerigars (on legal hygienic grounds, of course, rather than on cultural or racial ones), and quarantine regulations were waived. Toby's normal place was in the Old Man's bedroom, and it was one of the valet's main tasks every day to let the bird out of his cage. One of his favourite tricks was to hop on to my shoulder and peck away at my moustache, something Sir Winston did not have, and he also liked to nibble at the books his master read. Should members of the London Library find themselves handling books where the pages have ragged edges, let them not think that moths or rats have been at them, but rather that Sir Winston's budgerigar Toby once perched there.

When we travelled on the Onassis yacht *Christina*, Toby's cage would occupy a place of honour at the meal table, and from time to time he would be released to flutter around the lower decks. When we travelled by plane, then occasionally he would be allowed to stretch his wings.

We lost Toby in 1961, in Monte Carlo, when we were staying on the eighth floor in the Onassis suite at the Hotel de Paris. About 5 pm someone opened a French window in the lounge, when the budgie was just taking his exercise. Out of the window he flew. The alarm was given immediately by the secretary on duty at the time. I notified the general manager of the Hotel, Monsieur Broc, one of the most delightful men I have ever met, with a lovely wife to match. I also informed the local police, and indeed I think I told everybody who could possibly lend a hand to find the bird.

I dashed outside into the gardens between the hotel and the Café de Paris and began my search. I found him, sitting on a branch of a tree, just out of my reach. Calling a member of the hotel staff, I asked him to procure a ladder as soon as possible and bring it to me. Shortly afterwards I instructed him to place the ladder very carefully against the branch while I continued to chat to Toby to keep him calm. Bang went the ladder against the tree and off went Toby, heading very appropriately in the direction of the Casino. As I told Jimmy Horrocks, an old friend of my Indian days who was with the Hickey column of the *Daily Express* at the time, when he phoned me up in the middle of the night for news of the disappearance, 'when last seen he was disappearing in the direction of the Casino . . . probably for a flutter'.

Needless to say, Toby's disappearance made news in most European newspapers. Before long there came hundreds of phone calls and even telegrams from all over the south of France announcing that the bird had been seen in dozens of different places. The manager and I made numerous trips by car in the region to examine the birds, but without success. The most improbable of all the responses was a telegram from a woman in Manchester the day after the escape to inform us that at 9 pm the previous day the budgerigar had flown into her open bedroom window and she would keep it until Sir Winston returned to England. Four hours to fly home eight or nine hundred miles was probably a record.

It is perhaps a bitter comment upon old age to have to record that Sir Winston, eighty-seven years old then, was extremely upset at the loss of Toby and for several days afterwards he kept calling me in, asking for news, and his disappointment at my negative answers was very apparent. There were plenty of offers of other budgies to replace Toby – the *Daily Sketch* actually sent their local agent with a similar bird, but it was not accepted – nor was Mr Onassis's offer of a parrot which he himself had received from Prince Rainier and whose present home was on the yacht *Christina*.

Meanwhile, things were happening at home too, on the eve of the disappearance. I was supposed to be taking my wife to an important dinner and dance where she was to reply to the main toast of 'The Ladies'. As I was in France I telephoned my brother, who owned the Crown and Cushion public house in Windsor asking him to accompany my wife together with his own wife. The three of them were having an aperitif in the bar at Windsor, prior to leaving for the dinner. Carolyn, my brother's younger daughter, was in the sitting room doing her homework while she also listened to the radio. Suddenly she dashed into the bar in a very excited state. 'Daddie,' she blurted out, 'it's terrible it's awful. They've just announced it on the radio.'

'What have they just announced on the radio?' asked Tom.

'That Sir Winston's bodyguard has disappeared,' Carolyn said.

Urgent calls to the BBC quickly elicited the correct information and peace again returned to Windsor. My wife was very happy to be able to include the story in her reply later that evening.

Cats also featured on the list of pets, the only criterion for entry into the Churchill household being a readiness to be affectionate. A black cat, for instance, wandered into No 10 Downing Street the day that Mr Churchill returned to take up residence there in 1951. Such an omen was too auspicious to be ignored and that black cat became Whisky, and was a great favourite for a number of years until suddenly he disappeared just as mysteriously as he had arrived.

At Chartwell there was a huge, disreputable ginger cat, that was disliked intensely by Mrs Churchill who refused to have him in the house, but was a big favourite with the Old Man because of the way it had of rubbing itself against his legs when he sat in the garden. The cat, called Marmalade, was half-wild and in the early days lived largely on voles, birds and other small creatures, but later he did find himself a place on the household list. Mr Churchill would feed it fish when possible and at other times, the duty uniformed policeman would ensure that it did not go hungry. I know that I was a police-man myself, but I must say that I have always considered the men in blue to be the kindest people in the world where animals are con-cerned, and very often they extend their kindness to the human race as well! This largesse did not entirely satisfy the big beast, however, and it would still go off on its marauding patrols. One day Mrs Churchill and Mr Montague Browne, the Secretary, saw the cat raiding a nest of young birds. That really put the kybosh on it and it lingered in complete disgrace for months afterwards. Mr Churchill was, of course, only very rarely apprised of the misdemeanours of the animals, but I doubt whether his attitude towards them would have changed had he known.

If an animal was hurt, or became sick, in the vicinity of the Churchill household, there was always consternation. On one occa-sion, Norman, the valet, arrived rather late for duty and had to explain to the Old Man that his dog, a very nondescript mongrel, had caught his paw in a door and injured it. Mr Churchill called immediately for a car and a driver and had Norman hurry off to the vet; and he paid the bill too.

Mr Churchill was most loath to see any creature die and I remem-ber very clearly indeed the occasion when the lawn at Chartwell was causing some problems to Lady Churchill's croquet games because it became infested with worm casts. She had Mr Vincent put down some chemical worm-killer and the next day the whole lawn was covered with dead worms. She proudly escorted her husband to see the havoc and he was very, very cross. 'You know,' he said to his wife, 'it is very wrong to kill the poor worms for they all have their places in Nature's grand design.'

There was the time when two herons came to nest at Chartwell, and proceeded to help themselves to the golden orfe, the pride of his rambles in the garden round the ponds. I offered to scare them off by firing a .303 rifle in their direction. He agreed, on condition that I shot to scare and not to kill. I got the rifle out of his private armoury, which was examined regularly by local Police Sergeant Hort, lay down on the grass and took aim. Mr Churchill stood behind me to supervise the operation, insisting all the while that I must not hit either of the birds. I carefully squeezed the trigger and a spout of water shot up just at the feet of one of the birds, and off they flew. For the next three months at least we saw no sign of them.

The black swans at Chartwell, a gift to Mr Churchill from Western Australia, were a showpiece of which he was extremely proud. Any guest could expect to be taken to see the swans and the Old Man would usually feed them for the benefit of his visitors. But their numbers did decline over the years. Foxes got two of them and quite a number of cygnets disappeared the same way despite anti-fox wire and a flashing night light. Occasionally one or two would have a yen for pastures new and would fly off. On one occasion I actually enlisted the assistance of Interpol to try and find the wanderers, but the swan that was eventually recaptured in Holland proved to belong to a Dutchman and it was handed back to him.

The fish-ponds at Chartwell, especially the larger main one, were favourite spots for Mr Churchill and in fine sunny weather he would sit beside the water, a superbly peaceful place surrounded by flags, azaleas, rhododendrons and masses of colourful weeds, and watch the lazy movements of the golden orfe for quite long periods. He would be most contented there, alone – well almost, for I would also be there, unobtrusively – and reflective, and even his cigar would be forgotten for a while and would gradually peter out. Then suddenly, after such a silence, he would make some remark about national or international affairs, bringing himself, and me, abruptly back to the everyday world almost as if he felt a little guilty at having temporarily renounced it.

Those gold fish weighed up to 3 lb and were in some cases as much as twenty years old. Not long after I arrived, they were attacked by a fungal disease. Each fish had to be treated individually and it fell upon the staff at Chartwell to do the job, actively supervised of course by Mr Churchill himself, sitting there at the end of the pool where the operation was to take place. The goldfish had to be taken carefully out of the water and rubbed in a cloth impregnated with a mixture of permanganate of potash and saline solution. The expert from London Zoo who had been called in to advise on the matter was of the opinion that the top pond was too cold, so it was decided to put the fish in the middle pool, which received much more sunshine. There were about sixty of the large golden orfe and quite a lot of small common goldfish and everyone was expected to pitch in and help in the salvage operation. Even Diana, the eldest daughter who was married at that time to Duncan Sandys, without any hesitation at all, just lifted her skirt and tucked it cavalierly in to her bloomers before stepping in to do her bit. I found it too hilarious for words and I was certainly not going to comply with the boss's unspoken wish to take off my shoes and enter the freezing waters and risk catching cold. But then I always had to be prepared to do battle with intruders. It was a very slow task, for the fish had to be counted – there were 164 in all – and the netting being used to catch the things was rotten, and kept splitting when filled with fish. Everyone became rather bored with the occupation, even Mr Churchill.

'You are taking a long time,' he complained as the netting gave way for the umpteenth time, letting the fish fall back into the ice-cold water.

'Give us the tools, sir,' answered Johnnie Collins, the MOW driver, 'give us the tools and we'll finish the job.'

'What did he say?' the Old Man asked me, and I told him, repeating the words from his radio broadcast addressing President Roosevelt on 9 February 1941.

'Do you know,' he chortled, 'I seem to have heard that before.'

There were no complaints from his direction after that.

As a former cavalry officer, Mr Churchill was very fond of horses, especially of the racehorses he had at the stud farm at Lingfield, Surrey, not very far from Chartwell. Although he only became an owner in 1949, he rapidly acquired great enthusiasm, partly due to an early run of successes. Regularly he would drive along to his Newchapel stud farm to carry out his tour of inspection. The horses would be brought out one by one, on parade, and the details and progress of each animal would be recounted by the veterinary surgeon in charge, Major Carey-Foster. Mr Churchill would carefully inspect each horse as it passed, take the stud book and examine the details there, discussing the cost and probable current value. Then he would inspect the boxes of a chosen few.

One of the best horses he ever had, and certainly his favourite, was the big-hearted Colonist II. One or two experts had turned down the horse before Mr Churchill bought him from France for 1,500 guineas in 1949. That same year he rewarded the Old Man's faith in him by winning three times. In 1950, he won eight out of his eleven races and brought home more than seven thousand pounds in prize money. When he was finally sold to stud in 1951, Colonist II had won thirteen out of twenty-four races and brought his master more than twelve thousand pounds in prize money. In view of the fact that his selling price for stud was 7,000 guineas, he made quite a handsome sum of money for Mr Churchill.

Colonist II had two characteristics particularly which caught the public admiration and somehow indentified him with his owner. The first was his never-say-die spirit, for once the horse got his head in front, he never gave up until he was past the winning-post. The other was his remarkable reluctance to turn left and it was only on left-handed circuits, like Brighton, that he did badly.

14

FAMILY LIFE

CERTAIN CHARACTERISTICS STOOD OUT very clearly in the day to day pattern of Mr Churchill's life. There was his intense fondness for almost every type of animal, a trait entirely predictable. Then at a rather different level, there was his immense passion for every scrap of news regarding the world about him. It was a bad day for everyone in the Churchill household, at home or abroad, if the newspapers were not delivered.

Normally there would be two sets of all the morning newspapers, one for Mr Churchill, and one for his lady — both sets to be read in bed, of course. But if ever the occasion arose when only one set arrived (and Mrs Churchill did occasionally try to cut out one set as part of an economy drive) it created an acute problem for the staff, for demands for the papers would come from both bedrooms and the greatest diplomacy was required to ensure that harmony was maintained. Usually the Old Man got them first, and I have often seen Norman, or Walter, very busy ironing the newspapers that had been through Mr Churchill's hands, to remove the creases before passing them to Martha or the lady's maid at the time.

On those occasions when there were no papers at all, the Old Man would be very irritable throughout the day, and as he slowly withdrew more and more from public life the newspapers became increasingly important to him.

When we were abroad it was nearly always my responsibility to organize the supply of newspapers. Even when other people took it upon themselves to do the arranging, I felt it was my responsibility to double-check the arrangements. We went to the Château de Madrid, a very fine restaurant overlooking Beaulieu, near Nice, in the South of France, one Sunday for lunch. Having escorted Sir Winston, as he was by then, to the reserved table, and ensured that

Emery Reves and Wendy, Sir Winston's hosts at the time at Roquebrune and Mr Montague Browne, the aide from the Foreign Office, were in attendance, I went down to the forecourt to look round the gardens for security reasons. My colleagues from the 'Voyages Officiels' in Paris, were in the courtyard. I saw Mr Montague Browne speak with them, then he came to me and said, 'I asked them to go and fetch the newspapers from Nice, but they referred me to you.'

'How right they were, Mr Montague Browne,' I replied. 'Of course they cannot go to Nice for you. They are here to assist me in the protection of Sir Winston Churchill . . . not for the convenience of any of the members of his staff.'

'The newspapers are for Sir Winston, of course, not for me, Sergeant Murray.'

'Then do you not think that it would be a very good idea in such circumstances, to ask me to request my French colleagues to render a service, rather than tell them to do something for you?' He scowled, and grunted that he supposed I was right. I then went to l'Inspecteur Fournier and off he sped with his driver for the newspapers knowing that if they had an accident on the way, they could count on me to bear witness that they were just doing their duty. Mr Montague Browne was careful in future to ask me to do the asking.

The trouble with being on protection is that you are there more or less all the time and you are aware of so much that goes on that really has nothing at all to do with protection duties. Yet a protection officer has to keep his eyes open all the time and use his retentive mind to remember everything he sees. What the people surrounding a VIP, like in Mr Churchill's case, the secretaries, drivers, nurses and personal servants do not seem to realize is that their private lives must remain secret as far as the protection officer is concerned, unless their actions prejudice the protection. Though I saw many indiscreet things happen, I did not spy on people of the entourage, and anything I saw went into the strange, secret recesses of my memory, no threat to anybody.

I remember the time when I was checking on things in the former dining-room at Chartwell, which had been turned into a cinema as a gift from the Hollywood movie mogul, Spyros Skouras. It was in the afternoon and there was to be a film that evening. I went behind the heavy curtains at the very back of the room and shone my torch in the corners. I was not looking for anything in particular, just fulfilling part of my duties. Moments later I heard voices, and recognized them both as members of the staff. I considered what to do. Show myself and risk their thinking I was spying on them? or stay put until they left?

I decided to stay and hoped they would not remain long. The male voice began with quiet entreaties for favours, then as the female kept declining, he became more and more insistent and pleading that it would not take long and that he was madly in love with the lady. Eventually there came the sound of two bodies falling on the deep sofa in the middle of the room, heavy breathing and pleas for kindness and gentleness, and for a good half hour I was obliged to stand there unmoving, hardly breathing for fear of discovery and subsequent ill feeling. Eventually they separated and left the room and I continued my examination of the cinema, singing loudly to warn any other intruders of my presence. There had been no risk to the protection of Sir Winston, so there was no disclosure of the amorous dalliance, though I did feel a bit guilty at the time.

Returning to the subject of newspapers, the *Financial Times* was always one of the first to be read, for Sir Winston always followed very closely the fortunes of the shares in which he had his money invested. A good deal of this money was actually in American shares and so the *New York Herald Tribune* and the *New York Times* were also carefully studied. The evening papers were thoroughly perused too and whenever we travelled from London to Chartwell in the afternoon, a stop was made at either of two newsvendors, the one at the entrance to the House of Commons quadrangle, or the one at Crystal Palace.

The Times and *Guardian* naturally came high on the list of priority reading, but he always took an early look at that star product of his great friend Lord Beaverbrook, the *Daily Express*. Actually, when he was in London, a good deal of the day's news was available to him about eleven o'clock at night when the first editions of both the *Daily Express* and the *Daily Telegraph* were delivered to his home. When the Other Club was having its meeting at the Savoy, a copy of the *Telegraph* was always sent to the Savoy for him. The Other Club was a highly exclusive dining society whose rules were wreathed in mystery. Mr Churchill had founded it in 1911 with the celebrated F. E. Smith, later to be Lord Birkenhead, who is possibly best remembered for his remarkable tenure of the post of Lord Chancellor and one of the most important members of Lloyd George's post-World War I coalition government. He was one of the ablest and greatest lawyers and orators of his day, but also possessed qualities which made him many enemies. Lord Birkenhead died in 1930.

Mr Churchill devoured the newspapers avidly, but he was equally a most voracious reader of books. At least a dozen books would be selected for him from the London Library, and he often read the lot. Dickens, Kipling and Jane Austen figured prominently in his list of favourite authors, as did C. S. Forester.

I supposed that the feature which most marked his choice of reading was the strong stress on adventure contained in many of the books he chose, with authors such as Stevenson, Conrad, Fenimore Cooper and 'Sapper', the creator of Bulldog Drummond, well to the fore. Historical works also attracted him and very often he would turn for relaxation to William Shakespeare. In 1964 he returned to Arthur Conan Doyle's Sherlock Holmes.

Lady Churchill almost matched her husband as an ardent reader, but her choice was rather more wide-ranging than his. She would, for instance, read a book in German or French from time to time for in both these languages she was highly proficient. How often did I hear her make the Swiss or Austrian maids quake with her fluent German, and one of them once commented, 'I do not know where she could have learned such expressions.'

Mr Churchill could hardly be called a great lover of music, but like many other Englishmen he greatly enjoyed the works of Gilbert and Sullivan. However, when he raised his voice in song, it was usually something from the music-halls of the turn of the century which he chose. The old songs like 'A Little Bit Off the Top' and others like that, together with the classics of the First World War, constituted most of his repertoire, and it was always possible to tell whether he had enjoyed an evening out, because if he had, coming back in the car he would launch into one or another of these songs.

In his later years he certainly became much more interested in the cinema than the concert hall. Practically every night when he was at Chartwell a film would be shown in the small cinema and although he liked to give the impression that it was for the benefit of the staff, the real truth was that he enjoyed it more than anyone.

When we were at sea, too, he seldom missed the chance of seeing films. On board Mr Onassis's yacht, *Christina*, there was usually a film each evening and on one occasion when we paid a courtesy visit to a

British warship, anchored off Villefranche, Mr Churchill remained on board, much to the delight of the officers and men, until past 1 am watching a film called *Scaramouche*. Overnight stays at Windsor Castle always entitled him to a free film show as well. It was usually a historical adventure film, wherever he went, for it became common knowledge that this type was preferred. People were so nice to him generally and would often ask me in advance for some indication of the things he liked so as to accommodate him.

Whilst in the Middlesex Hospital after he had broken his thigh in Monte Carlo, I asked his doctors if they thought it advisable for Sir Winston to have entertainment in the shape of a film. They all agreed that it would be a good idea so I went to see the Rank Organisation people in London. They were delighted to arrange it, and would give no publicity to the matter. The apparatus and the films I had chosen duly arrived some hours later at the hospital and the Old Man invited all and sundry to come to the show. But with the night nurse, two gentlemen from the Rank Organisation, the apparatus and myself, there was hardly room for his cigar. Sir Winston did appreciate the trouble we had all taken to make his sojourn in the hospital as pleasant as possible. The Rank men certainly put in a lot of overtime and I do hope that they were recompensed, for when at last Sir Winston left hospital to spend a recuperation period at Hyde Part Gate, they even continued their film shows there. The arrangement came to an end when the Rank Organisation refused payment for the service and it was considered that the charitable performances should cease.

He also enjoyed the theatre, but going to a play was a much more formal business entailing dressing up and being in his seat at a certain time, to which I knew he secretly took exception. He much preferred to drop casually into his own private cinema and have the programme start when he was ready, though of course he lacked the applause he always received whenever he ventured into the theatre, when the audience would always rise to its feet and acclaim him.

Television did not really appeal to him very much. Although sets had been installed both at Chartwell and Hyde Park Gate, his viewing was extremely limited. He would watch an occasional evening programme when Lady Churchill would switch the set on and he would be more or less obliged to watch. Then there was also the occasional Party Political Broadcast delivered by former colleagues, for example, but his use of TV was mainly confined to watching racing . . . and then only if his own horses were running.

I remember so well one of the first times that he watched, or tried to watch. One of his horses was running at Sandown Park and he announced his intention of attending to watch the race at Sandown. But the weather was so vile that morning that he was reluctantly persuaded to watch it on TV instead. Then the weather changed and became fine and sunny, but it was by then too late to get to Sandown on time. He was shepherded after lunch to the front room at Chartwell, still his painting studio, where the television set stood, rather like an outcast.

We got him seated, deep down within an easy chair, his cigar well alight, and I switched on the set. But instead of the clear picture we expected there was only a misty blur and not a sound to be heard. Like a small boy denied some long-promised treat he began to complain. 'When will I see something . . . when are we going to see the race? I was told I would see the race, why can't I see anything?' but although I twisted the knobs vigorously and optimistically, and kicked the television a few times for good measure, neither picture nor sound was possible. To tell him that a perfect picture had been admired the night before did not help. He was furious, disappointed and he felt that he had been betrayed. The rest of that day was difficult for everyone. In cases such as this, I used to feel rather like the boy who 'stood on the burning deck, whence all but he had fled', for the regular fair-weather sailors seemed to disappear leaving me as protection officer, who had to remain close by whatever happened, to bear the brunt of the Old Man's wrath. However it soon petered out, really, because he knew it would be unfair to vent his displeasure on someone who was there on duty and innocent of any wrongdoing. He would leave me and look for his family who took great pains to placate him. He would sulk for minutes, or even hours, and the family would be babyishly sarcastic, or encouraging. Then suddenly his face would light up and he would chuckle, though usually rather shamefacedly, and he would be once more his usual happy self.

The Churchill family were very closely knit. No one having even the slightest association with the Churchills could fail to appreciate the great love he had for his wife, and his immense reliance upon her. They married in 1908, when he was thirty-four and she was but twenty-two, and in the early years, when his political views had made him something of a social outcast, life cannot have been easy for either of them. Perhaps it was those early tribulations which forged the inseparable links between the two. Whatever the bond, I know that without 'my darling Clemmie', Mr Churchill would have been like someone bereft of a limb.

In the house, Mrs Churchill ruled, if not supreme at least with a great deal of assurance. There were times when she and I found ourselves at loggerheads. Perhaps such events were inevitable when she was so acutely concerned with the welfare of her husband. But there was no denying the great charm she could exert over everyone, including her husband. However over the years I came to realize that even in the home he got his own way a good deal more often than at first appeared.

One feature that really marked the entire Churchill family was the curious animal language they used among themselves. The common family greeting was 'Wow! Wow!' and it was rather odd to enter Hyde Part Gate or Chartwell with Mr Churchill and hear him send forth that strange cry as soon as he stood in the hall, and odder still to hear it echoed, in the tones of his wife or one of the children, from somewhere in the house. How it originated I was never able to discover, although I suspect that it dated from the time when the children were very young. The Wow call-sign was firmly rooted in the family and even the youngest of the grandchildren soon picked it up and used it. If Sir Winston was in the garden, for example, they would cry 'Wow! Wow!' when they approached, and dutifully he would respond in a like manner.

This odd excursion into the world of animals did not stop there, though, and one of Mr Churchill's most endearing nicknames for his wife was 'Dear Cat', to which her reply, made tender despite its strange associations, was 'Dear Pig'. The other members of the family were also drawn into this 'animal' world, and Captain, now Lord Christopher Soames, husband of Mary, the youngest Churchill child, was often known as 'Christopher the Chimp', and Sarah, the actress, was 'Sarah the Mule'.

The great strength that Mr Churchill drew from his family was always characterized for me by the way in which he treasured their photographs. On trips abroad these photographs were an essential part of his luggage, and they were always placed in prominent positions in his bedroom.

Although he clearly sought to avoid having favourites among his children, I felt that the youngest daughter held a special attraction for him. Perhaps this was because Mary and her husband lived in the farmhouse on the estate at Chartwell for a number of years so that she was closer, in a physical sense, to her father and he was able to watch her family growing up about him through the years.

He and his son Randolph were also very close, of course. Randolph was just about as outspoken and uncompromising in his views when talking to his father as with anyone else. He made no concessions to eminence and his father respected him for this. In the case of his only son, he did, I know, make special efforts to ensure that there was a firm link. As a boy, his own relationship with his father, Lord Randolph Churchill, had been very formal and austere and by the time of his father's death, prematurely, the two barely knew each other. It is my opinion that it was that fact, as much as anything, which led him to develop and cherish the deep personal ties with his own family. Yet despite their closeness, he and his son often had terrible rows, usually over some headstrong criticism levelled at one or the other of his father's colleagues. In fourth estate circles, Randolph was appreciated as an excellent journalist and critic, but he was a 'loner' and discretion and diplomacy were never his strongest points.

Among his grandchildren, Randolph's son Winston was surely the one to whom he looked to continue the traditions of the name that he himself had made so great, and young Winston never left his grandfather without a substantial addition to his pocket-money. When he grew older, the two would chat together for very long periods. I would often see them, each with a cigar, conversing at the meal table long after everyone else had left. I myself have always had a great affection for young Winston and his wife, Minnie, but have yet to make the acquaintance of their offspring.

Personally I always had a sort of *entente* with Sarah Churchill, and found her gay and witty as a person, talented as a straight actress, and very human and kind with no trace of the affectation which some members of her profession acquire.

I remember well one occasion when I took my wife and the three children to the West End theatre where Sarah was playing 'Tinker Bell' in J. M. Barrie's evergreen *Peter Pan*. Though I had never mentioned to Sarah that we were going to see the show, I must have been seen by someone entering the theatre and the information had been passed on, for hardly had we settled in our seats when Sarah's secretary appeared bringing an invitation to take the children back-stage at the interval, an invitation which was eagerly accepted. When we all trooped round to her dressing-room, Sarah spent a good fifteen minutes talking to our children and showing them her fairy costumes.

Sarah was a lovely person, but very highly strung. There were times when she got into, dare I say, the wrong company, and her actions received too much publicity in the Press which caused her much pain and mind-searching. When this happened she would take a couple of drinks and that was fatal, for she was one of those people who after a few drinks find themselves in deep depression, causing them to act strangely. On a number of occasions I have been contacted by police and have taken action to get her out of trouble in order that the Press might know nothing and her father be spared reading it in the papers.

Once, for instance, in the middle of the night, the policeman on duty at Chartwell came to my room and told me that Sarah had gone out into the snow-covered garden, and he thought I should know. I dressed quickly and followed her footsteps in the snow till I found her. She was in her night-dress and barefoot. I picked her up and carried her back into the house where I awakened Mrs Churchill and, following her instructions, called the doctor. I told the police-man how grateful Mrs Churchill was and asked him to make no mention of the incident in his diary, nor to mention it to any other person. No one else ever found out and Sarah was her usual self the next day.

On another occasion, at the Hotel de Paris in Monte Carlo, she got very cross at the dinner table and stormed out of the room. Mr Mon-tague Browne asked me to help him keep an eye on her to see that she did not carry the matter further. She was by then in her room and Montague Browne sat for a while on the stairs below her room, and I sat on those above. After a while I decided that we could not spend the night there so I suggested a new course of action to Mon-tague Browne. We knocked on Sarah's door and I asked her if she would like to come out for something to eat, and perhaps dance awhile, in private.

She thought it was a fine idea, so we took the lift down to the foyer and I took them over to a bar opposite the police station which was owned by a Swiss friend of mine. I often used to spend many happy hours there with Aimé Barelli and his orchestra after their work was completed in the cabaret. We used to play liar dice and it was great fun for they always tried to ensure that I won while I tried, most of the time in vain, to lose.

There were half a dozen clients drinking in the bar when we got there, but a quiet word from my friend soon emptied the place and he put up a notice outside the door saying that the place was closed until further notice.

I then asked Sarah if she would like bacon and eggs and fried bread, one of the specialities of the house, and she told me that she would love some. Montague Browne said that he was not hungry, but I was. The food was ordered and I then put some coins in the music-box and suggested that Montague Browne dance with Sarah. He thought that I was exceeding my authority and should be back at the hotel protecting Mr Churchill, and he didn't dance. I took Sarah's arm and led her to the handkerchief-sized dance floor. For a quarter of an hour we swirled to cha-chas and French tangos without a break and then ate the delicious early breakfast, for it was past one o'clock in the morning. I put more coins in the machine and we danced again, till Sarah and I were perspiring profusely. Suddenly she stopped and looked at me, and smiled, 'Sergeant Murray, please take me back to the hotel . . . and thank you.' The crisis was over, we linked arms and went back, but not before I had thanked my Swiss friend for his kindness and consideration.

Winston Churchill's close contact with his family was obviously something of a link between the exalted, cosseted world in which he spent his latter years, and the mundane everyday life of most people. For instance, he hardly ever handled money personally and so had no idea of the cost of everyday things. On one occasion, his son-in-law, Christopher Soames, who was a director of the Bentley car firm, drove up to the door at Chartwell in a brand new Continental Bentley saloon, costing in the region of five thousand pounds at the time. The Old Man came out, for we were off to Hurst Park races, and I helped him up into the front seat. As Captain Soames drove off, he turned to the Old Man and asked him what he thought of the new car.

'It looks very nice,' said Mr Churchill. 'How much did it cost?'

'How much do you think?' said Christopher.

'A lot of money, I think. Maybe five hundred pounds.'

When he was told the actual price he just could not believe it.

On other occasions I have heard him complain quite strongly at the amount he had to pay at restaurants when he entertained abroad, on the French Riviera, for instance. Yet I know for a fact that many of the restaurants we went to invariably reduced their prices when he was there for they wanted him as a customer. Word quickly got round that he was either going to the place, or had been there, and it was an excellent recommendation that did not cost much.

For the day to day outlay of petty cash, I was his Chancellor of the Exchequer and I always kept between ten and twenty pounds in my pocket in case of emergencies. I always paid taxi-drivers, though he did not use them often, also hotel porters and attendants at the gaming-rooms in Monte Carlo or Nice or Cannes, and Mr Churchill was very conscientous about it and always asked me if the 'necessary' had been done. It was always up to me to settle his bill at the Other Club dinners as well, for according to the rules of the Club, payment had to be made on the spot.

At race meetings I would have to place a bet for him, just a modest fiver or tenner, with one of the course bookies who always asked me to convey his best wishes to the Old Man just to let me know, really, that they knew who I was and that it was lovely that Mr Churchill was trying to keep them in business.

His horses absorbed him and he would be very disappointed if one or the other ran badly when his trainer, Walter Nightingale, or his sister, had told him that it was to be expected to do well. Walter was known to be the most optimistic trainer that ever was, and terribly charming with it. But the amount his runners brought him from the bookmakers was not important and this was stressed on one occasion after he had watched a race on television. I was playing croquet with Mrs Churchill when he came on to the croquet lawn, calling out to me, 'Well, that was very exciting, did you see it?'

'See what?' I asked.

'My horse. It has just won a race at Goodwood. I was watching it on television.'

'I did not even know that you had a horse running,' I said. 'Had I known I might have had a bet on it. I suppose you did very well.'

'No,' he said, 'I did not put anything on because I'm not concerned in backing them. I just like to see them win.'

As a matter of fact I had been told not to back the horse as it had no chance at all. But there was one occasion, however, when our roles were reversed and I found him placing a bet for me. It was at Ascot, where one of his best horses, Le Prétendant, was running.

Mr Churchill was present and just before the off, I had to go to speak with the Duke of Norfolk to say that the Old Man thanked him for his kind invitation to join him in his box, and Mr Churchill would do just that after the next race. When I returned the race was running and of course, I did not have a bet on the horse. It won.

'Did you back it?' the Old Man asked me when he was getting out of the car later on at Chartwell. He was as exultant as a schoolboy.

'I did not have a chance of putting my own bet on,' I said, a trifle disgruntled, 'I was otherwise occupied.'

'Well, you are lucky,' he said to me, 'I managed to put one pound each way on for you. Let us collect your winnings from the office.' So we went there together and worked out how much he owed me, and it was settled immediately out of petty cash. This demonstrates just how responsive he was to 'atmosphere' generated by those close to him, and how quickly he could instinctively react.

When one of his horses did well he was on top of the world and I have known him dash off a telegram to Lady Churchill if she was abroad, for instance, just to let her know of the success. If he himself was out of the country and his horse won a race, he was immediately informed by telephone. 'Well, that has paid for its food for the next twelve months,' he would often say to me when he gave me the news, to keep me in the act.

What I consider to be one of the nicest stories about Mr Churchill was in connection with racehorses as well, and it happened at Lingfield where he occupied the Duke of Norfolk's box as the Duke was in attendance on Her Majesty the Queen, in her box. The Queen had a horse running in the same race as the horse belonging to Mr Churchill.

The race was run and the Queen's horse won, with Prince Arthur, I think it was, coming last of four. Mr Churchill, attended as usual by Captain Soames, called me to his side and handed me a message to be phoned to the Post Office at nearby Lingfield right away. I sent the telegram off. It read, 'Congratulations on your fine win. Your most humble servant, Winston S. Churchill', and was addressed to the Queen. A few minutes afterwards, a Post Office motor-cyclist delivered the telegram to the Queen's box and roared off back to Lingfield. Not for long, for before many minutes had elapsed he was roaring back again, this time to deliver into my hands, another telegram addressed to the Rt. Hon. Winston S. Churchill Esq. I took the message to the Boss and was shown it later. It read, 'Thank you very much for your kind message. Sorry you were not in closer attendance. Elizabeth R'. The next time we went to Lingfield, the two telegrams were in a frame hanging on the wall of the Duke of Norfolk's private box.

If gambling on horses held little attraction for Mr Churchill, gambling in the casinos of Europe took an increasing hold upon him as he grew older and the study of Mr Churchill at the casino is just as interesting as that of Churchill, the painter.

One aspect of the Old Man which I gradually learned to cope with was his curious periodic shift of mood. For instance, for a week or two he would appear to be particularly hard of hearing and comic interchanges of the following sort would occur.

Churchill to secretary: 'So you are going on holiday? Where are you going?'

'I'm going home.'

'Going to Rome. That's a very nice city.'

And, nurse to Churchill: 'May Frieda serve your lunch?'

'Share my lunch? Is there not enough in the kitchen?'

Churchill to nurse: 'Where's Sergeant Murray today?'

'Sergeant Murray has lumbago.'

'Oh! We must send a telegram to congratulate Mrs Murray.' (We think that he had heard 'baby' rather than lumbago.)

One had the feeling that he was deliberately mishearing and looking for the opportunity to twist things in this manner. Then the apparent deafness would pass, and we would run into a period when each day on arrival at the House of Commons, he would religiously check his watch against Big Ben. Or perhaps he would sit in the car checking the time taken to travel between Chartwell and Westminster, urging us to try and cut the time taken. He seemed to take the trip as a sort of challenge, a contest, an adventure, where he was on the sidelines and Bullock and I the participants. The trip was no longer just a familiar voyage, but a race along all-too-familiar roads.

This last quirk was all very well, but it led to one or two very narrow squeaks. As Prime Minister, Churchill's timing became meticulous, in contrast to his days as Leader of the Opposition, but it meant taking risks to achieve it. Our narrowest escape occurred at the junction of Constitution Hill and Hyde Park Corner while we made our way back from the House of Commons to Hyde Park Gate. The car was fitted with a police bell in those days, and this usually cleared a path for us when we were in a hurry, and I was the sole judge in using it. On this occasion, as we shot out of the Arch on the wrong side of the road, I'm afraid, a police car suddenly appeared with its own bell ringing furiously. Somehow we missed each other, only by millimetres, and we continued down Knightsbridge. I turned my head to look at Mr Churchill in the back of the car. He grinned widely and exhaled a cloud of cigar smoke.

15

THE OTHER CLUB

IN THE WINTER OF 1952 CAME an event which dealt a severe shock to Winston Churchill – the sudden death of King George the Sixth. The two had been personal friends for many years, the bonds between them forged unbreakably by five years of war. Together with friendship had gone a deep mutual respect. When the news came, shortly after breakfast on a bleak February morning, Mr Churchill was still in bed at No 10 Downing Street. Struggling up he made for his wife's bedroom, calling loudly for her in his distress. Later on, after his wife's ministrations, he appeared composed but thoroughly downcast, a state in which he remained for the following three weeks or so.

The funeral at Windsor, with all the historic weight of its pomp and circumstance, quite overwhelmed him. He would never attend a funeral unless he could not possibly avoid it, and, in fact, was not an ardent churchgoer at any time. On this occasion, with the highly moving pageantry of the funeral adding sombre undertones to the loss of a man he loved and admired, Mr Churchill was seen by his intimates to weep a great deal.

It seemed an indication of his state of mind that afterwards, he took not the usual whisky and soda, but a cup of tea. He was drinking this in the Deanery when suddenly General Eisenhower appeared.

'Say, Murray,' he demanded, 'where's Winston?'

'He's in there having a cup of tea, General,' I replied.

'A cup of tea?' he said in mock incredulity. 'I sure would like to see Winston drinking a cup of tea.' As I took him in to Mr Churchill, Ike turned to me and said, 'By the way Sarge, I'm having trouble finding my car – can you help me?' Telling him I would certainly do my best, I returned to the courtyard where the General's aides were searching furiously for the absent vehicle which did seem to have gone astray in the mass of VIP vehicles.

Within minutes I saw Inspector Smith of my own Special Branch who was there on anti-terrorist observation, and he directed me to the car. I escorted the driver to the Deanery door just as Ike came out. I got out and he climbed in, saying, It's just like they say, Mr Murray. If you want anything sorted out, get in touch with Scotland Yard.' This was not the only occasion I was to hear that sort of tribute to the Yard paid by some foreign dignitary.

During his second term as Prime Minister, there was little or no time for anything else but work for Mr Churchill. Holidays there were, of course, comparatively fleeting trips to the Continent, but these too, were greatly occupied by affairs of State. One function, however, which he strove never to miss, was the monthly meeting of the Other Club, whose members dined in the Pinafore Room of the Savoy Hotel on the first Thursday of each month that Parliament was in session.

His support of the club was really remarkable. On more than one occasion he returned to London from the South of France simply to attend the dinner, flying back to the Riviera a day or two later. When he fell ill in Roquebrune in 1958 he did his utmost to get the regular date changed in order that he might attend when he was fit again.

Such support was not really surprising as he was one of the two founders of the club, which came into being in 1911. He and F. E. Smith started it as a rival to a pompous group of Members of Parliament who had started The Club with a simple certainty of their own importance. Membership of the Other Club was restricted to fifty, not more than twenty-four of whom were to come from the House of Commons. Theoretically a club dinner was an occasion when men of varying political persuasions forgot their differences and mingled together. That was how it began, with twelve Tories and eleven Liberals from the House of Commons, with one Nationalist, T. P. O'Connor, who had the post of Secretary. But by the time I began escorting Mr Churchill there, only one Opposition member, the then Sir Hartley Shawcross, was on the books. He always attended in evening dress, complete with red silk-lined cloak and telescopic top hat.

The Other Club has always been a fascinating, yet little publicized, institution. Some of the best-known names in the land are always among its members. Of the forty men who were its original members in 1911, in addition to Churchill and F. E. Smith, there were names like Bonar Law, Admiral Lord Charles Beresford, who never spoke to Churchill anywhere else but at the Other Club dinners, in the course of a bitter feud, Lloyd George, Lord Kitchener, Beerbohm Tree, W. H. Massingham, who had been the editor of the *Daily Chronicle* until he lost his position because of his opposition to the South African War, and J. L. Garvin, editor of the *Observer* for some years until he resigned in 1942.

The long list of former members bears such names as Lord Asquith, Viscount Astor, Arnold Bennett, Viscount Camrose, the Duke of Devonshire, General Lord Gort, Henry Irving, Frederick Lonsdale, Sir Edwin Lutyens, Sir Desmond MacCarthy, Sir Oswald Mosley, Field Marshal Smuts, Lord Tweedsmuir and Brendan Bracken.

Such was the Old Man's enthusiasm that he was generally the first to put in an appearance at the Savoy for the monthly dinner where the ritual was always the same. Once out of the car he would allow the hotel's general manager, Mr Hofflin (who was to become a very good friend of myself and my wife because of our Swiss connections) then later Mr Contarini or Mr Griffin would take his arm and escort him to the Princess Ida room for the aperitif. Although he did not know it, the Savoy's own doctor was always on hand every time he went to the Other Club, but he was never called on to my knowledge. I would always have my aperitif there as well, and check each person as they entered. After a couple of meetings they used to treat me as an old friend and I enjoyed the meetings just about as much as the Boss.

The Club rules give the Executive Committee a great deal of power, and their decisions have never been subject to any form of appeal. To protect these men, whose precise number is never defined, one of the rules states that '. . . the names of the Executive Committee shall be wrapped in impenetrable mystery'.

Perhaps the most characteristic rule, however, is the last one, Number Twelve, which declares that 'nothing in the rules or intercourse of the Club shall interfere with the rancour or asperity of party politics'. To what extent that rancour and asperity persist is uncertain because, as I have said, the membership is now politically pretty one-sided. In any case this is something known only to a very few discreet waiters at the Savoy, and even they are required to leave the room when speeches begin.

The dinner always takes place in the Pinafore Room and I was allocated a special table in the Princess Ida room where I was served the same repast and drinks as the distinguished company next door. The door leading to the other room was always locked, so that access was only possible via the room where I sat in solitary splendour.

Marc Giachello was the manager of the private rooms in those days and he treated the Other Club as his own little private do, watching everything his waiters did and checking and rechecking that all was according to the traditions of the Club, and the Savoy. Marc had been at the Savoy for many years, working very hard to attain the supervision of the private rooms. He lived just outside London on the way towards St Albans, I think, and invited me several times to go rough shooting with him. I was never able to find the time but he used to tell me of the fine people who went with him.

Marc's great dream was to retire to the south of France where he would build his own house overlooking the Mediterranean. His wife's dream was to have a large kitchen with a great big window with a lovely view.

When he eventually retired in the early 1960s both dreams were realized; Marc had a lovely villa built at Cavalière, in the Var Region, not far from St Tropez and facing the Islands of Hyères, one of which is the Levant Island, a paradise of nudism. The Villa Mon Midi (my southern land) had all they wanted – the beautiful kitchen with picture windows facing the sea, garage under the kitchen with an English dartboard for visitors to amuse themselves, a very workable garden with all the fresh vegetables he required for his wife's cooking and a restaurant next door where their young son, André, was able to work, following in his father's footsteps. But their dreams were all shattered when his dear wife died only about six months after they had settled in.

When Beryl and I dropped in to see him on our way back by car from our stay at the Martinez in Cannes, thanks to Elleston and Jonquil Trevor, in 1965, it was still a depressed Marc who received us with open arms, *crudités* from the garden, canapés and champagne.

Whenever, during Marc's *séjour* at the Savoy, Beryl and I went to dine in the restaurant, although it was not his province, he never failed to appear towards the end of our meal with his bottle of vintage port which he would leave on the table for our benefit.

Even after Marc had left the Savoy, his successor bestowed upon us the same privilege on the rare occasions we went there.

The Old Man was always terribly superstitious about sitting down to a meal with thirteen people at the table, and to avoid this situation at the Other Club, a life-size wooden, or it might have been papier-mâché, model of a black cat was always there on a small shelf on the wall, ready to be placed in a fourteenth chair should it be necessary. Until this was done the Old Man would not even venture near the table.

On a couple of occasions the system almost broke down during the war. After a private party for members of a squadron of the Royal Australian Air Force in one of the private rooms, it was found that the cat was missing. Mr Churchill himself was informed and was so cross about it that he set an inquiry in motion and the cat was eventually recovered – minus tail and one ear – all the way from Singapore, though the offenders were never officially traced.

A few months later there was another party for the same squadron, and once more the cat disappeared at the end of it. Luckily one of the celebrants was found in the cloakroom trying to get the cat under his greatcoat. He was relieved of his prize which was then returned to his perch, only to disappear again a few minutes later. By a great stroke of luck, an off-duty waiter from the private rooms happened to be queuing for a bus in the Strand outside the Savoy, when he saw what was indubitably the cat's head sticking up out of an airman's coat. He took the cat from the man and returned it to its accustomed place where it continued to serve its purpose to lull Winston Churchill's superstitions for many years afterwards. In fact I hope that it is still there, even though he is gone.

Mr Churchill often took a guest to one of the dinners. On one particular occasion when his guest was Laurence Olivier, this led to some embarrassment. Every member of the Club is expected to pay his own bill at the end of the dinner, in cash. By some oversight, a waiter presented Mr Olivier, as he was then, with a bill. He paid, but was by no means very happy about the incident. I did not realize that he was Mr Churchill's guest for he came separately and was welcomed by all the diners, so when called upon, I just paid the Old Man's bill. Although Olivier and Vivien Leigh had been to Chartwell several times before that incident, henceforth we saw them not at all, and I have a vague feeling that it was a direct result of the non-payment of the bill. I was sure that Mr Olivier was later reimbursed by Mr Churchill.

I remember particularly an incident following another of the Club dinners, when Lord Montgomery was Mr Churchill's guest. This time his dinner was paid for as I knew he was not a member and we had collected him on the way to the Savoy at the Athenaeum where the Viscount stayed when he was in town. When we came to leave the Savoy to return to No 10, there was no sign of the official car outside the Savoy Hill entrance as it should have been, so I called one of the taxis standing near by. Mr Churchill and Monty climbed into the back and I jumped on to the luggage space beside the driver. We were in a hurry and I quickly silenced the driver's protests that no passengers were permitted in that place, by showing him my warrant card and informing him at the same time who his passengers were. The journey was a short one to Downing Street and when we arrived, the Prime Minister told me to pay the cabbie as usual.

But Monty protested. 'No, no,' he said, 'I will see to it, Sergeant Murray.'

'The Prime Minister instructed me to pay,' I said, reaching for my wallet, but Monty was adamant. I waited, while he searched high and low in all his pockets, eventually to discover only a halfpenny. I paid.

About the only other time I knew Sir Winston to travel by taxi was one evening in 1960, after he had been to the House of Commons for an evening session. Lady Churchill was using the car so, as instructed, and against my better judgement, I ordered a taxi to be at the Ladies' Gallery entrance at 10.15 pm. When Sir Winston had stated the time, I had pointed out that the cabbie would have to wait a long time because Sir Winston usually went to the Smoke Room on leaving the Chamber, but he would have none of it, so I complied.

The driver arrived at 10.15 pm. I told him it was for Sir Winston but he did not believe me and checked first with one of the policeman in the courtyard. Realizing that the illustrious person was indeed to be his passenger, he parked his cab and sat waiting patiently without even starting the meter . . . for the first twenty minutes anyhow, though it was another forty minutes before I managed to get Sir Winston to the cab, quite oblivious of the time.

On the way back to Hyde Park Gate, the taxi was driven with the sort of care that one associates with the carriage of eggs, and best new-laid at that, rare indeed for a London cabbie. At our destination

Churchill canvassing during the 1951 General Election campaign.
Behind him, to the left, is his protector, Sergeant Edmund Murray.
(*Magnum Photos*)

(*Above*) After casting his vote in the 1951 General Election, Churchill is escorted by Sergeant Murray (on his right) through an enthusiastic crowd. (*Associated Press*)

(*Below*) Leaving New York International Airport in 1952, Churchill is accompanied by Sergeant Murray (on his left) and the tall figure of Mr Bernard Baruch, financial adviser to numerous American Presidents.

(*Above*) Sir Winston and President Eisenhower during a visit to Washington in 1956.

(*following page*) The two great warriors, Sir Winston Churchill and Lord Montgomery, leaving Hyde Park Gate in 1962.

(*Below*) Nice Airport in 1957. Sir Winston is met by Emery Reeves (left), continental editor of Churchill's *The Second World War*, and M. Moatti, Prefect of the Maritime Alps Department.

Sir Winston gives his familiar V for Victory sign after having been made a
citoyen d'honneur at Roquebrune in the South of France, 1961.

(*Above*) On board Aristotle Onassis's yacht *Christina* during a Mediterranean cruise in 1960. From left: Sir Winston, Marshal Tito, Onassis, Tito's wife and Lady Churchill.

(*Below*) Monaco, 1962: Sergeant Murray representing Sir Winston upon the departure from the Principality of ex-Queen Victoria Eugenie of Spain. Also present are Prince Rainier and Princess Grace.

(*Above*) Sir Winston and Sergeant Murray survey Monte Carlo from the Grande Corniche on one of their frequent trips to the Principality. (*Pierre V-Manevy*)

(*Below*) January 17, 1965, just a few days before Churchill's death, Lord Moran, Sir Winston's private physician, issues a statement to the Press. (*UPI*)

the driver leapt out and opened the door, carefully helping his august passenger to alight. Having landed on the pavement, Sir Winston turned and gravely shook the driver by the hand. When, moments later, I pressed a pound note into the driver's hand, his face carried an almost trance-like expression, as if he had just seen a vision.

That was just one more example of the veneration with which the old Sir Winston was regarded by the majority of ordinary people in Britain.

To shake Sir Winston's hand, I might say, was an honour hundreds of people sought, although very few achieved. Many, many times on trips abroad, foreigners would come up to me and ask if they might be permitted to shake his hand, but I rarely allowed this of course. To have allowed one bystander to do so, would have been to open the way for numerous others to pester him. There were many highly persistent people, particularly Americans, who seemed to think that a simple act of courtesy like relinquishing a seat for him, for instance, in the Casino, entitled them to formal inclusion in his party.

In the summer of 1952, after an arduous ten months at No 10, the Churchills snatched a brief holiday in the south of France, staying at the Villa La Caponcina, belonging to their old friend Lord Beaverbrook, at Cap d'Ail, a charming little village a mile or so west of Monte Carlo. The villa, like a small monastery, was formerly owned by Captain Edward Molyneux, the famous dress designer, and was bought by the Beaver in 1939 – an act which clearly confirmed his personal faith in the 'There will be no war' thesis of the *Daily Express* in that year. Just to add to the irony of the situation later on, the Gestapo occupied the estate for part of the war.

On arriving there, the Old Man immediately issued instructions that I was the only person to handle his painting materials, a role assigned to me because of my own interest in painting.

Talking about Lord Beaverbrook reminds me of the day Sir Winston was invited to lunch at Cherkley, near Leatherhead, in Surrey. Owing to the fact that we had encountered very little traffic, we arrived half an hour early and as Sir Winston reached the door, assisted by the late Joe Bullock, his chauffeur hired from Rootes when Sir Winston was not in office, I had already rung the bell. The major-domo opened the door and, rather surprised to find us there, said, 'Good morning, Sir Winston. My Lord is in the garden.' Quick as a flash came the response, 'Walking on the lake, I presume.'

Quite by chance, my wife had presented me with the wherewithal to paint in oils shortly before I joined Sir Winston, to extend my range beyond the pastels and water-colours in which I had previously occasionally worked. Looking back I do remember that I had used oils when three of us, including Frank Southern as the sole collaborator I can remember, under the supervision of Joe Binks, the Art Master at my old Grammar School in Durham, painted a sort of fresco round the walls of the art room, many years before; and at Marrakesh, on our trip there in 1950, the Old Man questioned me very closely on my knowledge of oil painting, and I seemed to pass the inquisition. Thenceforth I was given the job of suggesting suitable painting sites first, then, when he realized that we had the same ideas about colour and composition, he relied upon me to set out the colours he would be needing at the spot I had chosen for him. This proved to save a lot of time, of course, but the enhanced collaboration between the two of us caused a certain amount of jealously on the part of my colleagues at the time.

In those days painting constituted a very important part of his life, there is no doubt about it, and for an amateur he was highly accomplished. Between 1950 and 1955 I feel that he painted some of his most acceptable paintings, many of them in the vicinity of the villa at Cap d'Ail, for it was one of his favourite spots.

Sir Winston's interest in painting all started when he was watching Sir John Lavery painting a Churchill portrait commissioned by the Armoured Car Division which he himself had created during the First World War. The job of making a picture, he thought, was very much like making a book, a job he knew something about, and he was immediately interested. Within minutes he was wearing Sir John's smock and splashing on oil paint. No more brooding, no more discussions or justifications. He was on his own and there was a complete withdrawal from all other matters. A different cluster of brain cells was being used and the relief was immense. He made rapid progress. Under a *nom de plume* or *nom de brush* as he once told me, four out of five paintings he exhibited at a Paris Exhibition in 1921 were sold for thirty pounds each. His painting equipment was to travel with him almost every time he travelled abroad afterwards. In his *Thoughts and Adventures* he wrote, 'Painting came to my rescue at a most trying time and I shall venture in a concluding chapter to express the gratitude I feel.' In that concluding chapter, which has also been published in book form as *Painting as a Pastime* he writes, 'When I get to Heaven I mean to spend a considerable portion of the first million years in painting and so getting to the bottom of the subject . . . but then I shall require a still gayer palette than I get here below. I expect orange and vermilion will be the dullest, darkest colours upon it, and beyond them will be a whole range of wonderful colours to delight the celestial eye.'

You might notice that he intended to get to Heaven. When he was asked on his seventy-fifth birthday if he had any fear of death, he said, 'I am prepared to meet my Maker. Whether my Maker is prepared for the ordeal of meeting me, is quite another matter . . .'

I was always very amused, and flattered, by the way he used to seek my advice – and then seemingly ignore it. He would say, for instance, 'Now where should I put the horizon – high or low?' I would suggest something and he would proceed to disregard my advice. Then later he would change his mind, and adopt surreptitiously, my own suggestion. By then, of course, it had become his own bright idea. I take no glory from this, I assure you, for we both knew that it was just a lovely little game we played.

Even so, it was not unusual for his paintings to contain tiny fragments of my hand, for on being asked for advice, I would take up a brush and deliberately introduce my own particular idea of colour or line, that he would find difficult to change. Well, put yourself in my place . . . it was more fun.

Sir Winston was a very quick painter and some of his best-known works, which have been exhibited at the Royal Academy, took only a couple of hours to complete. His method was to cover the canvas with a pale-blue outline of the scene and work up from that, sometimes from back to front, and at other times from the front backwards, making his rules and regulations as he went along, and often enough terminating the painting when he was back at Chartwell, in the studio.

As he filled the canvas with bold, courageous strokes, his concentration would be enormous, even his cigar being allowed to go out and remain out. He never minded people watching him because, while he was painting, he had no idea that they were there.

When he became immersed in a painting in that fashion it was the most difficult job in the world, almost, to drag him back for such a mundane thing as food. One classic episode during our visit in 1953 was on Frankfurt Beach, the private beach of silver sand belonging to Sir Harold Mitchell, at Montego Bay, in Jamaica. It was a beautiful situation, with the white breakers rolling in from a pure blue sea, to the feet of gently waving palm trees – an ideal site for the Old Man's boldly coloured pictures. He had been working for a couple of hours or so when Lady Churchill arrived. 'It's very good, my darling,' she pronounced, 'but lunch is in fifteen minutes.'

Her husband grunted in reply.

Some ten minutes elapsed, during which time he carried on working assiduously, then Christopher Soames came on the scene and said that he thought it 'very nice' . . . but we should be moving in five minutes. Another grunt was the only response.

Once more Lady Churchill appeared, this time with the usual family rallying call, 'Wow! Wow!' She stood looking at the painting over her husband's shoulder for a few strategic seconds, then said, 'Yes, it really is a beautiful picture, but we must be going now,' and moved away as if expecting him to follow immediately.

'Why can't she leave me alone,' I heard him say *sotto voce*. He was fairly boiling now. Then with his petulance mounting, 'You know nothing about it,' he called after her. She retired, defeated, to leave the field of battle to Mary, her daughter, who also drew a blank. I began to think that there might be a wager on who could get him to move. So I stepped in myself and told him that my lunch was waiting and could I leave him to fend for himself. He was only half an hour late for lunch, but it was I who had the black looks.

The therapeutic effect which painting had upon Sir Winston was a fact readily recognized by his family and staff. When we were abroad and he appeared to be bored or in a bad temper, or when he was recovering from an illness, I would always be urged to get him out painting. As an artist he was very susceptible to praise, and there was always plenty of that. His wife was usually quite a stern critic, however, and in a diplomatic way I, too, tried to make constructive criticism. He would ask me what I thought of a picture he was paint- ing and I would perhaps suggest that a certain tree, for example, would look better a little bit to the right, or the left, or not there at all. He would pointedly ignore my suggestion at the time. But at the next session I would find that the painting had been altered to fit in with my idea either during the time I had been to dinner, or when we were again on the site, when he would suddenly do the alter- ation while he turned to me and said, 'I think that tree will be better here, don't you think so?' I would agree, of course. There was also the odd occasion when he would hand me the brush he was using and suggest that I show him just where I thought the tree should be. A photographer from the *Daily Express* actually caught me doing just that, one day, in Marrakesh.

Sir Oswald Birley, I think, was his most honest critic, but however amateurish he might be, his tableaux were always a great attraction at the Royal Academy.

The Old Man was very keen to persuade his friends and acquaintances to take up the art of painting. His colleague 'RAB' Butler had, in fact, painted for some time, and he and members of his family joined the Churchills for a day at Cap d'Ail in 1952. Mr Butler, Chancellor of the Exchequer at the time, Sir Winston and I, all had easels set up in the blue-grass (imported from its native Kentucky by Lord Beaverbrook) garden, miles and miles away from the world of politics and finance.

Shortly afterwards, Willy Sax, who supplied ninety-five per cent of oil paints used by Sir Winston from his factory at Urdorf, near Zurich in Switzerland, and his wife, came to lunch at Cap d'Ail bringing with them to meet Sir Winston, a famous Swiss painter, M. Amiet, who showed us all how, according to him, the blue grass should be painted on canvas. It was really an instruction to see a master at work.

During a visit to the South of France in 1961, I was able to render a small service to a member of the Monte Carlo police. Later he told me that he had a cousin, called Marcel, who had a restaurant in Sloane Street, London. When I got back home, I telephoned Marcel to convey the good wishes of his cousin and he invited me to take my wife there for dinner, and arrangements were made.

The restaurant was just what Beryl and I had been looking for; the food was very good, the service excellent and the wine superb. Glancing round I concluded that the clientèle was upper middle class and they all seemed to be happy with the attention they were receiving. We were quite impressed. I suppose that we went back three or four times during the next twelve months and it was in March 1962 when Marcel decided to tell me a story.

In his beautiful English, beautiful because it was so Gallic, for Marcel would never wish to be anything but French, he recounted how a certain gentleman who had been to the restaurant several times had turned up one evening with a rather exuberant party of about a dozen people. They had been to the theatre, he gathered.

After a well-chosen meal of oysters, partridge à la Normandie, filet de boeuf à la Régence, salade Windsor, cheese and Poires Hélène the host asked for the bill, 'L'addition s'il vous plaît', for he spoke good French. Marcel gave him the bill.

The gentleman searched high and low for his cheque book but finally concluded that he had left it at home, and he did not have enough money in his pocket.

'Marcel,' he said, 'let me have a blank cheque please.' But Marcel did not understand, nor did his staff, so he asked the gentleman to explain. After the explanation and failing to find a blank cheque, Mr X asked for a sheet of paper.

Quite mystified, Marcel tore a clean sheet from his order book and handed it over. The man then wrote 'Please pay Marcel, for goods supplied, the sum of . . . pounds and charge to my personal account.' The man signed his name beneath, handed it to Marcel and told him to present it at the man's bank in Sloane Street the next morning. He then asked for their coats to be brought, gave Marcel a very good tip and departed with his friends.

'Monsieur Murray,' said Marcel, 'what was I to do? Call for help? Call the police? Would I ever be paid? I just prayed to le bon Dieu and went to bed.'

Marcel then told me that he had not slept a wink that night and that he was outside the bank the next morning, willing the doors to open quickly. At last the way was clear and he dashed to the *guichet* and pushed the piece of paper under the nose of the cashier. 'Is this good, can I have my money?'

The man behind the counter took a long look at the paper. 'Where did you get this?' he asked.

'The gentleman who came to supper last night gave it to me as he had no money. He called it a blank cheque. He said you would pay me,' gasped Marcel.

'Did you not recognize the man?' asked the cashier.

'No, of course I do not know him, but he has been to my restaurant several times. Can I have my money please?'

The cashier smiled broadly, and Marcel knew that all was going to be all right. The money was handed over.

'You might like to know the name of your client,' said the cashier. 'That is the signature of Mr Butler, the Chancellor of the Exchequer.' Marcel went his way back to the restaurant a very trusting, happy Frenchman.

Another member of the Government who painted with much skill was the then Chief Whip, Mr Patrick Buchan-Hepburn, later to become Lord Hailes when, in 1957, he was appointed the first Governor-General of the West Indies Federation. Dorothea, Viscountess Head, wife of another Churchill Cabinet Minister, the late Brigadier Anthony Head, PC, GCMG, CBE, MC, who was made a viscount in 1960, was also a very good painter, in fact in a letter to the *Sunday Telegraph* in October, 1985, she described herself as a professional artist, and we had long discussions on the subject of painting.

Sir Winston always took a great interest in my painting, and one day I received a deputation of Mr Butler and Mr Buchan-Hepburn in my office at No 10 Downing Street. They had been sent by Sir Winston from the Cabinet Room, after a meeting, to view my three entries for the Summer Exhibition at the Royal Academy. They expressed great surprise that they had not been accepted, but encouraged me to try again.

Lady Dorothy, wife of Mr Harold Macmillan, and the daughter of the 9th Duke of Devonshire, was uncommonly good as a painter. She loved to stop off at my office in No 10 when she was visiting, just to have a chat about our favourite hobby. After she died, my wife and I one day went to a reception at the Savoy, where, seeing Mr Macmillan sitting alone at a table in the corner, I went to him just to say hello. He asked my wife and me to join him and we chatted for a while as he reminisced about how his wife used to talk about Sir Winston's 'charming detective who painted so well and loved to talk about painting'. We were all very moved and there was not a dry eye at that particular table.

Sarah Churchill would sometimes paint, but the pastime was not shared by other members of the family, until Edwina Sandys, one of his granddaughters, made a name for herself as a painter in the US. On one occasion, also, young Julian Sandys, Edwina's brother, while on a visit to Chartwell, decided that he would like to have a go, and Sir Winston asked me to fix him up with an easel, brushes and paints, and to give him some instruction. Julian worked away rather laboriously but conscientiously over the weekend, but I do not think that he ever took it up as a serious hobby.

Although, naturally, except for that one occasion at Cap d'Ail, I never painted alongside Mr Churchill, I would often enough make a quick sketch of the scene he was working on, or very near to it, and then work on the canvas when conditions were more favourable. It was in this way that I came to produce the picture which I presented to Sir Winston and Lady Churchill on behalf of myself, my wife and family on the occasion of their golden wedding anniversary in 1958. The day before the anniversary which was to be celebrated *en famille* at La Caponcina at Cap d'Ail, I was pondering on the sort of gift we could offer, when I suddenly remembered the sketch I had done when we had visited Venice in 1951. This was a view of the Grand Canal and the Rialto Bridge and I felt that it would be particularly appropriate, because the Churchills had spent part of their honeymoon in that wonderful city. It took me three hours to complete from the sketch in the sketch-book that always accompanied me in those days – and I was content with the result. Next day, with the painting neatly framed, I handed it over, sti'l wet, to Mr Churchill. His reception of it was more than gratifying, for he instructed the valet to place it in his bedroom in such a way as to permit him to view it when he lay in bed. There it remained during the rest of the stay in France. When we returned to Chartwell, it was given a very favourable place in the studio – the only picture there that had not been painted by the Old Man himself.

In 1970 I wrote to Lady Churchill to suggest that if the painting was going to be somewhat lost or endangered when Chartwell was opened as a National Trust property, she might consider its return to its originator. She agreed to let me have it back and it is now a very important item in my collection.

On that brief holiday at Cap d'Ail in 1952, Mr Churchill spent most of his time painting, but there were also numerous social functions he had to attend. He was made Honorary Mayor of the village of Cap d'Ail and there was a 'duty' cocktail party to celebrate the event. There were also events in Nice and Monte Carlo which demanded his presence. During one of these at the Hotel de Ville in Nice, the Boss turned to the Prefect and said to him, 'This officer looks after me.' The Prefect, Mr Moatti, started to reply but he was stopped by Mr Churchill, who said, 'but wait and listen to the very important thing I have to tell you. This Scotland Yard officer spent eight years in your French Foreign Legion, and during the war at that.'

The Prefect immediately stepped forward and shook my hand, while the old warrior looked on approvingly like a schoolmaster introducing one of his brightest pupils.

I have it on the best possible authority that some time later, the Chief of the CID in Menton, near the Italian frontier, and the 'county town' of the district where, at Roquebrune, Sir Winston was to spend numerous holidays, proposed me for the great honour of the Legion of Honour, and M. Moatti was quite prepared to approve it for submission to Paris. However, he mentioned it to one of Sir Winston's staff who, for reasons quite obvious to myself, said that it was impossible, for Sir Winston himself did not have the honour.

16

THE PRYING PRESS

ON TRIPS ABROAD, ESPECIALLY TO the French Riviera, we invariably had trouble with too many enthusiastic photographers and reporters. On the 1952 trip, one of the newer weapons of the fourth estate, the helicopter, was employed to spy on Churchill while he painted in the seclusion of the Caponcina grounds. But he was quite unperturbed for, as he heard the chattering of the machine overhead, he commented, 'I may fly home in a helicopter too.'

'Would you wish to land in the Festival Grounds, Sir?'

'No,' said he, 'on the Horse Guards Parade. Why not?' chuckle, chuckle. He did not do so, however, and in fact, his first ride in a helicopter did not take place until some four or five years later when the American Navy picked us up at Nice Airport to carry us to the United States carrier *Randolph*, part of the Mediterranean Fleet, for dinner. It was a superb evening and I was told that permission had been obtained from the White House or the Pentagon, for champagne, whisky and cocktails to be served, probably for the very first time since the American Navy went dry.

Trouble with the Press was not, however, restricted to aerial observation. Walking in the gardens of the Caponcina once, after I had felt that there was something amiss in the area, a sort of sixth sense, which had often proved well founded, I suddenly spied a photographer hanging on the garden wall, just above a very small chalet where I could see four French police officers playing cards, supposedly on protection duty. (I had already warned them to be vigilant because of my presentiment.) I had encountered this same character in Marrakesh when I had confiscated a roll of film he had taken in dubious circumstances. To have reached his present position he must have passed the door where the policemen were seated, or else have climbed over the roof of the bungalow/chalet, without detection.

The photographer's intention was obviously to lie in wait until Sir Winston appeared and then to snatch some exclusive pictures for his magazine, *Paris Match* – just what I was there to prevent. I put my hand inside my jacket, on the butt of my pistol, and called out in menacing tones, 'Jacques . . . if you move another inch, you will find yourself limping for the rest of your life.' He froze, and when the Frenchmen dashed out of the building on hearing my voice, came down very slowly. There was great Gallic commotion. They were all for whisking him down to the police station, but he was my discovery, and so my responsibility. 'The best course for this gentleman, I think, is for him to leave Cap d'Ail and the Riviera and catch the first plane back to Paris.' Which was precisely what he did.

Often when the reporters were short of copy about Churchill, when the weather was bad, for instance, or it was cold, they would write stories about me and the facts about my life in the French Foreign Legion. For the most part they were quite flattering.

In the main, my relationship with the Press, British and foreign, was quite good. But the Old Man did not want publicity on his private visits, so it was part of my job to see that his wishes were carried out. It was all largely a battle of wits, a battle where I usually had the advantage, and frequently won.

Three months after returning to England from the Riviera, we were off abroad once more, to America and Jamaica this time. Our first stop was New York, the realization of a long-held dream for me, and we made the voyage by sea this time, travelling on the fabulous *Queen Mary* in the super luxury accorded all first-class passengers on that vessel. For me the high spot of the voyage was being allowed to steer the ship briefly on one of the several visits I paid to the bridge.

In bustling New York, Mr Churchill was the guest of a very old and dear friend, Bernard Baruch, the economist and banker. The two had first met during the First World War when Baruch visited England as the man in charge of munitions production in the United States, and Churchill was the newly appointed Minister of Munitions Production here. He was born in 1870 and his first job was in an office at the age of nineteen, but by very careful speculation on Wall Street he soon amassed a huge fortune. This permitted him to be generous to charities and public causes. In 1916, President Woodrow Wilson nominated him in an advisory capacity to the Council of National Defence and in 1919, he was a member of the Supreme Economic Council at Versailles, and personal economic adviser to President Wilson on the terms of peace.

Thenceforth he was financial and economic adviser to a succession of American presidents.

Every day the lofty figure of 'Bernie' – he was 6 ft 4 in tall – could be seen on the way from his apartment on East 66th Street to a bench in Central Park, where he would sit with his secretary-cum-nurse, Elizabeth Navarro, and watch the world go by. One day, to the delight of the Press, Mr Churchill accompanied Mr Baruch to his bench, but their conversation there was quite secret due to the noise of the clicking cameras.

Back at the apartment, one afternoon, the two old gentlemen had a visitor in the shape of Mrs Eleanor Roosevelt, an old friend of Baruch. As I whisked her up to the appropriate floor in the private lift, she turned to me and said, 'Mr Murray, you have a most enviable job, guarding the most wonderful statesman of all time.'

On this visit to the United States it was interesting to observe the scale on which American security precautions were based, compared with the British. At Baruch's apartment for instance, there were always half a dozen uniformed policemen and a dozen plain-clothes detectives and Secret Servicemen on hand. When General Eisenhower, the President-elect at the time, paid a visit to the place, it was simply alive with bodyguards. On the British side there were only two of us.

This was quite routine for the Americans as I discovered later. Compared with our arrangements, their security was always on a mammoth scale, a reflection, probably, on the police techniques of the two countries. The Americans work with a good deal of outward show, and in large numbers, whereas we do things on a much quieter and more modest scale – but achieve equally satisfying results.

To Baruch himself, all the fuss must have been amusing, for if there was one man who could never have needed a bodyguard, it was he. His easy-going, highly democratic nature was in fact an embarrassment at times because if I was around when he and Winston Churchill were having a drink – and I usually was in the vicinity – he would always expect me to join them, a practice which was rather unusual for a bodyguard, to say the least.

'Hi, Sarge,' he would greet me, 'how's the Boss?' and the inquiry was far more than a formal one. He would always demand to be told privately just how Mr Churchill was keeping, and he would always conclude our chat with the exhortation, 'Well, look after him. There's no one like him, never has been, never will be.'

When General Eisenhower was leaving after a long chat with Mr Churchill and Mr Baruch, a photographer took a picture showing the two statesmen and myself. When I saw it later that day, I thought it was an excellent photograph. I obtained a copy from the photographer and asked Mr Churchill to sign it. Then I gave it to one of Ike's men and he signed it as well. Unfortunately, due to a misunderstanding, I was obliged to let the picture go to a close friend. This friend had bought General Eisenhower's book *Crusade in Europe* and had asked me if I could get it signed by the General. This I did, but instead of just signing his name, the President-to-be had written, 'To Edmund Murray from Dwight D. Eisenhower'. The only thing I could do was to keep the book and relinquish the photograph to compensate.

The Duke of Windsor also paid a visit to the Old Man at Bernie's on that occasion. Shyly he shook hands with me as I took him to the lift, and he inquired about the state of health of his friend. In his unassuming way he told me that it always gave him the greatest pleasure to meet Mr Churchill, and I am sure that the pleasure was reciprocated. Their meetings were occasions of reflection, however, and they always left the two of them much moved, and as far as my boss was concerned, very close to tears.

Some five years were to elapse before I met the Duke of Windsor again, in the south of France. It was at the Villa La Pausa, at Roquebrune, above Menton, the home of Emery Reves, the Continental editor of Mr Churchill's *The Second World War*. Churchill was recovering from a bout of the flu and the Duke had come to visit him. I was standing at the entrance to the property when a chauffeur-driven car pulled up and the Duke stepped out of the back and came towards me with hand extended in greeting. 'Hallo there, Mr Murray, I haven't seen you since New York.' We shook hands. 'I don't think you've met my wife, the Duchess,' he said, and opening the car door, he said, 'Darling, this is Inspector Murray of Scotland Yard.' We shook hands. 'I'm so glad to see him still looking after my very best friend.' He climbed into the Rolls and I jumped in beside the driver to escort them to the 'presence'.

While in New York we made a very interesting visit to the birthplace of Mr Churchill's mother, in Henry Street, Brooklyn. To my surprise, I found as we drew up to the house with a screaming of sirens from eight police motor-cycle outriders, that Lady Randolph had been born in very modest surroundings indeed. The small house, with a garden the size of a postage stamp, was still inhabited and when half a dozen of us crowded in, it was very full.

Although Winston Churchill undoubtedly inherited his political capacity from his father's side of the family, I am sure that much of the dash and vigour exhibited throughout his life came from his mother's side. Before her marriage to Lord Randolph in 1874, she had been Jeanette Jerome, daughter of Leonard Jerome, a forceful and very independent-minded New York businessman who, by the time his daughter married, had become very wealthy. As proprietor and editor of the *New York Times*, during the American Civil War he had fortified his office with rifles and cannon against mobs who disagreed with the opinions expressed in his newspaper and rioted furiously outside the offices. Lady Randolph was much renowned for qualities which her son was later to show to a marked degree — wit, honour, loyalty, sincerity and above all, steadfast and pugnacious courage.

From New York we flew to Washington for a stay lasting just twenty-two hours. For two of those hours we were at the White House where the Boss had a conference with President Truman, then on the point of relinquishing office. It was a good time to visit the White House because it was really looking splendid after the several million dollar overhaul it had just received. For many, many years previous to that, it had simply been patched up, and when it was thoroughly surveyed after Miss Margaret Truman's piano had fallen clean through the floor into an empty (luckily) room below, it was found to be in a state of near collapse. It is interesting to note that in the Kennedy film, shown on the occasion of the twentieth anniversary of his assassination, a lot of prominence was given to Mrs Kennedy's redecorating to the tune of several million pounds more, after the departure of President Eisenhower and his wife Mamie.

A year or two later, one of my own paintings joined the Stevens collection on a wall of the White House, and remained on view until the retirement of President Eisenhower in 1961. No other collection had remained there as long. It was a still-life of carnations and ferns, painted during a slack spell at Roquebrune when I was there with Sir Winston. It found its way to the White House when Thomas E.

Stevens, who was the President's Appointments Secretary, asked me to contribute to the group of paintings he had assembled to hang in the corridor directly outside the President's office. Strangely enough there was no painting by Churchill, but Ike himself had contributed, and there were two by Averell Harriman, who was eventually to become the husband of young Winston Churchill's mother (Pamela Digby before her first marriage, to Randolph Churchill).

From Washington we took off for Jamaica in President Truman's personal plane, the *Independence* or *The Flying White House* as it was more commonly known. In those days pressurization in aircraft was a novelty and this plane was not pressurized. As a result, we had one of the roughest trips I remember.

On doctor's orders, Mr Churchill was not allowed to fly higher than around 17,000 feet, so that when we ran into a terrific storm, there was no way of going above it. In deference to their important passengers, the pilot tried to take the plane round the storm, but it was much too extensive so there was nothing they could do but plunge right through it and hope for the best. For hour after hour the blasted thing kept pace with us; lightning played all around and hailstones like cricket balls kept striking the fuselage and wings like shrapnel. Through it all the Old Man sat quite unperturbed drinking his whisky and soda and pulling regularly at his cigar, which by all rights should have been extinguished anyway. I do believe that he was actually enjoying it, and I suppose, as he had said on his seventy-fifth birthday, he was prepared to meet his Maker.

In some wonderful way, the crew managed to produce food, despite the constant rolling and pitching of the aircraft. In those days, when food was still rationed in Britain, the portions they gave us were of gigantic proportions, and some of it went untouched. In my own case, the beefsteak was much too large and I only ate half of it.

In Jamaica there were huge crowds, with big white smiles on shining black faces to welcome us and as our cars made their way via ramshackle villages – well, they seemed ramshackle to me then, but later I grew to love the warm, friendly imbroglio peculiar to the West Indies – the inhabitants would follow us as far as they could, on foot or on bicycles, waving madly all the while. Just one more example of the esteem in which Mr Churchill was held by great and small.

Our destination from Montego Bay, was Prospect, the home of Sir Harold and Lady Mitchell and although the comfort and hospitality accorded the party there was considerable, the weather was far from cooperative throughout our stay. It rained for a good part of the time. In fact, it was the wettest January they had had for many years, and in consequence Mr Churchill was robbed of much painting time, and he was correspondingly depressed. A direct result of the weather was that once he got cracking on a painting and the sun was giving him the light he enjoyed, he forgot all about food and other people, and when he had to perform those things that are necessary, especially in elderly gentlemen, the toilets very few and far between, the nearest tree had to suffice.

Lady Churchill would, of course, have to organize times for meals, though luckily, the Mitchells and Captain and Mrs Soames, who had been with us throughout, were the only guests. Getting him away from his canvas turned out to be a major operation. If only they had learned to leave it to me, for I also had to eat, it would have been much easier. But no, they had to come along and pester him, and he always reacted strongly to that. However, though tempers did flare pretty often, anger would collapse very quickly when faced with Mr Churchill's rosy, shamefaced, puckish, cheeky inquiry, 'Did I keep you waiting? I am sorry.'

Sir Harold Mitchell's estate was an extensive one, and he had a very fine herd of Brahman cattle which were guarded by drovers on horseback. I was issued with a grey horse to patrol the estate each morning for security reasons, of course, although I loved riding through the extensive woods surrounding the property.

Jamaica is a lovely island, 150 miles long by 50 miles wide, and when Queen Elizabeth I asked one of her prominent sailors, some sixty years after the island had been discovered by Columbus in 1494, what the island was like, he is said to have taken a large piece of brown paper, and, crumpling it up in his hands, dropped it on to a table to show his Queen the distinctly irregular formation of the island. One trip of great interest took us through the Green Forest, where the vegetation is very much like that of our own country and so abounds with all the trees, ferns and wild flowers with which we are familiar.

The Governor of the day was Sir Hugh Foot, later Lord Carradon (brother of Michael Foot), and of course he invited the Churchill party for dinner and to spend the night. During a reception in the afternoon in the grounds of Government House, the military band played. The uniform worn by the members of the band resembles very much that of the famous Zouave Regiment of France's pre-1962 army in North Africa, including a sort of white turban, white blouse, red bolero, black baggy pants, shoes and white spats. Queen Victoria was watching a parade in France one day when she noticed the uniform worn by the Zouaves taking part. She asked the aide if there was a similar uniform worn in the British Army and when she heard that there was not, she ordered one to be made for the oldest native regiment we had. It happened to be the Jamaican regiment and when it adopted a more conventional garb, years later, the colourful uniform was bestowed on the band and they still wear it.

While Winston and Captain and Mrs Soames stayed at Prospect, I stayed at the Rebellion Inn, having organized a twenty-four hour guard by members of the local constabulary, and from where I had a direct line connecting me with Prospect. It was a lovely hotel with the bedrooms just above ground level to make use of any small breeze that might be blowing to cool the nights, and the restaurant and other facilities were below ground level. A frequent visitor to the hotel at that time was the famous actor, Stewart Grainger, who was making a film just a short distance away. The film, if I remember rightly, was *All The Brothers Were Valiant*. The village there was Ochio Rios, probably a large town now for I know that several big hotels have since been erected around it, taking advantage of the fabulous beaches. It received its name from the fact that no less than eight rivers of the hundred to be found in Jamaica came down to the sea there. The film was being made on one of these rivers that ran by the side of a property whose owner was away. The agent, however, had given permission for Mr Churchill to use it for his painting. So his easel was erected and he began to paint in the knowledge that I was there to protect him from interruption. When Mr Grainger and his acolytes heard about this proximity they decided to go down in the boat they were using for the film, to meet, or at least observe, the Prime Minister at work, private holiday or not. But on the way down they came to a small bridge over the river, and I had organized a reception committee for all intruders. A strong net, attended by Jamaican police officers, was stretched across the waters interdicting all passage. Frustrated, they called upon me to allow them through, but I told them that it was all according to Mr Churchill's wishes. I was sorry, but there was no entry. They turned around, disappointed, but not before shouting as loudly as they could, 'Good luck, Winston. Happy holiday,' and went away.

Later that evening I was able to apologize to the film star, who was very nice about the incident. We had a drink and parted the best of friends. While with him, I was very struck by the way he could not ever pass a mirror without stopping and examining himself thoroughly to check that his tie was straight and his hair as it should be.

The remarkable thing about the river there, was that I could, and did, stand in the middle of it, with one bare foot in fresh water and the other in salt water.

The party made a tour of the island and the whole of the Jamaican population seemed to have turned out, because of course the trip had to be announced beforehand. For most of the trip Mr Churchill sat on the folded-down canvas roof of the car in a very uncomfortable position.

As Prime Minister he naturally had to keep in touch with events in Britain throughout the world. There was a lot of labour unrest in Jamaica at the time and the telephone and post office workers were due to come out on strike. But when they heard that Mr Churchill was coming to their island they called it off. They even laid a telephone line from Kingston, the capital, to Prospect, a distance of seventy-five miles, and set up a small exchange in the grounds for good measure.

At the end of the stay, the Prime Minister had more or less promised to stop off for a few minutes at Noël Coward's property, as it was on the way between Prospect and Montego Bay Airport, but it was abandoned as the heavens opened and the rain poured down as it only can in tropical places. Mr Coward however sent his staff to line the route outside the property and wave palm fronds as the cavalcade went past.

17

ILLNESS STRIKES

IN MARCH 1953 THERE WAS an event of some considerable international importance. Marshal Tito, President of Yugoslavia decided to visit Britain. The security precautions for the visit were particularly rigorous, and like so many people in this country, I was slightly taken aback by the heavy escort of motor-cycle outriders which Tito and his entourage were given, and the high speed at which they were driven around, as if anticipating that somewhere, someone would take a shot at them. However, things went off very smoothly, to the relief of everybody including, not least, Mr Churchill.

Mr Churchill had a very real liking for Tito, based largely, I imagine, on the President's wartime exploits as leader of the partisans in Yugoslavia. Randolph Churchill had been parachuted into the country to join Tito, of course, which lent a strong family link to the sentiments. In fact, I was led to understand, though I could never check the information, that Tito had in some way saved Randolph's life during the guerrilla warfare against the Germans.

The emotion stirred in Mr Churchill in his encounters with other wartime leaders, such as Tito, was made very plain to me during another meeting at which I was again present, in 1959. On that occasion we were aboard the Onassis yacht, and we had called at Split, in Yugoslavia, in the course of a cruise in the Adriatic, en route for Greece. For a long time the Old Man regarded Tito after their first words of greeting, and finally, with tears rolling down his cheeks, he said, 'When I look at you, the past all comes flooding back to me.'

Then, with President Tito holding one arm, and Mr Churchill holding my arm on the other side, we slowly walked round the grounds of the President's villa close to the rocky coast. They talked about what a struggle it had been; how people in both countries had been made to suffer; that Tito had perhaps been happier than the people in London, for he had been fighting the aggressor actively, whereas Londoners had had to just sit there waiting for the dreaded bombs to fall on their heads and homes and children, unable to retaliate; and about how there was no peace in the world. Neither of them could restrain the tears that fell, and there was a mist in my eyes as well.

When President Tito paid his visit to England I was able to perform a service which earned me a standing invitation to Belgrade – an invitation I have, as yet, been unable to take up. At a reception at the Yugoslav Embassy in Kensington Gore I was introduced to Tito's head of security, a colonel, and pretty soon our conversation turned to the qualities possessed by English gun-dogs. The colonel announced that Marshal Tito was anxious to acquire some long-haired dogs, because the short-haired animals they used in Yugoslavia tended to collect burrs on their coats which caused skin irritation, with the result that they continually had to stop and scratch instead of chasing after the game.

It so happened that I visited a pet shop in Chelsea just a few days earlier to discuss, on behalf of Mr Churchill, a possible shampoo visit by Rufus, and I had had a long chat with the owner about dogs. She apparently had kennels out in the Kentish countryside and was very well known in doggy circles. I immediately thought about that lady when the colonel told me about the President's wish, and the very next day, accompanied by the Yugoslav military attaché from the embassy, I went back to the shop where the owner had procured a fine setter in superb condition. The attaché knew quite a lot about dogs and was absolutely delighted with the animal and bought it at once. A few days later he was in touch with me again. A bitch was now required for breeding purposes and the demand was very quickly fulfilled from the same source. To show his personal appreciation President Tito sent me an autographed copy of his book about Yugoslavia at war. It was signed with his real name of Josip Broz, not with the name under which he had become famous as the leader of the Yugoslavian partisans, Tito. With the book came the standing invitation to visit Belgrade, and this was renewed at Split, in 1959, when once again I met, with Tito and a number of other members of the entourage, the military attaché who had accompanied me to the dog shop in Chelsea. He reported that the setter kennels they had established in Yugoslavia were very successful.

*   *   *

A month after President Tito's visit, in April 1953, there was a highly significant event in the life of Mr Churchill – he was knighted by the Queen. The honour was a very well-kept secret, quite as closely guarded as the engagement of Princess Margaret and Tony Armstong-Jones, and it certainly took most people by surprise including myself. It had always seemed that he was determined to remain plain Mr Churchill and in this connection I remember an amusing conversation which had taken place about a year earlier. We were driving along a muddy rutted, pot-holed Puddledock Lane, which skirts the estate at Chartwell, when Christopher Soames, who was riding with him in the back of the estate wagon said, 'So you have decided not to accept a peerage then?'

'No, I'm not accepting one,' was the reply, and suddenly the Old Man was laughing loudly.

'What is so funny about that?' asked Christopher.

'I was just thinking,' Mr Churchill spluttered as we bounced along the awful lane, 'that if I became Lord this and Lord that, Randolph would probably become Lord of Puddledock Lane,' and he bubbled with laughter, joined very quickly by his son-in-law.

I am sure that the reason he did not accept a peerage was because his strong sense of history and tradition led him to hope that the name and fame of the Churchills would be perpetuated in the House of Commons, possibly by the grandson who bears, and proudly so, his own name. It is rather intriguing to note, however, that shortly after Sir Winston died, his wife accepted a life peerage, bestowed on her by a Labour government under Harold Wilson.

The first hint I had of impending advancement for him was as we were about to set off for Windsor, from Downing Street, on the day he was knighted. When he climbed into the car, his Private Secretary, Mr Jock Colville, who was soon to be knighted himself, said as he helped him in, 'Goodbye Mr Churchill – for the last time,' and Mr Churchill replied, 'Oh yes, of course.' This gave me food for thought on the way west to Windsor. I surmised from the conversation that something was in the wind, and when I went for lunch in the steward's room at the Castle, half an hour or so after our arrival, the facts were revealed. The Queen, I was told, had just bestowed the accolade upon him and he would henceforth be Sir Winston Churchill, Knight of the Garter.

His own reaction was one of modest pleasure, though he said nothing to reveal his feelings in answer to the congratulations of the staff. The only remark he made to me was, rather strangely I thought, 'My wife is very pleased. She will be Lady Churchill now.'

Less than three months later the pendulum of fate had swung in the reverse direction and serious illness struck, dispelling a sense of well-being and replacing it with weeks of anxiety. Sir Winston was then seventy-eight years old and had been back in office as Prime Minister for some twenty months. To the strain of office was added the arduous ritual of the Coronation of Her Majesty Queen Elizabeth II which had taken place just a month earlier.

The malady which struck him down in July 1953 was, in fact, a stroke, although it was not to be made public until 1983, under the thirty-year rule. The Press was simply told that the Prime Minister was in need of a complete rest. So successful was the blackout on the true nature of the situation that some papers suggested that it was a 'diplomatic illness' designed to make it possible to avoid the impending Big Three Conference between the leaders of Great Britain, America and France, which was due to begin in Bermuda a few weeks later. But there was no question of his avoiding the conference and it was actually held five months later.

As soon as I was informed of the stroke, I telephoned my colleague in Barnet and told him that Sir Winston was in a bad state but not a word of the illness was to leak out to the Press. I suggested that he get down to Chartwell as quickly as possible for it was going to be a two-man job. Sir Winston had been found blue in the face and speechless by the valet when he went in to wake him in the morning. He had at once given him the prescribed tablet and had summoned the local doctor. The effects of the stroke began to pass off after an hour or so and he regained the power of speech. Later that same day, true to his bulldog spirit, he was again dictating letters.

My colleague and I kept the Press and the public at bay, with the garden gates closed and by carrying out patrols a bit more often than usual. We were very noncommittal to all inquiries when we went to lunch in Westerham or Brasted.

But the illness was serious. He remained in bed for four days and when he did get up, he found that his right leg was partially paralysed and his right arm and the side of his face were also affected. But it was impossible to treat him as a normal invalid. He refused to stay indoors, for example, and since the doctors had advised him to use his legs and arms as much as possible, his wishes were acceded to.

Luckily the weather was fine and warm and my colleague and I went to great trouble to see that there were no possible onlookers when we carried him into the garden to enjoy the sunshine. The secrecy regarding the illness was maintained throughout and it certainly proved something about the devotion of police and staff of the time to the old gentleman.

Any acute observer might well have guessed the nature of his illness when Sir Winston returned to active duty, though, for the stroke was to affect his right leg permanently. It always dragged slightly making it rather difficult to climb in and out of motor cars, for instance. In fact, Rootes Garage who supplied the driver, Joe Bullock, during the years when he was not at No 10 Downing Street, converted the back seat so that half of it could be moved forward and swung round in order to facilitate his movements into, and out of, the vehicle.

Throughout his illness he never relinquished his cigars, however, smoking them in bed just as avidly as out of bed. He had long had the habit of smoking in bed and at one time used to wear a kind of bib in towelling designed by Lady Churchill and made by a member of the staff, to keep the ash from the cigars from falling on to his pyjamas, or rather the top of his pyjamas or silk vest, for it was very rarely indeed that he wore the trouser part. The main reason for the bib, however, was because when he had previously used handkerchiefs for the same purpose, he had burned holes in several of them, and there was a distinct risk that one day he might set himself on fire.

It was not until the middle of September that Sir Winston was fit enough to convalesce, and once more he chose to do it at Cap d'Ail. The secrecy in which his illness had been veiled continued at this time, and instead of being booked on to the flight to Nice in his own name, he travelled as 'Mr Hyde'. Such precaution was justified, though, because it diverted a lot of attention which the Press would otherwise have paid to him had his real name appeared in advance on the passenger manifesto. As it was I had considerable trouble with a French woman journalist, but I was able to checkmate her plan to approach Mr Churchill. The day before we set off she arrived at No 10 Downing Street and handed in a letter for the Prime Minister, and was allowed into the hall while she waited for a reply from the Private Secretary. I saw her there and recognized her as someone with whom I had previously had some trouble at Cap d'Ail when she had tried to force her attentions upon my protégé. She did not recognize me, however, and did not realize that I understood

French. In consequence, she chatted away in her own language with the man who accompanied her, and told him that if she could not get the interview she sought here, she planned to confront the Prime Minister on the aircraft to Nice. How she had the information about the flight did not emerge, but apparently she already had a seat booked on the plane.

I made certain that she was not received at Downing Street, and she and her companion left. I also contacted my colleagues of the Special Branch giving a full description, and her name, of course, and officers were on duty to watch her at London Airport. British European Airways were also informed and cooperated fully, so that when she tried to check in, she was politely informed that there was no room on the plane for Nice. She created quite a stir at the news and had to be escorted to a private office accompanied by Special Branch detectives. When Sir Winston and his party arrived, all was calm. I had told Sir Winston and Lady Churchill that there was the faint possibility of trouble, and they were really disappointed when nothing happened as they were curious to see the lady in question, but they certainly did not wish to be interviewed. The journalist had been successfully dealt with and we never heard from her again.

The holiday at Cap d'Ail passed peacefully and uneventfully, the Old Man wishing to do nothing else but paint for most of the time, which meant that I was much in demand setting out his easel, paints and brushes, and discussing subjects and the state of the weather, and going out to find suitable sites.

'If only you could order and arrange the weather as you do my painting material, it would be wonderful,' he said to me on one occasion with that boyish, yet satanic, smile which from time to time illumined his features.

The highspot of that particular period at Cap d'Ail was a most magnificent firework display staged one evening at the Sporting Club of Monte Carlo, when the Churchills were dining there. Sir Winston was a most enthusiastic lover of fireworks and in fact on numerous occasions we would arrive from Chartwell or Hyde Park Gate at Edenbridge for the annual 5th November bonfire celebrations, and, of course, he had really enjoyed the Coronation fireworks festival in London. He also enjoyed a good fire when he could find one to watch, as on the occasion we were driving from the House of Commons to Chartwell, rather late at night. At Crystal

Palace we found our passage blocked by crowds of people, fire engines and hoses. Part of the derelict Crystal Palace was on fire.

'If it's a fire I should like to see it,' said the Boss from the back seat. 'I shall get out.' Undaunted by the fact that he was only wearing his blue carpet slippers, his usual footwear when on his way from London to Chartwell for the weekend, he got out of the car and picked his way through the hoses along the water-covered road to a vantage point. He surveyed the proceedings for a good ten minutes before he returned to the car. 'That was a very nice fire,' he said appreciatively as he climbed into the back seat.

Then there was the afternoon when we were again on our way to Chartwell, via Purley, Woldingham and the B2024, so we must have been returning from the races to the west of London, rather than the usual road through Crystal Palace and Biggin Hill which we used when coming from Kensington or Westminster. About two miles from Westerham, at a sharp right-hand bend of the road, there stood, in those days, a couple of houses. As we approached the bend, a cloud of smoke could be seen coming from the chimney of one of the houses and as soon as we drew level, Sir Winston called on Bullock to stop the car.

'You had better go and see if they know about it,' he said to me. I went over and knocked on the door and an elderly woman appeared.

'Yes, I do know my chimney is on fire, but what can I do about it?' she asked.

Going round to the back of the house, I found some old sacks and quickly drenching a couple of them with water from an outside tap, I hurried in and held them over the front of the fireplace. Within ten minutes the flames subsided, the smoke disappeared and I was able to leave and go back to the car. The woman began to thank me profusely, but I said, 'Don't thank me, thank Sir Winston Churchill.'' She looked surprised at this, so I told her it was on his instructions that I had come to help. Clearly, she would have liked to thank him personally, but she was very dishevelled and dirty from the soot and dust and resisted the urge, so she asked me to do it for her.

Back in the car I put him in the picture as to what had been done and how the lady was very grateful. He puffed patiently at his cigar with a look on his face like that of a Boy Scout who had performed his good deed for the day.

*　　*　　*

Every week during the period that Parliament was in session, Sir Winston, as Prime Minister, would report to the Queen at Buckingham Palace. His respect for royalty in general, and for the Queen in particular, was quite immense, as was clearly demonstrated when, for example, he met her at race meetings. He would be ushered up to the Royal Box where he would shake hands, very tenderly, with Her Majesty, making a deep bow and keeping his eyes twinklingly fixed on a point somewhere between her knees and her ankles. At the conclusion of the conversation there would be another deep bow of respect, and then he would back slowly away in such a rapt and concentrated manner that I would always prepare myself to jump to him should he fall backwards down the steps.

On one of our visits to Buckingham Palace I got a fascinating glimpse behind the scenes, such as few people ever have. Sir Winston's Humber Pullman was parked in the inner courtyard and the driver and I sat waiting for him to return from his audience with the Queen, when a second car drove up and Prince Philip got out. He disappeared through a swing door into the Palace. Seconds later a small boy emerged. It was Prince Charles. He stood there for a short while, then a strident voice called out, 'Come in'. The Prince took not the slightest bit of notice, and the command was repeated, but still the Prince ignored it. Suddenly the door partly opened and a hand reached out to take Prince Charles roughly by the ear. 'When I tell you to come in, I mean just that,' said Prince Philip, as he drew his lamenting son, very unceremoniously, back into the building.

The caste system among royal servants was always very carefully observed, I discovered the very first time I had lunch in the staff quarters at Windsor Castle. Everyone there was seated according to rank, with the Chief Steward at the head of the table. Uniformed flunkeys moved discreetly around giving me the impression that I was at a State Banquet, and from the oppressive silence which prevailed as we began to eat, it seemed as if a meal at Windsor Castle was some constraint-laden ritual. When I asked if I could have a bottle of beer or something to drink with my meal, there was immediate unspoken consternation, for I was well down the table, below the salt I am sure, had there been only one salt cellar. Eventually, a bottle of beer was produced, though I was given to understand that it was very unusual. However, as I was a guest. . . .

The meal progressed to the accompaniment of very subdued and intermittent remarks at the top of the table, as if the lower ranks were not allowed to speak. Soon the whole thing became a bit too much for me. To nobody in particular I suggested that a telephone line should be installed in order that I might speak to my friend at the top of the table, and I indicated the Chief Steward whom I had known for a number of years. All along the line, heads swivelled in my direction in frozen silence, and then they turned toward the Chief Steward to watch the great man's reaction. To his credit, he responded: 'Well, you see, Mr Murray, we've never needed one in the past, but I can see that it could prove useful.' But the ice was broken, and the rest of the meal proceeded in an atmosphere that was almost warm, with quite a number of inquiries directed towards me on the subject of Sir Winston.

A ritual of another kind was the annual visit to his old school, Harrow, for Songs, each November. It was a function he enjoyed immensely, and one which he made great efforts to attend regularly following an initial visit there in 1940. It was always a splendid occasion for the school too, as the boys demonstrated by their wonderful enthusiasm. My job became virtually superfluous as soon as we reached the school, because the senior boys linked arms to protect the Headmaster and Sir Winston from the brush of the rest of the school in a sort of slow-moving chain as we approached the Hall. The function usually lasted a couple of hours, during which time the monitors would be introduced, as would foreign royal students or ex-students, like King Hussein of Jordan and King Faisal of Iraq, who might be present.

The songs always stirred him deeply, especially when an extra verse was added to the old favourite, 'Forty Years On', so that it became henceforth 'Sixty Years On', to mark his eightieth birthday. Speaking to the students once, he said, 'It gives me immense pleasure to listen to these tunes and words which touch my heart and which have inspired my actions and my life,' and he clearly meant every word he spoke.

I always enjoyed those visits to Harrow because I had friends, a master and his wife, at the school. Not long after the war I had met them on a train travelling across Europe, when I was actually on my way to Lucerne to get married. The next time we met, to our intense surprise, was some four years later when I arrived at Harrow in the company of Winston Churchill.

The Old Man's determination not to miss this annual pilgrimage to Harrow was such that he would not be deterred by even the worst weather. On one occasion, emerging from the school at the end of the songs and the get-together for drinks and canapés afterwards, we found the fog so thick that we could hardly see a yard ahead. The journey back to Kensington was a complete nightmare, with my having to walk in front of the car three parts of the way keeping to the kerb and shining my electric torch behind me so that the driver could follow, until we came to the main street lighting of London proper. Eventually we reached Hyde Park Gate, greatly relieved to have avoided becoming completely stranded, but with my eyes tired and sore, my feet aching. The relief was shared by the passengers, Jock Coville, Lady Churchill and Sir Winston. The instant the car stopped, Lady Churchill got out and disappeared into the house through the door I had just opened; a moment or two later she reappeared, bearing two bottles of champagne. Smiling broadly she handed one to Mr Bullock and the other one to me, while her husband looked on approvingly.

At the beginning of December 1953 came the Bermuda Conference, postponed earlier in the year because of Sir Winston's illness. Both he and Mr Eden, the Foreign Secretary, were there to represent the British Government, while the American contingent was led by President Eisenhower, of course, and the French team was headed by the current Premier, Monsieur Laniel, a man, as far as I was concerned, notable only for the fact that he resembled the actor, Jack Warner.

I should like to digress here for a short story concerning the actor I have just mentioned. It happened when I was on reserve duties for a spell in Special Branch at Scotland Yard when I was being plagued by a 'nut-case' who kept phoning up at precisely nine o'clock every morning. He called himself 'Jack Horner' and the conversation would go something like this.

'Special Branch. Good morning.'

'This is Jack Horner. Hurry up and get the squad car here – they're just going into the jeweller's shop.'

'Who is going into the shop?'

'Them of course.'

'Who is them?'

'Oh, never mind, they've gone now. But you better get the squad car down. I'm off, Mother's just got here.'

Sometimes it was a bank, sometimes a silversmith's, but his

mother always turned up to finish the conversation.

On the Thursday morning, the telephone rang at exactly nine o'clock, and having had a very busy night with several visits to CRO (Criminal Records Office) and the dusty Special Branch files rooms in the attics, I picked up the receiver and hearing, mistakenly, the name of Jack Horner at the other end of the line I told Jack Horner to get back into his corner or sing for his supper, or even go up the blooming hill with his mother, but to leave us in peace. A very surprised, and rather irate, male voice on the other end of the line said, 'I beg your pardon! Is there any need to speak to me in that manner?'

'Who is speaking please?' I asked, for I was quite sure he had said Jack Horner.

'This is Jack Warner and I should very much like to speak to Inspector Jarvis.' Now Joe Jarvis was a Masonic friend of mine and I went to see him to explain the situation. He told me that Mr Warner was on his way over about a passport for an Indian friend and I could explain the mistake to Mr Warner himself in about half an hour. I did this and we had a big laugh together.

The other Jack Horner was discovered when my CID colleagues managed to trace the next call he made. He was just a poor fellow, living with his mother, and suffering from delusions. The visit by big uniformed officers from the local police station must have put the fear of God into the man and his mother, and the phone calls ceased forthwith. Ever since, however, the mention of that great courageous actor's name, now no longer with us unfortunately, reminds me of Jack Horner.

18

TRAVELS AGAIN

IT WAS A GREAT THRILL TO be quitting England in that grey, cold December and heading for the sun-soaked island of Bermuda. This, the oldest of the self-governing British colonies, actually consists of a group of about a hundred and fifty coral islands of varying sizes, clustering together in the Atlantic, six hundred miles from any other land. With its pink and silver sands, blue skies and crystal-clear water, it proved to be a truly enchanting place. It was more American in character, I thought, but this is not surprising since it is within two or three hours' flying time from many parts of eastern America.

The place was first discovered, I learned, by a Spaniard, Juan de Bermudez, in 1515, but the Spanish made no attempt to capitalize on the discovery. Almost a century passed before an Englishman, Sir George Somers, came upon it in 1609. Three years later a British company, the Virginia Company, had begun to colonize it, and two years after that, a second British organization, the Bermuda Company, was also on the scene. There was plenty of evidence of these early settlers: St Peter's Church for example, in Hamilton, is a rather austere, low-roofed building over three hundred and fifty years old, and St George, the oldest settlement on Bermuda, was another place exuding the atmosphere of the seventeenth century; and it was strange to note the names of some of the nine parishes of Bermuda, or Great Bermuda as it should properly be called; Southampton, Warwick, Pembroke and Devonshire, for instance.

It is interesting to note that Somers was taking colonists to the plantations in Virginia, in the United States, when his ship, the *Sea Venture*, was wrecked off the Bermudas, and his story of the event in 1609 was one of the sources used by Shakespeare in 1611 for *The Tempest* which mentions '. . . the still vexed Bermoothes'.

Our journey began at the House of Commons, where, true to form, Sir Winston lingered until the very last minute. It was 20.45 when we at last swung out of Palace Yard, yet fifty-five minutes later we were rumbling down the runway at London Airport on board a BOAC Stratocruiser. Even today, when the route to the airport is made easy by a dual carriageway, that would be very good going, but in 1953, with dual carriageways merely drawings on paper, it was almost a miracle.

Flying westwards we were very soon battling against strong headwinds, so it was decided to divert to Shannon to take on extra fuel. There was a duty-free shop so I took the opportunity to buy a couple of bottles of whisky and gin. The barman asked me for my name and address, whereupon I told him my name and said that I was from London, and that sufficed. When I came back from washing my hands, he had my parcel ready, and pushed it part way over the counter. 'Oh! Mr Murray isn't it?'

'Yes,' I said, 'that's right.'

'But I hear yer from Scotland Yard . . . and yer look after Mr Churchill.'

'Yes, it is my honour and privilege to do so,' I said.

'Well tell me one thing, sor,' he said, 'with a name like Murray [and of course there are many of that name in Ireland] what the hell are ye doing looking after an old bastard like Churchill?'

I took my parcel which by this time had completed the crossing of the counter, aided by the steward's rather reluctant hand, and went back on to the plane. At the first opportunity I told Sir Winston my story and he laughed and laughed and laughed.

When next I heard the story, it was Sir Winston who was telling it to Lady Churchill as they sat in the back of the car on the way to Woodford, and Lady Churchill's only comment was, 'But you do know the name of your father, my dear, so he was wrong wasn't he?'

On arrival in Bermuda some eighteen hours after leaving London, I soon observed the scale on which the security precautions were based. The Mid-Ocean Club at Tucker's Town, where the conference was to be held, seemed more like a fortress than an exclusive club. There were inner and outer perimeters, both heavily guarded, and the guards themselves were so zealous that passes had to be produced if one so much as stepped out of the front door for a breath of fresh air. When a signals officer and a sergeant turned up at the club to repair a telephone, they were firmly turned away, even though they were in uniform, until they had been issued with passes.

I also had my part to play, of course, in the security procedures which always took place when we were on foreign soil. The first task on these occasions was always to search for hidden microphones or cameras and generally to ensure that the buildings in which we were living and working were secure, not only from the viewpoint of the personal safety of my protégé, but also to ensure that no conversations leaked out to those who had no right to hear them. As in fact happened later on, in Sicily, until I had traced the source of the leak.

It was on occasions like these that the American Secret Service men came into their own. When we had visited the United States before, I had had a foretaste of their technique and the manner in which they swarmed at every conceivable point of potential trouble. On the occasion of the Bermuda Conference they ran true to form, and whereas the Prime Minister's protection squad consisted of just two officers from Scotland Yard, President Eisenhower arrived with a bodyguard of no fewer than 28 Secret Service men. I really do not know how many men came with Monsieur Laniel for we had no time to fraternize and each party kept themselves to themselves.

With such strict precautions it was not surprising that things ran smoothly enough, although there was one moment of drama affecting the conference as a whole. The three delegations had just got down to a secret evening session in one of the large, faintly old-fashioned rooms of the Mid-Ocean Club, when suddenly the whole place was plunged into darkness. From the conference room came the scraping of chairs and aides emerged asking urgently for candles. These were quickly forthcoming, together with reinforcements in the shape of oil lamps, and for half an hour this emergency lighting sufficed until the power was restored. The extra power needed for all the radios and other apparatus connected with the conference had been too much for the local power station, and a fuse had blown.

Most of the guard duties were undertaken by a British regiment, the Royal Welch Fusiliers, and their presence in Bermuda enabled Sir Winston to renew his acquaintance with their mascot, a billy-goat, that he had previously met in Jamaica at the beginning of the year. The goat was taken in to meet the Prime Minister one evening, but did not appear to be very impressed by what he saw.

He graciously accepted a glass of champagne, and then munched a handful of cigarettes in an absent-minded sort of way, but soon lost all further interest in the proceedings, much to the chagrin of his famous host.

One incident during the visit to Bermuda illustrated again the extra-curricular duties I found myself performing from time to time on behalf of the celebrated politician and statesman's peace of mind. He had been walking on the beach with only Inspector Davies and me as companions, when we came to a sand-dune which had to be climbed in order to leave the beach. For a man of his age, for he was then seventy-eight, this was rather a formidable obstacle, and Inspector Davies and I took him by the arms, and assisted him up the sand-dune. As we approached the summit, one of the indefatigable *Paris Match* photographers suddenly appeared and took a picture. Now in my years as Churchill's bodyguard, I had more trouble from *Paris Match* photographers than from the rest of the world's Press put together. At the same time I had always had to admire their resourcefulness, and in the course of my many struggles of pitting my wits against theirs, I had come to know most of them pretty well.

I knew that this picture of Sir Winston being assisted rather unceremoniously through the sand would present a most embarrassing view of Britain's Prime Minister at a Summit Conference. So, as soon as I could, I sought out the photographer (who had bribed a Mid-Ocean Club employee to let him out on to the beach) and asked him to let me have the photograph and I would see that he did not lose by handing it over.

'It's too late,' he told me, 'I have already sent if off by air to Paris. But it will not appear this weekend for there is a Press strike there.'

'If it can be kept out of the magazine,' I told him, 'I will get you a very good, exclusive photo to replace it in time for the next issue.'

After some hesitation, he agreed to telegraph the Paris office for authority to do a deal. Later on he told me that it was all arranged for someone to meet me in Whitehall for the other photo. On returning to London, I kept my part of the bargain and presented the *Paris Match* representative in London with an exclusive photo I myself had taken, with Sir Winston's own Leica camera, when we went for a drive before leaving Bermuda. Sir Winston was standing up in the car, gazing out over the dockyard at Tucker's Town, which had just been, or was just about to be, given up by Britain, so there was some political interest in the picture. The other picture was never, to my knowledge, published, so there is some substance, I suppose, in the matter of 'honour among thieves'.

The Bermuda Conference lasted only four days, and all too soon we were back in London again, Sir Winston once more with his nose to the grindstone with very few breaks to relieve the strain of official duty.

Occasionally, however, there would be time for a dinner and a game of cards with old friends, and it was on just such an occasion, a visit to the town house of Lord Salisbury in Swan Walk, Chelsea, that I found myself participating in a contretemps with a certain well-known Tory politician.

We knew that Sir Winston, after dinner, would spend an hour or so playing bézique, or another of his favourite card games, though I assumed that as Her Majesty, Queen Elizabeth the Queen Mother, was present on this occasion, she would choose the game to be played. So when we had dropped him off, and I had checked that a uniformed officer from the local police station was there outside during my absence, the chauffeur Mr Collins and I drove off to the House of Commons staff canteen for dinner. We came back about 10.30 pm, and as we drove down Swan Walk, a very narrow lane, a small car came towards us, with lights flashing and horn hooting. Mr Collins sat there impassive in Sir Winston's car. The other driver stopped his vehicle and jumped out. 'Come on, come on,' he called out to Mr Collins, 'Back up, back up!'

'Why should I?' retorted Collins, never the easiest person to order about. 'It's much easier for you to reverse your small car than it is for me.'

'I should like you to understand that I am a Junior Minister in the Government,' said the other driver, though I felt that this was not going to help at all, for Collins was not really Conservative-minded.

I suddenly looked towards the driver's window, and recognized Mr Ernest Marples.

The chauffeur stuck to his guns, adamantly declining to move, so Mr Marples made for my side of the car, the while proclaiming, 'Perhaps you can do something about your driver.' As he passed in front of the car, however, the breeze stirred the flag of the Cinque Ports which as Lord Warden, Sir Winston was entitled to fly from the flagstaff on the bonnet of the car, and which moments before Collins had unveiled by removing its plastic cover. Approaching Collins, he said with bated breath, 'Well, you might have told me the Queen was here. Of course I shall now go the other way to the Palace of Westminster.' Before we could enlighten him as to the real owner of the flag, he was in his car and reversing rapidly away from us.

There was a sequel to this event for at the House of Commons the very next day, after I had escorted Sir Winston to his room, I returned to the car in Palace Yard. On the way, just outside the Ladies' Gallery entrance was Mr Marples. I held the door open for him to enter, and smiled at him pleasantly. He returned the smile, then suddenly checked in his stride and said, 'Haven't we met before?'

'Yes, Mr Marples,' I said. 'It was about 11 pm last night, and it was not the Queen's flag, it was Sir Winston's flag of the Cinque Ports.'

He stood still with a surprised look on his face for a moment, then passed on with a rather embarrassed laugh. Many times afterwards we met in the corridors of the House, and most times he asked me if I had seen any good flags recently.

I have already mentioned the way in which Sir Winston would become hard of hearing when the mood was upon him, and I had another good example of this foible at Chartwell about this time. We were walking in the garden and both of us stopped momentarily to look at a splendid laburnum tree in full bloom. As we slowly carried on walking, I said, referring to the tree, 'It's rather magnificent.'

'What?' said Sir Winston.

'That tree,' I said, 'it's magnificent.'

'What?' he repeated.

'It's a very nice tree,' I said, speaking slowly and distinctly, thinking that I had perhaps overstated the case by describing it as magnificent.

He cocked an eye at me. 'You were right the first time,' he said impishly, 'it's magnificent.'

This particular tree was in fact especially noteworthy that year because, in addition to the normal yellow blooms, it produced pink ones as well. This aroused Sir Winston's interest for as we walked past it one morning he turned to the Private Secretary at the time, David Pitblado, and said, 'You might find out for me why it has yellow flowers and pink flowers.'

A few days later we passed the tree again and Sir Winston's, 'Well?' was answered by Mr Pitblado's, 'I am told by the Royal Horticultural Society that it is a freak.'

'I could have bloody well told them that. But why?'

I quickly restored the peace by telling him that Mr Vincent, the gardener, and I had studied the matter in various books and we had found that it often happened with plants. When they grew old, instead of losing their hair like we do, they revert to their original colour in the wild state, in this case from the purplish-pink first developed from a graft made by a gardener in Vichy, France, about 1826, back to the common yellow which is its colour in the wild state.

Sir Winston was much impressed by this information, and said to Mr Pitblado, 'There now, we know where we are.'

It was in this year, 1954, that the controversial picture of the Prime Minister was painted by Graham Sutherland, showing him square-jawed and grim. The picture was widely criticized, mainly by critics who had only seen photographs of it, for not many people actually saw the finished portrait. I know that the Churchill family did not like it, and Sir Winston himself, though he did not say so in so many words, felt that it was a good likeness, but that Sutherland could have been kinder in his treatment. Sir Winston's speech when he accepted the painting, a gift from Lords and Commons, on the occasion of his eightieth birthday, 30 November 1954, was a model of diplomacy for he described the work as 'a great example of modern art . . . it certainly combines force and candour'.

Graham Sutherland began work in September on the picture, and I remember the Prime Minister saying to me, 'I have told Mr Sutherland about your being one of the profession.' I found the painter to be an extremely pleasant man, although rather shy, and faintly overawed in the presence of Sir Winston, as were most painters and sculptors to whom he gave sittings. Sir Winston could always sense when a person stood in awe of him, and he would begin by putting on an act, to appear to live up to the reputation of a man to be feared. At the outset he would be awkward and uncooperative (he would behave in the same way to members of the staff when he thought they were nervous of him) then he would suddenly change and be all reasonableness.

There were surprisingly few sittings for this picture, only four or five in all, during which time the artist executed a series of sketches concentrating largely on aspects of the face and hands, while Mrs

Sutherland, a very pleasant, approachable lady, took a number of photographs. To while away his time as a sitter, Sir Winston asked me to provide him with an easel, brushes and paints, and he began to paint a portrait of the artist's wife. He did not get very far with this portrait and I'm sure nothing remains of it, for most of the work was executed away from Chartwell, from sketches and photographs. I took a photograph of Mrs Sutherland so that Sir Winston could finish it in his studio, should he ever wish to do so.

When Sir Winston's portrait was completed, it was not shown to him until the day before the presentation. First it was at Hyde Park Gate to be seen by members of the family, and then it went, at the request of Her Majesty the Queen, to Buckingham Palace. Then according to the *Sunday Telegraph* who had a couple of their best reporters trying to track it down, in late December 1954, it was taken to Chartwell. In February or March of the next year, it was taken to London to be photographed by Mrs Elspeth Juda, before being again crated and returned to Chartwell. The painting, unfortunately, for I consider it to have been a fine study, by an excellent painter who was known to have his own particular way of presenting greatness on canvas, has not been seen since.

Some time later, in the south of France, I met Graham Sutherland again in the International Bar in Menton, not far from the villa he had there. He wanted to know exactly what Sir Winston thought of the painting and I had to say that I was of the opinion that Sir Winston had not been very flattered by it. His aim, he told me, had been to try and capture the force and power of the Prime Minister's personality, and he maintained that people viewing it stood much too close to get the full effect.

Back in England I put his words to the test, and at a distance of ten or twelve feet I had to admit that the work acquired new aspects. The figure then revealed an air of virility which just did not exist when viewed at close range. At a distance it was indeed the Churchill I knew. When I discussed the painting later with the artist, once more in Menton, I agreed that it was much better from a distance, but I could see no reason at all for giving such a romantic, courageous, unique character, such a common, unexciting background of khaki, which had been the colour chosen for the army because it is so drab and nondescript. We argued about it well into the night.

The following is an extract from the Hickey column of the *Daily*

Express dated 3 May 1982 and entitled *Sir Harold (Wilson) dabbles in a mystery* (i.e. the disappearance of the Sutherland portrait of Sir Winston). '. . . he [Wilson] surmises that Sir Winston's personal detective, to whom the grisly task was entrusted, felt unable to do it. The detective, now dead, was an amateur painter, and may have lacked the resolve to perform the act of vandalism. So he could have stored it in a vault, or hidden it behind another painting in a frame, or anything . . . and nobody else would have known'.

Yet here I am telling the story, a very live and active 'dead' man.

A significant fact about the picture, though, was that Sir Winston normally discussed with me any portrait or sculpture he was sitting for, but he never spoke a word to me about this portrait from start to finish.

As I have said, the Churchill family disliked the Sutherland portrait intensely, but I am quite sure that there are many things in the life of the great man that did not meet with the approval of the clan and I find it quite impossible to believe that the story in the *Sunday Telegraph* by Charles Laurence and Richard Holliday who came to Bath to see me about the business, is absolutely true. A former employee of the family said that the portrait was smashed to pieces by Lady Churchill, then he was told to burn it. I do not believe the man . . . but on the other hand, Lady Soames also stated that it had been burnt and this is quite a different matter and, very much against my better judgement, I must concede that the Sutherland portrait is no longer with us, that Lady Churchill had it destroyed without any assistance from outsiders, and the National Portrait Gallery is poorer, as is the country, for the loss.

One of the best works portraying Sir Winston, in my opinion, was that by Oscar Nemon. It was a sculpted figure which went to the Guildhall, in the City of London. Perhaps I am a bit biased, however, because I had a small hand in the work, for while Nemon was at work on it I used to go along to his studio in Chelsea to act as a sort of adviser and spent some time demonstrating the distinctive slope of the Old Man's shoulders, a factor reflected very successfully in the finished masterpiece.

At a meeting to commemorate the twentieth anniversary of the death of Sir Winston, on 24 January 1985, his nephew, John Churchill, laid a wreath on his grave on behalf of the International Churchill Society. About a couple of dozen members, including my wife and I, attended and then repaired to The Bear in Woodstock for lunch. Neighbours of Oscar Nemon were there and we chatted about the famous sculptor. I obtained his address and wrote to him as soon as I was able. There was an immediate reply on a postcard of his statue of Sir Winston and Lady Churchill in the Ashmolean Museum, Oxford. It was dated 25 March 1985, and was quite short:

'Dear friend, the famous Sergeant Murray,

It was very kind of you to remember me for the good old days' sake – I remember your painting ambitions – have you pursued them? Perhaps since we got in touch by letter, we shall also meet. Are you ever in the Oxford region? Do come and visit me for a long chat. Hopefully, see you soon. Yours, Oscar Nemon.'

My wife and I began to make preparations to visit Oxford, but the day after we had made our decision to go in a couple of days' time, Beryl was reading the *Daily Telegraph* of Tuesday 16 April 1985, and suddenly called out that he was dead.

Oscar's mention of my painting reminds me of a letter I received from Donald McLachlan dated 21.1.65, when he was Editor of the *Sunday Telegraph* . . .

'Dear Sergeant Murray,' it began, 'you may be interested to know that Mr Graham Sutherland, when I was interviewing him yesterday afternoon about Sir Winston's portrait, referred in terms of admiration to your own paintings and the fact that Sir Winston used to talk about them.'

I also, or should I say, we, for my wife was involved as well, became friendly with another artist who did a portrait of Sir Winston. This was Max Nauta, a Dutchman commissioned by the Dutch Government to paint his portrait for the Parliament Building in the Hague. Despite our friendship, I had to criticize the finished product for I considered that the artist had made the original much too square-faced. The last time we met Max Nauta was when he came to the Wembley area of Middlesex, as it was in those days, to the blessing of a stained-glass window he had made, for this was his real forte.

After he died Mrs Nauta married another Dutchman, Feike de Boer, who had been the first Mayor of Amsterdam after the war. My wife and I had great pleasure in having lunch with them on one occasion at the Amsterdam Hilton.

On the whole, Sir Winston was a reasonable sitter – for up to about an hour, that is. After that he would become restless and the going would become increasingly difficult for the artist. Most of the time during the session he would be attending to business, of course, dictating letters and so on, while he sat.

Since 1913, the Old Man had been an Elder Brother of Trinity House, so that a dinner of that august body was something not be missed by him. Thus we set off from Hyde Park Gate one evening in December 1954, for just such an event, but as we were about to leave the house, Lady Churchill hurried down the inside steps to me.

'Sir Winston has a small hole in the front of his trousers,' she announced to me, 'and I should very much like you to take this piece of cloth and stick it into his trousers so that the hole no longer shows, please.' She handed me a small square of cloth, but how she expected me to fix it without needle and cotton I don't know. Suddenly another method occurred to me, and I told her that I would put a blob of ink on the white spot showing through the trousers as soon as we got to Trinity Hosue, near the Tower of London. Meanwhile Sir Winston had clambered into the car, quite oblivious of the hole in his trousers or of the plans laid to put things right.

At Trinity House, Sir Winston was ushered into a room where cocktails were being served, and as soon as possible I found the Master of Trinity House and asked for the use of a private room, explaining my reasons. The Master looked dubious and said that he had noticed nothing untoward in Sir Winston's dress. He took a closer look and agreed that there was a hole and it was visible. I tactfully shepherded Sir Winston into the toilets and informed him that I was going to ink in the offending part of his underwear to hide the hole. He protested vehemently, but I told him I had promised Lady Churchill, who had been much concerned, and took out my fountain pen. Crouching, while the Master stood by the door to preclude interruption and any possibility of misconstruction of the performance, I took the piece of white cloth and applied my pen to it. Nothing happened – the pen was quite dry.

Somewhat embarrassed I got to my feet again, and as Sir Winston rumbled away like an angry volcano, I asked the Master if I could borrow his pen, which he didn't have. After a further delay – I was finding it quite amusing to be holding up such an important dinner for such an 'important repair job' – a pen was borrowed from the head waiter (or was it the toastmaster?) and I completed the work quite satisfactorily, to the obvious relief of the Master.

The hitch had no effect on the Lord Warden of the Cinque Ports' enjoyment of the evening, however, for he returned to Hyde Park Gate singing his old favourite songs lustily in the back of the car.

Trinity House is a fraternity of seamen connected from early times with the River Thames and was granted a Charter of Incorporation in the name of the Holy Trinity by King Henry VIII on 20 May 1514. Its present charter, granted by King James II on 8 July 1685, describes it as the 'Guild, Fraternity or Brotherhood of the Most Glorious and Undivided Trinity and of St Clement in the Parish of Deptford Stronde in the County of Kent'. The first Master and founder was Sir Thomas Spert, Controller of the Navy to Henry VIII, and the corporation developed rapidly. Queen Elizabeth I granted it power to erect seamarks at its own expense, and also to erect and place beacons and buoys. James I made considerable changes to the charter and added a number of 'Elder Brethren' as distinct from the remaining brethren who were designated 'Younger Brethren', whose sole rights consisted of having a vote in the election of the Master and Wardens. The corporation is now the general lighthouse authority for England and Wales, the Channel Islands and Gibraltar. It is also the principal pilotage authority for England and Wales, and its functions in both respects are controlled by statute. The Elder Brethren act as nautical assessors in the House of Lords, the Admiralty Division of the High Court of Justice, and the Court of Session in Scotland.

It was at this time that I showed Sir Winston and his lady a series of pictures and slides I had taken of them during various trips abroad. As we were walking downstairs afterwards, Sir Winston asked me if I had thought of publishing the pictures I had just shown them.

I told him that I had not given the matter any thought at all, and to this he replied that I might think about it for he could see no inconvenience to himself in having them published. I thanked him for the thought and the suggestion.

By his eighty-first birthday the strain of the Premiership was beginning to tell on Sir Winston, so it came as no surprise when, in April 1955, he decided to resign his great office. As was usual on such important occasions, the actual day of the event was a well-kept secret. There had been a certain amount of newspaper speculation, but when, on 4 April, we learned that the Queen and the Duke of Edinburgh were to dine at No 10 Downing Street, I for one felt that resignation was in the offing. By next morning it was generally guessed what he had in mind, and in consequence, Downing Street was tightly packed with watching, expectant crowds.

The Old Man was exceptionally grave and downcast that day and when, at 4.30 pm, he left to visit the Queen at Buckingham Palace, his sombre mood had further deepened. He remained there for two hours, and then went direct to Harley Street to see his doctor.

An hour later, no longer the tenant of No 10, he left London on the two-hour drive to his beloved Chartwell. In future his life would be lived in semi-retirement, with visits now and then to the House of Commons, but with more and more time spent in sunnier climes.

19

IN RETIREMENT

As PRIME MINISTER, AND EARLIER as Leader of the Opposition Party,
even though this was most unusual, Winston Churchill always had
two officers from the Special Branch as bodyguards – personal protection as it was called. When he retired as Prime Minister it was
decided that one officer only would be sufficient.

Commander Burt of the Special Branch accordingly made a visit
to Chartwell to inform Sir Winston that he could retain one, if he so
desired. In view of the faintly amused attitude he had always
adopted when referring to his bodyguards, it was perhaps surprising
to find that Sir Winston was now anxious to keep one of them in his
service.

My colleague and I were standing a few yards away from Sir
Winston and the Commander when the question was put to him.

'Yes,' he said, 'I would like to have one officer with me. I would
very much like Sergeant Murray to remain,' and he turned towards
me, 'that is should Sergeant Murray care to remain with me.'

Commander Burt and the Old Gentleman approached us and the
Commander informed me of the decision. There was really no question of whether I wanted to stay or not, but the result would have
been the same had I been asked. I thanked Sir Winston for the
honour which I was gratified to accept, and he turned from Commander Burt and added, as if for my ears alone, 'I think I can manage
another four years or so.'

In the event, of course, it lasted almost another ten years.

Our mutual interest in painting was presumably one reason why
Sir Winston chose me to remain with him in preference to any of the
other Special Branch officers who had acted as protection officers,
but another reason, I am quite sure, was my usefulness as interpreter. Quite soon after being appointed to his staff I came to realize

the reliance he was placing upon me in this respect.

It was during a visit to Cap d'Ail when Sir Winston was dining at the Hôtel de Paris in Monte Carlo. There were some twelve people in the party. Half-way through dinner the restaurant manager, Monsieur Henri, came to the table where I was having dinner with my colleague, Inspector Davies, my superior of course in rank, and two colleagues from Les Voyages Officiels, the Paris-based plain-clothes police department who protected VIPs in France. M. Albert announced that Sir Winston had asked to speak to his detective. Davies got up and went to the Prime Minister's table, but after a short conversation he returned to say that Sir Winston would like a word with me. Sir Winston required me to act as his interpreter in a small matter, and Davies spoke no French.

The next day we visited San Remo in Italy, to dine at a famous restaurant, 'La Lanterna', where one could usually choose one's lobster, for instance, from a huge tank just outside the entrance. Unfortunately when we got there, the tank was all but empty, and Sir Winston was terribly disappointed for he loved to watch goldfish and the like in tanks and ponds, as we know. I had a go at the manager who happened to be a friend of some three or four year's standing as he had been head waiter at the Hôtel de Paris, in Monte Carlo. He told me that the lobsters for the tanks were still in the pots in the middle of the harbour, the weather being much too rough for the boat to go out and collect them. When I told him that the honour of the restaurant was at stake, he promised to do his best by sending someone to the local fishmonger, and filling the tank by the time he had finished dinner. This would be all right since I knew that none of the party wanted lobster, for it took too long to prepare, and the fish on the menu was excellent.

I then went to sit down with Inspector Davies and our French colleagues and prepared to enjoy a very good meal. Once again the detective was called – Winston was now doing this deliberately to annoy Davies, who was rather 'toffee-nosed' he once told me. Again my superior went through the restaurant to obey the summons, but this time the Prime Minister burst out with the words, heard throughout the restaurant, 'Well I told you yesterday that you were no bloody good to me. You only speak English and I speak the language quite well myself thank you. Do ask Sergeant Murray to come to me. He's my interpreter.'

Episodes like that did nothing to help me vis-à-vis Inspector

Davies.

My story now goes back to the Three-Power Conference in Bermuda, where, on the very first day that we were there, the Chief Officer of Police invited Inspector Davies and me to join him and other people intimately concerned in security arrangements in Hamilton. There was to be a sort of *apéritif d'honneur* afterwards. Davies suffered from ulcers and did not usually drink spirits, or even wine, and insisted that I go to represent the British contingent. There was also a Sergeant Robinson who had come with Mr Eden. He decided to stay at the Hôtel with Inspector Davies.

Off I went to Hamilton and met the Chief of Police and presented the apologies of my colleagues. We talked of security arrangements and I had one rum punch, one solitary rum punch, and not a drop more. Then the Chief of Police called his own driver and instructed him to take his Jeep and drive me back to the Mid-Ocean Club without delay, because he himself wanted the Jeep as soon as possible.

Now the maximum speed limit in Bermuda was twenty-five mph in those days, principally because of the very narrow, very winding, roads on the island. The driver thought that he was under orders to do it as quickly as possible and hardly drove less than forty mph during the trip back to the hotel. When we arrived there, I was violently sick and was obliged to lie down. Davies and Robinson, under the impression that I was drunk, called an army doctor, who immediately agreed, after an examination of at least thirty seconds. About half an hour later I was fit as a fiddle and carrying out my duties, including a full report of the circumstances leading up to my illness and suggesting that if corroborative evidence was required, the Chief of Police could substantiate my statement. This was never done and naïvely, I thought that it was because I was believed. How wrong I was, for as soon as Inspector Davies got back to Scotland Yard, he typed out a very harmful report of my being 'drunk on duty', and Sergeant Robinson signed the report as a witness. I was called in by the Chief Superintendent and given a rollicking, but there was no question of my being taken off protection.

A few months later, down in Cap d'Ail, Sir Winston's medico, Dr David Roberts, obtained permission for me to drive his ageing mother-in-law, Mrs Riley, to San Remo, in her Rolls-Royce. The matter was quite urgent, for there were tablets to collect there and they were only obtainable in San Remo, unless the doctor waited for the promised delivery in two or three days, by mail from Paris. All went well on the tortuous road between Monaco and San Remo, and even on the way back, for I am considered to be a good driver. In my early days of protection, I had passed a police driving test at Hendon, in order that I might be proved efficient enough to drive Mr Churchill during his peregrinations at Chartwell, or in emergencies.

But as soon as I put the Rolls-Royce into the garage at Mrs Riley's home, I was again taken ill with exactly the same symptoms that I had had in Bermuda. Dr Roberts sent me to bed, with medication, and told me that I suffered from a common enough complaint – vertigo, a feeling of whirling or propulsion, often accompanied by sweating, nausea, vomiting and inability to stand.

Before that interview with Commander Burt at Chartwell and immediately after Sir Winston's resignation, in fact, there was another trip abroad – to Sicily. Sir Winston and his entourage made the trip by air, a hop of just a few hours. For me there was no such luxury, though I am not complaining, for I went all the way by train. Two and a half days in a train from Victoria to Syracuse, by way of Paris and Rome, was really my idea of travelling. So many things to see, so many people to meet, so little responsibility.

I was accompanied by Sir Winston's valet, Jock Kirkwood, and the reason we went by train was because of the luggage Sir Winston required to take, including his painting material. It would have cost a small fortune by plane. There were other considerations to take into account. Arrangements for the security of Sir Winston in what had always been considered the home of the Mafia had to be made, in cooperation with the local police. Given sufficient reason, I knew that I could make myself understood in Italian and had swotted up on useful expressions before I left.

We duly arrived at Syracuse, soon after noon on a blazing Monday, and there was work to be done with no fewer than four types of police organizations to be grappled with – the Carabinieri, the elite of Italian, or Sicilian, policemen, then the street patrolmen, the Strada, the Guardia who were to do sentry duties at the hotel, as well as the local version of the CID, the Questura.

Finally it was all arranged and Sir Winston and his party arrived at

Taormina, in the shade of Mount Etna, the very next day, to find that he was the target of attention for an even larger than usual army of photographers and Pressmen. Tourists also turned out in great numbers whenever he emerged from, or returned to, the hotel, so that keeping an eye on his security became an almost bigger problem than it had been when he was Prime Minister.

Such was the interest of the Press that it became necessary to issue communiqués to them at frequent intervals, although not a great deal occurred to make them interesting. However, it became apparent that some Italian papers were getting information not being issued from official sources, and in conversation with some of the journalists, I found they were much better informed of Sir Winston's movements and plans and the people he was in contact with, than they had a right to be.

The English journalists were, of course, jealous of the fact that their Italian colleagues were receiving inside information withheld from themselves, and one of them who had brought his wife along as his photographer, one day whispered in my ear that every telegram sent by Sir Winston or his staff was being copied and given to members of the local Press.

Telegrams were being sent from a basement room of the hotel where a temporary exchange had been set up. The next time one was being dispatched, I took one of the Syracuse inspectors down to the exchange. There, in the very act, was one of the girl operators carefully making a copy of the telegram. At first she refused to say why she was copying it, then admitted coyly that she wanted it as a souvenir. There appeared to be no point in creating a scene, since I was quite sure she was not the only operator concerned, so the whole staff manning the exchange was transferred elsewhere, and a policeman kept guard on the new staff henceforth to ensure that the practice was discontinued.

Needless to say, my action found no favour with the Italian journalists, but quite soon afterwards I was back in favour with the Press corps as a whole when I convinced the manager of the Villa Politi, the hotel where we were all staying, that some entertainment was called for to amuse the journalists. He managed to find an ancient gramophone and even more ancient collection of records. This livened things up considerably, because the place had previously been like a morgue after dinner, and it was now possible to dance. My action inspired an Italian journalist, short of copy now on Sir

Winston, to do an article on me instead. I was, he wrote, like a chestnut tree, very strong and very silent, when accompanying Sir Winston, but once off duty an entirely different man, which was I suppose, a pretty fair assessment.

In Britain at this time, a newspaper strike was in progress and this meant that Sir Winston was short of home news. It made him very irritable. There were foreign papers, of course, including American ones, but that was not quite the same thing. For such a prodigious student of newspapers as Churchill, to be denied the bulk of his supply just when he had plenty of leisure, was nothing short of a minor disaster. It left him more time to paint, but bad weather further contributed to his irritation, and I must confess that I sometimes welcomed a rest from the boring task of washing brushes and cleaning his palette while others just sat and read their books while they sipped their beers.

Among his guests during this period was Clare Booth Luce, then the American Ambassador in Rome, who came with her husband, the owner of *Time*, *Life* and a number of other publications.

I had, as usual, erected Sir Winston's easel in a room adjoining the dining-room, together with palette and paints and brushes and a number of photographs I had taken of the rope-makers' caves, his most recent subject, in the hope that he might like to carry on painting there. During lunch, his great enthusiasm for the art of painting transmitted itself to Mrs Luce. As soon as the meal was finished we went next door and she found herself undergoing instruction. I soon provided her with a small easel, a canvas, brushes, paints and a palette, and when everything was ready, there I was on one side of the easel, and Sir Winston on the other, and the Lady Ambassador began work under our joint instruction.

'It's really quite easy,' said the Old Man, in that annoying way the experts have when talking to rank amateurs. 'All you have to do is just take up your brush and start splashing on the paint. Start where you like, at the top, or at the bottom.'

With that perversity which typifies her sex, or did in those far-off days when women knew they were different to men, she began plumb in the middle of the canvas. For a good hour we stood over her, giving detailed instructions. I'm afraid that after that period of tuition her enthusiasm proved short-lived, and the work did not progress very far. In fact, both she and her tutor then retired to the card table to play bézique.

She was accompanied at the time by her Air Aide, a colonel in the American Air Force, and I told him how thankful I had been to the 14th USAAF in China after I had left the Foreign Legion and could he possibly express my gratitude in the Air Force News Sheet. He said that he would be delighted to do so. Months later, I had the letter from the son of my old friend Lieutenant Elyseev, whom I have mentioned before in a previous chapter.

In Sicily, I found the cooperation of the Sicilian police force much better than that of the Venice police, except for that occasion when they had found the ointment I wanted for Sir Winston, and when one of the Detective-Inspectors, who even spoke a little English, went out and bought a few small things as gifts for our three children at home. I remember being very moved by the gesture, offered at the very last minute, and I managed to get Sir Winston to sign a photograph for him.

On our return to England, life became far more placid for Sir Winston than he had known it for very many years. Retirement from active political leadership meant that there was time now to sit apart from the restless mainstream of life, time to paint, time to read, and time to meet in leisurely fashion, old friends of long standing.

One place he could now visit more frequently was the stately home which had been his birthplace, Blenheim Palace, near Woodstock, in Oxfordshire. His attachment to this magnificent house, built by Queen Anne for his illustrious forebear John Churchill, First Duke of Marlborough, sprang from three sources. There was firstly the historical compulsion of Blenheim, the overpowering appeal to Sir Winston's dramatic imagination which the Palace represented. Secondly there was the simple fact that he had been born there. Thirdly, it was the place where he had proposed marriage to Miss Clementine Hozier when she was twenty-two and he was thirty-four years old.

Having met Miss Hozier at a dinner party at the London home of Clementine's great-aunt, Lady St Helier, in the spring of 1908, in August he persuaded his cousin, the Duke of Marlborough, to invite Mrs Blanche Hozier and her daughter Clementine, to Blenheim Palace.

One day he strolled with the young lady from the front entrance of the Palace where he had been born, towards Diana's Temple, a stone tower set among the yew trees near the lake. Inside, a bas-relief shows Hippolytus offering flowers to Diana, and it was there that Winston proposed marriage to Clementine and was immediately accepted. They were married on 12 September 1908. In typical Churchillian style, he referred to the significance of Blenheim Palace in these words: 'At Blenheim Palace I took two very important decisions – to be born, and to marry. I am happily content with the decisions I took on both these occasions.'

His birth at Blenheim had in it a distinct dash of drama, for his American mother, Lady Randolph Churchill, was actually dancing at a private party to celebrate St Andrew's Day in 1874, when he showed signs that he was going to arrive sooner than expected and she had to leave hurriedly. As it was, she did not reach her bedroom and the birth took place in a small room on the ground floor at the Palace. This had once been the bedroom of the Chaplain to the First Duke of Marlborough, one Dean Jones, and it still bore his name. However, on this particular occasion it was being used as a cloakroom for guests at the party, so Winston Leonard Spencer Churchill arrived in the world in a room filled with men's capes and ladies' extravagant Victorian finery.

His association with Blenheim Palace and its owners, first his cousin the Ninth Duke, then his second cousin, the Tenth Duke, remained exceptionally close throughout his long life, and when I came to know him, I quickly noticed the pleasurable anticipation with which he would embark on a visit to Woodstock.

The routine on these visits was always very much the same. For a start, for some reason I could never establish, he would invariably take along his own bottle of Napoleon brandy. Then there would be a drive around the Blenheim estate, acre upon acre of majestic parkland, during which he would meet and chat briefly with estate workers and gamekeepers. Then there would always be a short visit to St Martin's Church, in the nearby village of Bladon, where both his parents lay buried, and upon whose grave he would usually place some flowers. The first time that my wife saw the Churchill graves she remarked on the extreme simplicity and dignity of the ensemble, particularly the grave of Sir Winston. Most people who visit the place and speak to me about it, remark how surprised they are that there is no grander display of a nation's sorrow and loss.

Each evening, of course, there would be a game of cards with the Duchess, normally his favourite game of bézique. His luck as a gambler, whether it was at the gaming tables in famous casinos, or simply in small after-dinner card games with friends, was good as a general rule, but I can remember at least one occasion when his good fortune deserted him.

We had had a short spell at the Palace, and were on the point of departure when I was told that Sir Winston wanted to see me urgently. I was having breakfast in the staff-room, blissfully unaware of the fact that the Duke, the Duchess, her maid and about half a dozen other people were searching for me.

The message finally got to me and I hurried up to his room, to find him being helped to dress by his valet.

'Good morning, my dear Murray,' he said affably, 'can you let me have six pounds, sixteen shillings?'

I took out my wallet and began to count out the pound notes, then into my trouser pocket for the silver to make up the exact amount.

'You must be asking yourself why I want this money,' he said, a trifle naïvely, I thought.

'I can guess,' I replied.

'What for?'

'You've been losing at cards.'

'Well, it is not very often that I have to ask you for money to pay my gambling debts is it?' I had to agree.

As Sir Winston drew on into his eighties, gambling began increasingly to fascinate him and I think the reason for the growing frequency of his visits to the south of France and Monte Carlo, was very largely the lure of the casinos. When he played, it was as if his skirmish with Lady Luck ranked equal in importance with the battles he had had during his long political career. He seemed to bring to the gaming-tables in his last years the same fierce concentration, the same grim determination to succeed, that he had demonstrated in the darkest days of the last war. The regular encounter with fickle Chance absorbed him, and it gave him a kind of satisfaction. It was something to grapple with, something over which to triumph, just as, less than twenty years earlier he had grappled with, and triumphed over, tyranny.

When we were down in Monte Carlo in 1960, there was a lovely incident to illustrate what I am trying to explain. It was a Sunday evening, and after dinner he called me in to the lounge where he and Lady Churchill were chatting with Montague Browne, the secretary. He had his brandy glass in his hand when I arrived, and swirling the brandy round he looked up at me, smiling, and said, 'I think I shall go to the Caniso' (yes it was always the Caniso rather than the Casino, to Sir Winston and Lady Churchill) 'now'.

But Lady Churchill protested in shocked tones, 'Dear Winston, you cannot gamble tonight. It is Sunday.'

Sir Winston looked nonplussed, and distinctly crestfallen, but only for a moment, then his face brightened. 'Oh! Oh very well,' he announced, 'Come and fetch me in forty-five minutes [he was looking at his watch]. Then it will be after midnight and Monday, not Sunday.' For all his eighty-six years we went off to the Casino after midnight and stayed there for a good couple of hours.

There was something quite ritualistic about going to the Casino, so let me describe the formal procedure in order that this small, but rather important, aspect of Sir Winston's declining years may be glimpsed with authenticity.

During, or after, dinner Sir Winston would call for me, and he would say, 'I shall be going to the Casino later on, my dear.' I would then warn my French colleagues and Monsieur Broc, the general manager of the Hôtel de Paris, who would ensure that security officers in the Casino were informed and a new table started with a few selected players for roulette.

The party usually included two or three friends or relatives, although quite often he would decide to go with only myself as company, and we would make our way to the two lifts of the hotel to go down to the basement, then along the underground passage to another lift that would take us up to the gaming-rooms. If he was dining in the hotel restaurant, of course, we would just make our way across the road to the main entrance, and then through the gaming-rooms used by the ordinary public, the 'kitchen' as it was called, to the select rooms at the back where one had to be correctly dressed to be admitted. One of the principal officials of the Société des Bains de Mer would meet us at some point to escort Sir Winston to the chosen table where play would already have begun to give the impression that no special favours were being accorded. On the way to the table, the procession would go to the change desk where Sir Winston would trade a roll of French banknotes for a pile of chips.

Once he was on his way, of course, he would have to pass through an aisle of visitors, applauding spontaneously and respectfully, many with tears in their eyes.

Before even getting properly seated he would throw a chip on the table. 'Le dix-sept,' he would call, and the lovely thing is that the croupier would accept the bet, whether or not he had called *'rien ne va plus'*. In fact, I have seen the occasion when Sir Winston has thrown his chip on the table and called and the croupier has seen the ball drop into some other number and put his rake on the chip to indicate that it was not valid – just to save Sir Winston the cost of a chip. People in Monte Carlo were always superb in their attention to Sir Winston, and me, as a result of reflected love. As his attention riveted upon the small spinning ball I would call one of the Casino's blue and red uniformed employees who, warned in advance, was ready with score cards where the last winning numbers would be marked in red and black for Sir Winston's guidance.

So intense would his concentration become that before long his half-smoked cigar would fall unnoticed on the carpet and an attendant would retrieve it and offer it back to him. I would then take it and wrap it in a paper serviette before sticking it into my pocket, for it was time for a new cigar. After placing his next bet, slowly and deliberately, deep in thought, he would reach for his gold cigar case and select a new one. Then would begin the ritual of lighting it.

Taking the match protruding from the box which I had just set beside him on the table, he would pierce the end of the cigar with it, blow through the cigar from the opposite end to ensure that it was smokable, then strike the match, oblivious the while of the players and the mass of visitors congregated on the far side of the table to watch the performance. Waving the match around to get rid of the sulphurous fumes he would then apply it to the cigar, which he would carefully revolve to ensure that it was properly lit, holding the match under it until only an infinitesimal part remained unburnt and he was forced hurriedly to drop the match into the capacious ashtray placed near his right hand.

With an attendant carefully marking his score card to check the run of winning numbers, he would return his entire attention to the table, perhaps turning now and then to ask me what colour I reckoned would turn up next – and occasionally even accepting that I could be right. With his noticeably elegant hands he would caress the chips in front of him into neat piles, and decide perhaps two or three times in a successful evening, to throw a chip across the table and call out, 'Pour les employés,' and a very loud 'merci Monsieur' would ring out from the croupiers. Sir Winston was never generous on these occasions because he had no idea at all how much he was giving away, and very unknowledgeable about the amount of money that was usually given by rich people 'pour les employés'.

After an hour or so, he would suddenly stand up and march through the throng which parted respectfully before him, towards a special cloakroom, reserved for VIPs, close by. I would tip the attendant who unlocked the room anticipating the inevitable question, 'Did you give him something?'

Then he would return to the table for another hour or so, until at last he would push across the final chip for the croupiers, carefully gather up the remainder then make his way to the change desk. There he would carefully convert his chips into cash, which, very slowly and very proudly, he would put away in an inside pocket of his jacket.

On the way out several people would probably approach me asking for permission to shake Mr Churchill's hand, but my reply was always the same, 'Very sorry, but no handshakes.'

Back in the car, if we were not at the Hôtel de Paris, otherwise on the way back to his room, he would be tired perhaps, but very contented. 'That was very enjoyable, my dear. Thank you very much for looking after me so well.' Had he been obliged to shake hands with all and sundry, I am sure those people to whom I refused the honour will realize that he would not have been able to say that – and mean it to the same degree.

Just occasionally, however, his enthusiasm would become momentarily dampened by a sharp loss of a hundred or so pounds, but it did happen very infrequently and he was usually lucky enough to get it all back within a few days. While I am writing this, I suddenly realize how fortunate I was on occasions, to have the trust of the casino directors. The cashier – a very powerful man indeed – told me that if ever Sir Winston wanted money or chips, I was the only person, other than Sir Winston himself, who would be permitted to sign for any amount.

I myself gambled but very, very rarely, and never when I was with Sir Winston. I would often go to the Casino of an evening, but just to have a drink, which was always on the house. There was inevitably someone who would come up and introduce himself, just to have a friendly chat, and very often there were people who knew me through their own associations with Sir Winston.

But back to my gambling. One night I was in the Private Rooms just looking round really, when I decided suddenly to play a chip I had, worth about two pounds. There were always several Inspecteurs des Jeux hovering round the gaming-tables looking for behaviour unbecoming to the dignity of the Casino, and I was known to all of them. Looks of utter amazement came to several faces when I placed my chip on the eighteen. They waited, and even joined me at the edge of the table as the ball rolled round on its allotted journey. Then it dropped, and bounced, and bounced, and stopped – in the eighteen slot.

The croupier looked towards me and called out, 'à qui?' knowing full well that it was mine.

Suddenly there came a voice from an old lady, all paint and powder, sitting at the table, 'C'est à moi.' Cameras should have been there to photograph the looks of astonishment on the faces of the Inspectors, gamblers and croupiers, for there was only one chip, mine, on the eighteen. I knew that something was expected of me. 'Madame,' I said in her own French language, 'I would never, ever contradict a lady . . .' I paused, 'Monsieur le Croupier . . . c'est à moi.' Sudden laughter broke out from the crowd, for unknown to me, the 'lady' in question was the 'Duchess', and she was a well-known *habituée* for ever trying to pinch other people's winnings. I gave a big wink to the croupier, and he pushed the small pile of chips towards the woman. Then the Inspector at my side also gave a nod to the croupier, and he pushed a similar pile of chips towards me. Such is life in Monte Carlo.

One evening Sir Winston decided to go to the Casino after dinner. It was about 11 pm and my French colleagues had gone home, or at least to their hotel in Menton. There were just the two of us as we made our way by car from Cap d'Ail to the Sporting Club d'Été, only open during the summer months. As we went towards the gaming-rooms, Sir Winston saw the bar on the right-hand side and decided he would like to sit awhile in one of the very comfortable easy chairs, some four or five yards from the actual bar. The place was almost empty, except for one man at the bar. I got a whisky and soda for Sir Winston and placed it on the table by his chair and then went to fetch my own drink. I looked at the Old Man as he sat there and thought that he looked rather sad and lonely. Just as I was about to go and sit beside him, I saw a friend enter the club. It was the Queen's doctor, Lord Horace Evans, with whom I had spent many happy moments in the Casino with is wife and delightful daughter. Just the person, I thought, and hurried to ask him if he would care to have a whisky and soda with Sir Winston. He was delighted and I made the re-introduction as Lord Horace shook hands and sat down beside Sir Winston. Happy, I retired to the bar where I prepared to keep watch. The two men were chatting amiably together and Sir Winston became his usual cheery self. I replenished the glasses and sat at the bar once more. I had taken the trouble, I must point out, to remove to a considerable distance all the chairs and tables close to my protégé to preclude anyone listening in on the conversation between the two men, but I still kept myself ready for emergencies.

Then I saw out of the corner of my eye that the man at the bar had put down his drink. He turned to walk towards Sir Winston's table. Casually I rose and, without looking in the man's direction, went towards Sir Winston. When only a few feet from him I turned towards the man approaching. He was in a dinner jacket, and I recognized him immediately but I had already begun to ask him very politely, if I could help him.

'That's OK,' he said, 'I'm just going to say hello to my friend Sir Winston.' The voice was very American.

'Well, sir,' I said, 'I'm from Scotland Yard and as you can see, Sir Winston is engaged in conversation at the present moment and cannot be disturbed. Could I have your name please?'

If looks could kill, I would have been dead immediately, as the man glared at me, then turned and walked out of the Casino. It was Frank Sinatra.

Still in Monte Carlo, every time Sir Winston went into the fine old restaurant of the Hôtel de Paris, the leader of the orchestra, Lartigo, would always get his musicians to strike up immediately with 'For he's a jolly good fellow'. The whole room would re-echo to the song as the diners already there stood up and joined in. Sir Winston would bow to left and right as he made his way to his table, where Monsieur Albert would be waiting reverently. Lartigo would always come along to see me at my table to ask what he could play for the Old Gentleman, and naturally I would suggest any of the 1914–18 soldiers' songs.

20

MEETING WITH ONASSIS . . .

DURING A VISIT TO MONACO in the autumn of 1955, the motor-yacht
Aronia, owned by a shipping magnate called Jack Billmeir, was put
at the disposal of Sir Winston and Lady Churchill, and it was aboard
this yacht that I found myself involved in investigations into a murder that had shocked both Britain and France.

A few weeks earlier, an English school-teacher, Janet Marshall,
had been found strangled in a wood while on a cycling tour of
France. Her killer at the time was untraced, so, when checking on
the crew of the yacht for routine security reasons, I was told by the
Captain that one of his crew claimed to have met Janet Marshall a
few days before the date on which she was supposed to have been
murdered, I at once felt that I should investigate a little further.

The man was an Englishman and he also claimed to have been in
the French Foreign Legion. When we were on the way towards San
Remo with Sir Winston and Lady Churchill, I walked casually along
the deck, whistling the famous Legion song, 'Voilà du boudin',
known to all legionnaires. The man was swabbing the deck at the
time and the tune seemed to draw no response at all. I decided to
have a chat with him. He was about thirty-two years old, tall, fair
and good-looking, I suppose, but very unfriendly. I concluded from
our conversation that he probably had been in the Legion, but for
just a few months, rather than the three years he claimed. I also
suspected that most of that time had been spent in hospital. Later
investigations proved how right I was for it was discovered that he
had been in the Legion for three months only and had then been
discharged on medical grounds.

His attitude when I talked to him of the Legion was one of wari-
ness, but when I turned the conversation to Janet Marshall and
murders of English people abroad in a general sort of a way, he

[207]

became rather hostile and, without mincing his words, told me to mind my own business. I had found out that he had neither passport nor any identity papers, though he had told the Captain that they were on their way from England. He had only been with *Aronia* a few days. I telephoned the Chief of Police in Monaco, Monsieur Delavenne, a good friend who had made me an Honorary Policeman of Monaco, complete with badge, and he asked me to arrange with the Captain that the man in question should be sent to collect the mail for *Aronia* from the Agent as soon as they returned to Monte Carlo.

Nothing untoward happened on the return journey, although Sir Winston and Lady Churchill did not care much for the yacht as it was rather ancient, smelly and smoky. On arrival in port, I watched as the Englishman left the ship. When he arrived at the Agent's, the local police asked to see his papers and when he could not produce them, he was taken along to the central police station, where I was waiting to act as interpreter.

His story was that he had met Janet Marshall two or three days before she was murdered, when he was hitch-hiking through France, but that at the time she was actually killed, he had been in Brussels. It all seemed highly suspicious to the Chief of Police, so he was held in custody while inquiries were made in London and Brussels. From the latter city came news that suggested that he had been staying at a hotel there *after* the murder. There still seemed to be a number of loopholes in his story, so although the Chief did not like his tale, as they could only keep him there for twenty-four hours (the real truth really being that they do not like dirty things like murders in the Principality), he was released and placed on a bus to Nice. But the French CID in Nice, having been warned about his departure, had sent two detectives to get on the same bus to keep an eye on him. On arrival at Nice he was arrested as he still had no identity papers. It was suggested that I attend as interpreter, but the Englishman would have none of that, so a man came along from the Consulate.

The following day a French Inspector of Detectives who was working on the case came post-haste from the Amiens district where the murder had taken place. The Englishman spoke no French and the Inspector spoke no English, and when they met in the middle of the night in the cell at Nice Police Station, there was no interpreter. The Englishman further extended his story, apparently, at this stage and claimed to have been in Germany the day before the murder. While the interrogation was taking place, his cabin on the *Aronia*, now also in Nice, was searched and suspicion was further heightened by the discovery beneath his bunk of some fifteen to twenty English newspapers all dating the day after the murder, and all featuring the case prominently.

The French detective came to the conclusion that the man had not been concerned with the death of Janet Marshall, and went back to Amiens. However, the Nice police telephoned me to let me know that the man was wanted for questioning about a razor attack on a solider in Liverpool, and they were sending him back. Would I please assist them and see the British Consul in order to have him returned by plane? The British Consul in Nice wanted to put the man on a train because it was cheaper, but there was distinct evidence that he had been put on trains to London before when he had no money, by several other British Consulates in Europe, and had always skipped off before reaching his destination, and had simply disappeared. There was only one course, I argued, and that was to have him escorted to a London-bound plane to ensure that he would be met by police on arrival. After some hesitation the Consul decided to adopt my plan and the man was eventually picked up at London Airport, finishing up in jail for his attack on the Liverpool soldier.

The murderer of Janet Marshall was later declared to have been a French tramp who had come upon her by chance. He had confessed to the murder, I read in a newspaper later, but subsequently withdrew his confession, and no other person has been found to pay for the crime.

There was a sequel to this matter, because the arrest of the man from the *Aronia* leaked out to the Press, and my part in the affair, although I had been most discreet about it all, and had even climbed through a window at the back of Nice police station in order to avoid the Press at the front entrance, was well documented.

When Sir Winston read the story, it was his first intimation of what had been going on. The weather had been bad and there had been no fear of his going out painting, and I had spoken to no one of the matter. He was therefore rather surprised to read in the Press that he himself had suggested the line of action to be taken, and was very peeved that he had not been informed so that he could take charge of things.

'You really ought to talk to me about these things,' he said reproachfully, 'I might have been able to help.'

It was about this time that I realized that I had been told that General Alessandri, who had been my regimental colonel in Indochina, lived in the area and I found his name and address in the telephone book. I rang and the phone was answered by a young male voice which, in answer to my query, said that neither the General nor his wife was there, but one of his daughters was. He was the son-in-law. Now you may remember that I had given English lessons to the young daughters in Indochina and when the elder came to the phone, speaking French, I explained to her that I was M. Murray, her English teacher.

She laughed and said, 'Go on . . . pull the other one.' I told her that I was in Cap d'Ail on the staff of Sir Winston Churchill, and this caused her to laugh even more. She thought that it was one of the lads from her university pulling her leg. I asked her to ask her father to ring me at Cap d'Ail, the home of Lord Beaverbrook, when he returned, and rang off.

Later that afternoon, I was called to the telephone. It was the General, who was in no doubt at all of the truth of my statements and invited me to lunch the next day. The whole family would be ordered to attend in my honour.

Sir Winston immediately gave me permission to go, and as the weather at the time was not very good, I knew that he would certainly not be painting, and my colleague would have no trouble coping without me.

The next day I borrowed Sir Winston's car and drove to Les Croisettes in Cannes and received a wonderful welcome from the Alessandri family, the elder daughter now convinced that I had really telephoned. Sir Winston had asked me to convey his special regards to my one-time chief and the General and his lady were very much moved. I was told that there would always be room at their table for myself and my family, in Cannes or in Paris. Alas, they are both dead now, and I have lost touch with the girls, so I have not been able to take up his invitation.

In the twelve months after his retirement, Sir Winston spent a great deal of his time abroad, mostly in the Riviera sunshine, as if wishing to make up some of the vacation time lost during his long years of command at Westminster. From Cap d'Ail he returned to London in time to celebrate his eighty-second birthday there, but within a few weeks he was back again in the south of France, at a new location this time, the Villa La Pausa, at Roquebrune, just above Menton and the Italian frontier at Ventimiglia. The place was to become famous throughout the world, because twice while staying there, in the autumn of 1957, and in the winter of 1958, Sir Winston became seriously ill, with the result that the world's Press congregated there in large numbers to report on his illnesses.

La Pausa, the home of his Continental editor of the *War Memoirs*, Emery Reves, was, in its way, quite as beautiful as Lord Beaverbrook's villa, La Caponcina, at Cap d'Ail, although it had a certain formality, a certain coldness, that I never associated with La Caponcina. Its setting, in green and well-tended gardens full of Mediterranean flowers and lavender, shaded by olive trees, was quite superb. It was perched several hundred feet above sea-level, adjacent to the medieval village of Roquebrune, a noted tourist attraction, with to the east a fine view towards the Italian mountains, and to the west, the white and red buildings of Monte Carlo.

It was a house furnished with an eye to taste of a high order, but, despite this and the Rodin statues and the highly valuable paintings, a sense of coldness, or soullessness, was always present, to me, at least. Maybe it was this that kept Lady Churchill away from La Pausa, or maybe it was because she could not get on with the occupants, Emery Reves and his girlfriend, American Wendy Russell. Whatever the reason her visits were limited to the two occasions when her husband was sick.

Emery Reves was a man of Central European origin who had been naturalized in Britain during the early part of the war.

Sir Winston appeared to enjoy his visits there well enough, though the first one did not get off to an auspicious start because he found that his bedroom not only had a fine view of Menton and the Italian mountains, but an unobstructed view of Roquebrune cemetery as well. His room was quickly changed to give him a scene overlooking the gardens. But I must say that I shared the lack of enthusiasm which I knew Lady Churchill had for the place. The host, in my opinion, was not a particularly prepossessing man, and it was always difficult to work out what the famous guest could see in him. I know that people have said much the same about Sir Winston's friendship with Aristotle Onassis, with which I shall shortly deal, but I infinitely preferred Ari to Emery. Maybe my first

[211]

visit to La Pausa led me to expect too much, and this, at least, is a charitable explanation.

On that first occasion the Churchills were staying at Cap d'Ail when they drove to La Pausa to visit Mr Reves and Wendy. One got the impression at that time that the villa's residents were very keen to have the Old Man as a guest, a keenness which was reflected in their treatment of myself and my two French colleagues. For us Wendy placed a magnum of excellent cognac on the table in a small room, and there were cigarettes and a jug of coffee. The next time that Sir Winston went there to stay the atmosphere altered very considerably and we almost felt compelled to give up drink and cigarettes, and even take our shoes off when in the villa, so changed was the attitude of the occupants now that their wish was fulfilled. I and my colleagues had no reason to expect hospitality, of course, but there was much more to it than that. I also found it rather strange that a person of such apparent affluence should himself, after Sir Winston had gone to bed, turn off the central heating, so that when his guest woke up the next morning, usually about 6 am, according to the valet at that time, he was freezing. I was lodged in a rather nice room over the garage opposite, but there was no heating even though the snow fell fast and furious, until I borrowed a small oil heater from a friend in Roquebrune.

Of course, I could not really sit on Sir Winston's doorstep twenty-four hours a day, and I had to eat, for Mr Reves did not provide anything now that he had Sir Winston staying at La Pausa. So I used to go down to Menton taking it in turns with my French colleagues so that the Old Man was always protected. I owe a great deal to the citizens of Roquebrune-sur-Mer, as opposed to Roquebrune Village, for the way they accepted me as a friend, especially as a member of the bowling club. Not the slow, friendly, concentrated, 'don't drop the wood' game we play on billiard-table greens in this country, but the happy, talkative, Latin and explosive game of *boules*. I earned a certain reputation as *pointeur* or 'lead' or 'No 1', as we call it in our game, and I still fill this role today. The *après boules* in the minuscule bar was mainly a post-mortem on the game just played, and quite as exciting.

As I say, I much preferred Aristotle Onassis to Emery Reves, but they are both gone now, and none of their money and possessions went with them. I am convinced that Mr Onassis had much more pleasure out of his wealth than Mr Reves. Mr Onassis appeared to be very happy to entertain Sir Winston and his entourage, lavishly and often, simply because of the immense esteem in which he held him. There was no ulterior motive that I was ever aware of, although many people felt that there must be one. I personally think that the way in which Sir Winston himself appreciated Mr Onassis's kindness and companionship may be judged from the fact that in his will, made in his mid-eighties, he left the budgerigar Toby to him, and Sir Winston was very, very fond of Toby. It was a highly significant gesture although Mr Onassis never got Toby, because, as I have already mentioned, the bird disappeared through an open window at Monte Carlo in February 1961.

'What can I leave you in my will?' the Old Man said to Mr Onassis, 'I want to mark your kindness with something, but what? You are a millionaire and you have everything that I could possibly give you.' Then his face lit up. 'I know. You shall have Toby.'

How did Mr Onassis and Sir Winston meet in the first place? And how did that meeting blossom into the firm friendship which flourished between the two men? These questions have been asked me many times, so I now set down the facts, as I know them.

It was during the winter of 1955–6, in the south of France, that Mr Onassis made the acquaintance of Sir Winston for the first time. Press reports had it that Sir Winston and Lady Churchill were seriously contemplating the purchase of a villa somewhere along the coast. I repeat that it was from Press reports. Mr Montague Browne, detached from the Foreign Office as Personal Secretary, considered that Mr Onassis was an expert on property in the area. He made himself known to the Greek financier and then brought the two men together. They hit it off right from the start and when I helped Sir Winston up to his bedroom following their first dinner together he declared that Mr Onassis 'was a fine man'. Under Ari's guidance, Sir Winston and Lady Churchill were shown a large number of houses in the Cannes–Monaco area.

During that same visit to the South of France, there was the usual visit to another octogenarian, also a very famous man, the writer Somerset Maugham, who lived in the Villa Mauresque, on Cap Ferrat. On this particular occasion, Mr RAB Butler was there. Mr Maugham's villa was a magnificent building standing in beautifully kept grounds, overlooking the sea at the tip of a spit of land between Villefranche and Beaulieu. It was a place of which any man would have been proud, but Somerset Maugham had particular reason for pride, because, as he told me, 'Everything you see here I earned by my pen, every stick and every stone.' It was a well secluded place, but when one actually reached the vicinity, the villa itself was easily identifiable, since outside, not only on the wall at the entrance to the drive, but also above the entrance door, was the curious Moorish emblem which appeared on all of his books. This was really a disadvantage to him because it meant that tourists could easily find the house once they had made the pilgrimage to Cap Ferrat. Regularly each summer he would be bothered, if that is the correct word for it, especially by rather brash Americans wanting to interview and photograph the famous author in order, so Mr Maugham stated, to earn a few dollars from their hometown papers.

There was another encounter of a very different sort during that rather exciting visit, an encounter which began with hot words but ended with handshakes and free hair-do's for my wife at one of the West End's leading hairdressers. I was accompanying Sir Winston and Lady Churchill, together with a small party of friends, to lunch at a well-known restaurant not far from Grasse. As we entered, Sir Winston shook hands with the manager and his wife, and then I noticed two men, English-looking, come forward and try also to shake his hand. They clearly had nothing to do with the restaurant, and from their behaviour they seemed a little the worse for drink, so I firmly put myself between them and Sir Winston, who passed on to his table in a far corner of the room.

The two men, one in his fifties, I judged, and the other probably twenty years younger, were extremely annoyed at my intervention, but I told them in plain language that Sir Winston was there privately and had no desire to meet anybody other than the management. The men returned to their table near the entrance. Half-way through lunch, the younger man suddenly left his table and began to make his way towards where Sir Winston and his party were sitting. As I started up to intercept, the manager signalled that the man was going to the toilet, the entrance to which was near the Old Man's table but concealed from it by a screen. Actually he had been given the table because of its proximity to the toilets, just in case. I watched the man cross the restaurant towards the lavatory, but as he was about a couple of yards from the door, he suddenly made a dash towards Sir Winston. Just as he reached the table, I had him by the back of the collar and the seat of his trousers and he was on his way back to his own table and his recently vacated seat. As I regained my own table, Sir Winston looked towards me with an inquiring look, so I went and told him that everything was all right and that a man had just become a bit of a nuisance.

'Oh, but do not be too rough on him, my dear.'

The sudden shock the young man had experienced at the hands of a Scotland Yard officer – for I had told him who I was during his trip across the restaurant in my grip – had clearly proved salutary, and after about half an hour he had sobered up sufficiently to write a note which he handed to a waiter to bring to me. He wished to apologize and invited me to take coffee with them. Not wishing to prove more unfriendly than my job forced me to be, I moved to their table, to the unveiled curiosity of Sir Winston and his party. They could not take their eyes off me for the rest of the time we were there.

It transpired that the young man was a well-known London hairdresser among whose customers was Mary Soames, Sir Winston's youngest daughter, and he wanted to make known to Sir Winston his acquaintance with Mrs Soames. I explained that, as his protection officer, I could not allow Sir Winston to be disturbed by every man or woman who happened to recognize him. The upshot of the incident was that my wife was invited to his London salon for free treatment. This she accepted later, and received most excellent service.

During this spell at La Pausa, Sir Winston was invited to become a *Citoyen d'Honneur* of Roquebrune, the local district, which he was happy to accept. The ceremony took place in Roquebrune's tiny town hall and, thanks largely to a horde of photographers, it looked very much as if the affair would turn out to be a shambles. Nobody sat on the chairs provided, for they could see nothing because of the photographers at the front. The only answer was to stand on the chairs. There was a lot of pushing and shoving and arguing, with a huge din. When our small party arrived, the place was so packed that there was literally no room for us, so by brute force, my French colleagues and I made a space just in front of the platform. As they stood there an irate Englishman, whose view was blocked by Miss Russell, put his hands on her shoulders and pushed her down on to her chair, quite forcibly saying, 'Now you will sit down.'

He had no idea, of course, who she was, but I stepped in very quickly and protested at his discourtesy. 'But I'm General X,' he said as though he had some divine right by reason of his military rank to order the situation to his own taste. I very soon told him that if he did not stop throwing his weight about he would find himself outside.

Sir Winston's friendship with Aristotle Onassis grew steadily from the first meeting. In the following months quite a number of houses were examined with a view either to renting or buying, and Mr Onassis was always on hand to guide and advise. Needless to say, there were a large number of people anxious to offer their villas for letting to the Churchills, for to have them stay would have enhanced the value of any property.

Mr Onassis actually wanted to buy a house for Sir Winston and Lady Churchill to use whenever they felt like it. The place he had provisionally selected was called La Vigie, a few hundred yards from the tennis club, the sea, and the railway line from Italy to Monaco and France. It had been owned by an absent Scotsman for a long time, but the Germans had used it during the war and it had not been renovated for many years. It was in rather a dilapidated state, but I think that the other factors, and because it was overlooked by the houses and villas of Roquebrune Village and the Little and Grand Corniche mountain roads, were the reasons why the offer was declined.

It was at this stage that we made our first visit to the famous Onassis yacht *Christina*, a vessel I was to come to know very well indeed over the next few years. That initial visit certainly made an impression on me because the standard of luxury was breathtaking as, I suppose, one might expect on a millionaire's yacht, especially a millionaire who made his money out of shipping. There were, for instance, lapis lazuli baths, huge hand-carved images of jade, onyx tables, numerous valuable pictures, gold icons, and a bar with models of ships sailing around beneath a glass-topped counter, each model representing a century of shipping. It is interesting to note that the covers of the bar stools were made from the skin of whales' testicles, and the supports for the feet were whales' teeth.

There were, for good measure, eleven motor-boats and a hydro-plane on board and facilities for film shows, much used when Sir Winston was in residence, and a fully equipped operating theatre, complete with X-ray equipment. On each occasion that Sir Winston used the yacht, Mr Onassis's brother-in-law, Mr Theodor Garofalidis, who was the chief surgeon at Athens Hospital, was always one of the guests — just in case.

The story goes that Mr Onassis married the daughter of the rich Greek shipowner, Mr Livanos, to further his ambitions to become also a rich man. But he had no need of help at the time for he had several million dollars in the bank, and since 1931, had owned six cargo boats bought in Canada for some 120,000 dollars, circulating about the world as 'tramps' on non-regular shipping lines. In 1939 he ordered his first oil tanker, the *Aristophane*, in Sweden.

On 17 April 1943, Mr Onassis met Mr Livanos to talk business in the Plaza Hotel in New York. He was thirty-seven years old, and they were meeting for the third time, but Mr Onassis had never met the Livanos daughters. There were three of them, and Mr Onassis immediately fell in love with the youngest, Christina, or 'Tina' as she was usually known. She was then fourteen. He courted the young Tina with flowers and presents and letters for forty-four months, till on 28 December 1946, Tina Livanos became the first Mrs Aristotle Onassis.

On 5 August 1959 a very remarkable thing happened on the *Christina*. The yacht was about to depart, a couple of days later, to the Greek islands, when Mr Onassis, hearing that Mr and Mrs John F. Kennedy were in the area, invited them to a cocktail party on *Christina*, having previously asked Sir Winston, of course, if he would like to meet the young Senator and his lovely wife, Jackie. Sir Winston had said that he would very much like to meet the son of the one-time American Ambassador to England, and he would also like to see how he was going to conduct his fight for the Presidency, due to end in his becoming the thirty-fifth President of the United States of America the following year. For his part, the young Kennedy, who was just my own age, forty-two at the time, expressed his delight at meeting the renowned ex-Prime Minister, and he was also happy to make the acquaintance of one of the richest men in the world.

Maria Callas and her husband Mr Ménéghini had already arrived from their home in Northern Italy to go on the cruise which was to prove so important in their future. So we can now see how, on 5 August 1959, Mr Onassis had on the yacht, not only the wife from whom he separated a month later, the woman who was going to be his partner for the next nine years, and also the one who was to become his second wife afterwards. How astonishing it is that on that first visit by Jackie Kennedy, Mr Onassis did not have more than a dozen or so words with her, and no one thought to introduce the famous opera singer to the future First Lady of the United States. Mr Onassis was deep in conversation the whole time with Sir Winston and Mr Kennedy. The Kennedys left the yacht about 7.30 pm and four years were to pass before Jackie and Ari met again. They were married on 20 October 1968, and the contract that was signed by Mr Onassis at the time is a most remarkable one.

'Mr Onassis was not to force her to have a child by him.

'Mrs Kennedy-Onassis was to spend all Catholic feast days with her new husband, and all the recognized main holidays as well.

'She was permitted, outside the above holidays, to visit her friends and relatives without being obliged to inform her husband.

'Mr Onassis was obliged to have a separate room from his wife. On the yacht he gave up his owner's suite on the upper deck and retired to "Lesvos", one of the guest cabins.'

As far as the monetary settlement was concerned, these arrangements were very complicated and intended to protect the ex-First Lady and her two children by her previous marriage, Caroline and John-John, until their majority. If Mr Onassis were to 'disappear' before their majority, then the sister and brother-in-law of Jackie, Prince and Princess Radzivil, would assume the same responsibilities as Mr Onassis, automatically.

Jackie was also looked after, of course, and received 5,000 dollars a month until the children became adults, as well as her allowance covering taxes, rates and expenses for house, car, doctors, masseuses, coiffeuses and a multitude of other requirements amounting to at least 17,000 dollars a month. These at the time of the contract were paid by Mr Onassis's New York secretary. She had an allowance also of 10,000 dollars a month for clothes, and besides another 6,000 dollars to pay for a bodyguard, she was allowed *six* seats on normal air flights so that the seats at her side, and those behind, remained unoccupied. As she went to Europe at least forty times each year, this meant another bill of some 30,000 or 40,000 dollars a year.

Servants considered her to be the toughest and most demanding mistress they had ever encountered.

21

. . . AND OTHER STARS

DURING 1956, SIR WINSTON MADE two separate visits to Germany, his first since the Conference at Potsdam between himself, Stalin and Harry Truman, immediately after the end of the war in 1945. The reasons for the two visits were completely different, the first being principally to collect the Charlemagne Prize at Aachen (Aix-la-Chapelle) and the second to see his horse, Le Prétendant, run at Düsseldorf. Perhaps it was not surprising that the two receptions he received were very different too.

The first occasion got off to a pretty inauspicious start when, on leaving the airport at Bonn, we passed a spectator who ostentatiously turned his back, dropped his trousers and revealed his bare behind as our car drove past. This kind of reaction from a few Germans was not particularly surprising, of course, because some sections of the Press in Germany, especially those run by the Christian Democrats, had begun to generate a 'hate Churchill' campaign from the moment it was announced he was to receive the famous Charlemagne Prize granted for his service to Europe. One weekly newspaper, whose editor had been a high-ranking Nazi official in the wartime administration of occupied Czechoslovakia, devoted an entire page to Sir Winston's alleged mistakes and misdeeds, and illustrated it with photographs of bomb-shattered German towns.

However, such conduct could never deter the Old Man. In fact on that particular occasion I could sense that he went in a definite mood of defiance, almost of bravado. It was very interesting to observe the reactions of the Germans on this, the first encounter for the great majority, with the man principally responsible for thwarting the megalomaniac designs of their own leader. When Sir Winston spoke in the ancient Rathaus of Aachen, with an overflow of over three thousand in the square outside listening to a relay of his speech, there was some derisive whistling from extremist rowdies, but most Germans seemed simply puzzled, quite uncertain whether to applaud or boo. This reaction was evident on the faces of the crowds wherever we went on that particular visit.

Sir Winston's speech was itself worthy of note, because it was one of the last major pronouncements he ever made, and certainly the very last uttered abroad. His main theme was that salvation for the world lay in a grand alliance of the European powers, the British Commonwealth and the United States not excluded. It was an old man's vision, perhaps, but not an inappropriate swansong for one who had rid the world of the menace of Fascism, thus ensuring some peace.

What a difference there was on our next trip to Germany, two months later. The visit was a fleeting one indeed, for we stayed for just part of a race meeting at which Le Prétendant, one of his better horses, was running. From that point of view the visit was not a success, because Le Prétendant could finish no better than fifth out of seven horses, but at the same time, there was tremendous evidence at Düsseldorf of the affection and esteem in which the race-going public held Sir Winston. Although they did not quite mob him in the way he was liable to be mobbed at race meetings in Britain, they nevertheless crowded round very enthusiastically, much in the manner of an English crowd, and there were hand-claps and cries of 'Good Luck'. There were also loud groans when it became apparent that on the very soft going at Düsseldorf that day, Le Prétendant was not going to be in the first three. The response of the crowd moved him in a way he had not been moved on the earlier visit, and to a large extent it did compensate for the very keen disappointment he felt at the poor showing of his horse.

The fact that he ever visited Germany at all on that occasion was a great surprise to me, because of the weather. On the morning of the trip (we were to fly from Biggin Hill, the famous Battle of Britain airfield just a few miles from Chartwell) the weather was appalling, with gale force winds and torrential rain. Conditions were so bad when I left my home in Hendon to travel down to Chartwell by car, that I was convinced the trip would be cancelled and so did not bother to take my passport with me. We drove to Biggin Hill, however – Sir Winston, Captain Christopher Soames, the stud manager and vet, Major Carey-Foster, Walter Nightingale, the trainer, the jockey, Doug Smith and myself – but it seemed that this drive was being made more out of hope than expectation because by then the weather was even worse. At the airfield, Captain Soames tried to charter a bigger aircraft than the six-seater Dove, but none was forthcoming at such short notice. He also tried very hard to talk his father-in-law out of the trip, but without success. The thought of cancelling had obviously not occurred to Sir Winston, and even I, who loved him greatly, must admit that on occasions like this, he could be extremely stubborn and inconsiderate.

'Well,' he declared irritably after the delay in trying to find a bigger aircraft. 'What are we waiting for? I can see no reason for further postponement. Come along, let us be on our way.'

At that moment I remembered that I had no passport, and hardly had the fact registered when Major Carey-Foster came to me and said, 'I haven't got my passport for I did not think that we could possibly fly in this weather. My wife is on her way here with it, but she cannot possibly be here before another half hour.'

'Don't worry,' I told him, 'I haven't got mine either but I am quite sure that I can arrange things with the German authorities.' So we duly took off, and after a terrible flight during which the Old Man did not bat an eyelid, we reached Düsseldorf. I made straight for the German airport official with the most gold braid on his uniform, and explained the situation, promising on my authority as a Scotland Yard officer that if we were allowed through without passports, Major Carey-Foster and I would stay with the rest of the party throughout. The Germans are real sticklers for law and order, and for documents to be signed and sealed on every occasion, but in this case they readily agreed to waive all formalities, and we were ushered through. Despite their willingness to assist on that occasion, I got the impression that had the guest of honour been anyone but Sir Winston Churchill, things might not have been so easy.

Life at this period, as I have already said, consisted largely of trips abroad, with brief intervals in England sandwiched between. One of these was in February 1956, a sentimental journey back to Westminster for Sir Winston to celebrate, very quietly, the fiftieth anniversary of the day when he first took his seat on the Treasury Bench as a member of the Government. On that far-off occasion in 1906 he held the post of Under–Secretary of State for the Colonies.

Then once more, we were off again to the south of France, and here he was invited to a private showing of *The Silent World*, the beautiful colour film of undersea life, which had just been completed by the French underwater explorer Jacques Cousteau. He was Curator of the Marine Museum run by Prince Rainier a few hundred yards from the Palace at Monaco. Now, another somewhat important person in the vicinity at the same time was Brigitte Bardot, and what better publicity could a film star get, and I mean any film star, no matter how famous, than to have her photograph taken with Sir Winston Churchill? That was certainly the way the Bardot publicity men were thinking when it became known that Sir Winston was to visit the film studios in Nice to see *The Silent World* — but things did not quite work out that way.

Our journey to the studios got off to a not very successful start when the French police motor-cyclist deputed to lead us to the location became somewhat overwhelmed by the importance of his mission and took a wrong turning, landing us up in the goods yard of Nice railway station. However, we eventually reached our destination and after we were introduced to the Commandant and several others concerned in the actual making of the film, we settled down to enjoy it. Half-way through, an attendant came to me to say that none other than Miss Bardot was outside with two friends requesting admittance. I told him to tell the would-be intruders that it was a private viewing and, in any case, in such a small theatre, any intrusion would cause a lot of disturbance and it would be unfair to the august guest. The answer was: no entry.

When the film was over we filed out into the narrow corridor outside. Someone introduced Miss Bardot to Sir Winston who did not seem very impressed and quite clearly did not know who she was at all. As he moved towards the door, about twenty yards away, I fell in behind him as Lady Churchill paused for a moment to exchange a few words with the film star. Suddenly, as the Old Man moved on slowly, I felt someone try to squeeze past me and I realized that it was the actress herself, anxious to appear at the door alongside Sir Winston, for the benefit of the Press photographers and the enhancement of her own image. I knew that Sir Winston did not take favourably to that sort of publicity, so I decided that when we emerged from the studio, it would be me, not Miss Bardot, who would be following at Sir Winston's shoulder. All along the corridor, however, she kept trying to get past, while her colleagues and friends urged her on and vainly tried to make me stand aside. Needless to say she did not succeed, much to the chagrin of herself and her friends.

Afterwards I noticed my two French colleagues with stupefied looks on their faces. 'Just imagine,' said one of them, 'her dress brushed against me as she walked past me. BB's dress touched me.' I then hastened to point out that a prominent part of the anatomy of France's 'Queen of Sex' had been insistently pressing into my back during our progress down the corridor, and it had had no effect on me whatsoever.

There was a sequel to this incident about a year later, when Miss Bardot was about to visit England. The gossip columnist of one of our national newspapers announced for her benefit the fact that when she was in England, I would be absent – in the south of France again with Sir Winston.

As the Suez crisis loomed, Sir Winston was back in England. So perturbed was he by the course that events were taking that he made a special, secret trip to Chequers to talk things over with the Prime Minister, Sir Anthony Eden. All the way there from Chartwell, a secretary sat beside him in the back of the car with a typewriter on her knees, making last-minute notes. This was a procedure only followed in the most important circumstances. Although, by then, he had been retired for well over a year, he was still closely in touch with things, and Foreign Office dispatches were still being delivered to him in ever-increasing numbers as the crisis deepened. Prior to his taking over the reins of power, Sir Anthony had been a most frequent visitor to wherever Sir Winston was staying. As Foreign Secretary, Sir Anthony always seemed to be hanging on to every word Sir Winston uttered, I used to think. At parties and similar gatherings he would invariably leave whoever he was talking to and make straight for Sir Winston when the latter appeared on the scene. Once he became Prime Minister, I noticed that the visits seemed to stop abruptly and I sometimes thought that perhaps this was the reason for Sir Anthony's remaining only twenty-one months at No 10, although I suppose that it could have been because of his poor health. What passed between the two statesmen at that time, remained, of course, a mystery to me, but at the end of the meeting I got a firm idea of the trend that events were taking when Sir Anthony said, as they emerged from the house, 'I don't know if that's where Napoleon landed . . . I shall have to find out.'

With Harold Macmillan it was quite different. On almost every occasion when he was about to leave Britain on an official foreign trip, or had returned from some conference overseas, or if Sir Winston himself was about to go abroad, then the two men would meet – and most times it was Mr Macmillan who came to see Sir Winston. Their meetings were always conducted in a spirit of complete and genuine friendliness.

On the occasion of the centenary of Sir Winston's birth, a magnificent luncheon was held at the Savoy Hotel on Wednesday, 5 December 1973. It also marked the publication of the first collected works of Sir Winston and the first volume of the beautifully bound edition was presented to Lady Spencer-Churchill by the Prime Minister, Mr Edward Heath.

The collected works contained all fifty of the recognized books by Sir Winston and the limited edition of 3,000 sets worldwide was published by the Library of Imperial History in association with the Churchill Centenary Trust.

The luncheon, to which my wife and I were invited, was held in the Lancaster Room and my wife was delighted to be seated next to the Captain of the tall ship *Winston Churchill*, a most charming officer.

After the lunch, while the guests partook of their digestive potions, I was interrupted by young Miss Edwina Sandys, the daughter of Mr Duncan Sandys and Sir Winston's eldest daughter, Diana, who asked me if I could help them with Sarah. I went with her to a small side room where I found Sarah rather the worse for wear, once again as a result of perhaps a couple of glasses of wine. Edwina asked for a few minutes to get her car to the Savoy Hill entrance of the hotel. Then I carried Sarah, bodily, and as discreetly as possible, with the manager of the Savoy preceding me to check that the way ahead was clear of indiscreet eyes. She was placed in Edwina's car, who then drove her favourite aunt away to a safe refuge, and I returned to the Lancaster Room.

It was possibly the worry of the Suez business which precipitated Sir Winston's next illness, in October 1956, a most disturbing time for all of us on the spot at that moment. It happened when we were yet again in the south of France, and once more at the Villa La Pausa, at Roquebrune. At about 8.30 am, Sir Winston got out of bed to go to the bathroom. A few minutes later, the male nurse who had been on hand since his illness a year or more earlier, went into the bathroom and found him sitting on the floor, blue in the face and unable to move. The nurse quickly got him back into bed, piled hot water bottles round him and administered the prescribed treatment decided on by his doctor, Lord Moran, at the time of the earlier stroke. The nurse immediately telephoned Dr David Roberts, the English doctor who attended Lord Beaverbrook when he was at La Caponcina, and who was also one of the doctors in attendance on Prince Rainier and his family in Monaco. Sir Winston very quickly returned to his usual self, and when I went in to see him I found him sitting up in bed, a grave look on his face, but reasonably well.

'I've just had one,' he announced rather cryptically, 'it was the real thing, you know. The real thing.' Then his face broke into a broad smile and he added defiantly, 'But I'm all right now.'

I told him that no one could possibly imagine that half an hour earlier he had had 'one of those things', and that I hoped he would be up and about soon. 'I get very bored when I am out on my own,' I told him, and he smiled. 'I shall have to stay in bed for three or four days, I'm afraid,' he said in a disgruntled fashion, rather like a schoolboy who had been told he must remain behind after school.

This illness drew the inevitable reaction from the Press all over the world, and life became tiresome as we contended with hordes of international reporters and constantly ringing telephones. I did my best to cope with my side, but it was impossible to stop bits of idle gossip, much of it incorrect, appearing in the newspapers. Life with the Old Man himself was almost as difficult, because, frankly, he was not cut out to be an ideal patient. Luckily his diet was only slightly restricted by his illness, but at lunch-time on the first day, when his doctor was just playing safe, his meal consisted of nothing but a piece of cheese, and he reacted strongly.

'Only cheese for lunch,' I heard him complain bitterly. 'Only cheese for lunch.' After that, however, he insisted on eating much more normally and even went downstairs like everybody else, so the male nurse and I had the task of carrying him up and down the stairs several times each day. Fractious as his illness sometimes made him, he was always appreciative of the help I gave, and never failed to thank me for it. It was only very rarely that he thanked his staff in words as he did me, but then they were paid to do what he wanted them to do, whereas the help I gave on occasion was quite outside my duties of protection, however willingly it was given.

This stroke delayed our return to England by more than a week, and although I was naturally unhappy at the thought of this extra separation from my wife and three children, the longer I stayed at Roquebrune, or rather at Cap Martin, the village, the more I became accepted by the locals. I usually managed to get a daily game of *boules* when I was there, becoming very adept with the metal balls which take the place of our English 'woods'. There is a world of difference between the rough or smooth patches of ground on which the French game is played, and the smooth velvet-like bowling greens of my native land. I would quite often manage a game of cards as well, either *belote* or *la manie*, with my French colleagues, to pass the time, when we were waiting for Sir Winston to move, or during our meal breaks.

In the sharpest possible contrast to the simplicity of the local café was the sophisticated restaurant a couple of miles away where I was also frequently welcomed. This place, perched just above the reach of the Mediterranean waves a short distance from Menton, was called the Pirate's restaurant because the proprietor always dressed as a pirate during business hours. His establishment was certainly popular with the rich and famous who throng to the Riviera. Prince Rainier and his Princess were regular visitors, as was Mr Onassis. Sarah Churchill also enjoyed a visit there when she was staying with her father at the Villa La Pausa and I rang up to entrust her to the Pirate and his very beautiful wife, Yvonne, who had been a dancer with the Bluebell Girls at the Casino Cabaret in Monte Carlo. Other people I have seen there include Frank Sinatra and Harry Belafonte.

As a result of my long association with things French, I had accumulated a fairly extensive repertoire of French songs, and quite often when I was dining there, I was called upon by the Pirate to entertain, just as I had been wont to do on the tours to Europe I had made in 1946 when I was a courier. In fact, he used to announce me as the 'only man who could keep Mr Onassis quiet for a whole evening', a claim based on fact. It had happened one evening when Mr Onassis, Sarah Churchill and several others were at the restaurant, sitting at a table removed from the bulk of the other diners. The Pirate asked me to sing, explaining that while I sang, people would listen to the two of us, for we often sang duets together, instead of eavesdropping on Mr Onassis and his guests who could thus be in a sort of world of their own. After working through quite a number of songs, in English and French, I realized that instead of talking, the party were actually listening to our songs, a fact quickly noticed by the Pirate himself.

It was at the Pirate's that I encountered the Dutch Royal family, in somewhat unusual circumstances. My brother and his wife and two daughters were on a touring holiday in the area at that time, and I had made arrangements for them to come with me, and the French detectives, to the Pirate's for dinner. Unfortunately, one of the children was not feeling well, and Beryl, my wife, ever kind, offered to stay at the flat we had rented to look after her.

When I went to dine at the restaurant, we were met as usual by the Pirate himself at the entrance, his guitar and violin players with him. Then he fired off two barrels of the shotgun he was carrying to inform all and sundry that a VIP had arrived. The Pirate told me on the way in that the man standing at the side was a senior Dutch detective, and that he was the protection officer with the Dutch Royal family. Naturally I invited him to come in to have a drink, but he declined as he was on duty.

We had been eating and drinking for some time when the Pirate, whose real name was Robert, came to me and told me that Prince Bernhard of the Netherlands wanted something done, and the Pirate considered that I was the only man in France to be able to do it. Would I please come into his private rooms where the Prince was waiting for me. He actually wanted to contact someone by telephone. I made three phone calls while he sat beside me on the Pirate's bed and chatted. I asked him if he was planning to visit Sir Winston, but he was not sure. 'We're on our yacht, you see,' he said, 'and my daughters decide really what we do. I am never sure when we are leaving, or even where we are going to.'

I thought with some compassion of his bodyguard, anchored uncomfortably outside, trying to make arrangements for the security of the Royal family on the basis of such capricious planning by the ladies, so, encouraged by the Pirate's very good wine, I said in a tone of mock astonishment, 'How on earth, sir, can your protection officer look after your safety when he doesn't know when you are next off, or where you are going?'

Prince Bernhard looked thoughtful. 'Yes, it must make a hard life for the detective. I do not think we consider him enough. I must see what I can do about it.' We were then interrupted by a voice I immediately recognized as the one we were waiting for, at the other end of the line. 'Prince Bernhard of the Netherlands would like to speak to you, Mr Onassis,' and I handed over the receiver and left the small room. When he had ended his conversation, the Prince came to thank me at the table saying, 'It is wonderful. I know now that whenever one wants anything, and it does not matter, I am sure, in which country one happens to be, one just has to ask for Scotland Yard.'

Later that evening, a good deal later, in fact, because we all stayed on until early morning, I was introduced to the Queen of the Netherlands, Queen Juliana, and the three princesses, and danced with them all. Once more it had been a wonderful evening at the Pirate's. My one great regret was that Beryl had not been there to share it.

The following Christmas I received a small Christmas card, a plain, tiny card devoid of any royal insignia, the sort that could have cost ten pence in any store. Except that in addition to the printed Christmas greeting inside, was written one solitary word – Bernhard.

It took Sir Winston some eight days to recover from his stroke at Roquebrune, until he was fit enough to return to England. Pretty soon he was back in action, making his way regularly to his special seat in the House of Commons, immediately below the Treasury Bench, after question time each day. But despite this activity, his latest stroke had thrown a shadow of doubt across his path, as I realized soon afterwards from an incident at Chartwell.

I was called into the drawing-room one afternoon and asked by Sir Winston to collect the painting he had been working on immediately before his illness, a view of Menton and the long sweep of the Italian coast as seen from La Pausa. I went off to the studio to find the painting, and when I returned, Lady Churchill was putting another painting on the sofa where Sir Winston was sitting.

'No, not that one,' he said, 'I want the last one I did.' Then after a pause, '. . . it will probably be the last one I shall ever do.' Happily, that gloomy prophecy proved incorrect, and he managed to paint at least half a dozen others before advancing age sapped his ability and interest.

There were frequently times when he could completely forget this uneasiness about his health, times when the essential, questing, adventuring spirit of Winston Churchill would come to the surface, refusing to stay submerged despite his great weight of years. I remember one very clear instance of this and although the incident itself might appear trivial, it has to be remembered that by now he was over eighty-two years old.

The builders were at work at Chartwell, adding an extension to his studio, a building set some distance away from the house itself, across the orchard. The platform was about sixteen or eighteen feet above the ground, so when I saw him place a foot on the first rung of the ladder, I said hurriedly, 'You can't go up there, Sir Winston.'

'Why can't I?' he demanded.

'Well, it's a long way up,' I answered, 'and after all I am supposed to be looking after you. If you were to fall, there would not be much that I could do to save you, and that would be very bad for both of us.'

He gave me an old-fashioned look. 'You know,' he said, 'this is not the first time I have gone up a ladder.' Without further ado he began to ascend, slowly but with great determination. At the top, when we got there – almost together, because I matched every little step with one of mine – I expected him merely to gaze round before coming straight down again. But not a bit of it. Instead, he carefully stepped off the ladder and on to the narrow plank which, as I have indicated, went round two sides of the building, and went right round to the further end, stopping to compliment the workmen on the way they were tackling the job, talking with the air of a man who himself had laid bricks in his day, as he in fact reminded them. At last, as I hovered anxiously around with arms and hands ready to stop any fall, he finally condescended to return to terra firma, where he smiled at me with a mischievous glint in his eyes.

That was not the end of the matter, for on the next two days as well, as if to say 'I'll show you if I can climb ladders or not,' he repeated the excursion to inspect the progress of the builders. As he slowly climbed the ladder on each occasion, I knew that it was just an adventure to put a little spice into the daily routine of old age, just as the journey to the siege of Sidney Street had brought flavour during his middle years, and the Boer War to his youth.

Before long we were again off to France and once more the examination of villas proceeded for Sir Winston and his wife. Most places they turned down after a single viewing. Only two houses interested them sufficiently to view more than once. One of these was particularly notable for it was the house at Cap d'Ail owned by Greta Garbo.

Miss Garbo lived in the south of France in the kind of seclusion which she sought wherever she went. Her villa was single-storeyed, set on a small rocky spit of land. It was virtually unapproachable from the sea because of the cruel rocks, and surrounded with barbed wire on the landward side. Entrance to the property was by way of a very narrow, tortuous lane, well away from the main road between Monaco and Nice.

Despite this protection, her house was invaded at least on one occasion, with distressing consequences to her. A woman journalist from a German magazine managed to bribe a local post office employee to hide her in his van when he went to the house to repair the telephone. The housekeeper, of Russian origin, let the man into the house and, having offered him a cup of tea, went off to prepare it. At that stage the woman in the van slipped out and into the house, where she proceeded to take photographs, particularly of the bedrooms. Her work was soon done, for she was a professional and she was able to slip away again undetected. A week later the bombshell burst. The German magazine, a scandal sheet, carried an article entitled *A Night with Garbo* which purported to show that, although a man friend of the Swedish actress was staying at the house at the time (it was in fact Mr Schlee, a very faithful companion and counsellor for many years), only one bed had been used that night, the evidence being photographs of one unmade bed, and a communicating door open between the two bedrooms.

Now the housekeeper was the wife of Miss Garbo's bodyguard whose name was — Murray. This was too good a chance for the woman journalist to miss and she finished her scurrilous article with the statement that it had been easy for Mr Murray to become Miss Garbo's bodyguard because he was a brother of Sir Winston's protection officer.

I heard this story from Mr Murray himself, a long time after it happened, when we first met in rather a strange way.

I was having an aperitif in our local *bistro* in Cap d'Ail with my French colleagues and the mayor of the village, Mr Gramaglia, when a middle-aged woman entered and asked the proprietor if she could use the telephone. This is, of course, the usual practice in France, where, at that time, telephone booths like the ones we have in England were virtually unknown. The proprietor said, 'Yes of course. Who do you wish to phone?' Meaning where, really.

'I wish to speak to Mr Murray,' she said.

'Mr Murray?' he echoed in surprise, for I was standing right by her side. She also appeared to be surprised by his reaction.

'Where is Mr Murray, Madam?' he asked.

'At the villa,' she answered.

I too was liable to be at the villa, for we were staying at the Villa Caponcina, Lord Beaverbrook's place, at the time.

'What is he like, this Mr Murray, may I ask?' asked the proprietor, persisting.

By then the woman was completely mystified by the questioning but being a foreigner she thought it best to remain calm. 'Well, he is tall, good-looking and he used to be in the English Royal Guards.' (Remember I was once in the Irish Guards.)

The proprietor, Robert, still seemed rather bemused, or amused so she tried to put the matter beyond doubt, 'And he's my husband.'

At this stage I intervened. 'Excuse me, Madam, are you Mrs Murray?'

'Yes,' she said, rather aggressively now. 'I am Mrs Murray.'

'That is rather strange,' I countered, 'for I am *Mr* Murray.'

'But you are not my husband,' she said emphatically, 'my husband is with Greta Garbo.'

At last the true facts came out, and soon we had arranged to meet for a drink with her husband that same evening. It was then that he told me of the disgraceful story in the German magazine.

I myself met Miss Garbo on a number of occasions and once attended a cocktail party at her villa after I had called there with flowers from Lady Churchill. She gave me a note thanking Lady Churchill and said, 'This is just a note inviting Lady Churchill and her husband to a cocktail party. You come along too.' I went but Sir Winston did not.

On that occasion it appeared that she was throwing a kind of 'duty' party for a few notables in and around Monte Carlo. She was very charming, but I got the impression that the proceedings held little interest for her and her friend. Mr Schlee confirmed my opinion that she did really 'want to be alone'. I saw her then as few of the general public ever saw her off the screen – without her dark glasses. Why she should wish to hide herself away behind glasses in public, I just could not fathom out, because even though she was in her fifties then, she still retained so much of her deeply alluring loveliness. She certainly did not look her age and her great attraction was enhanced by a deep, brooding, inner quality, almost a mysticism which invested her with an indefinable magnetic beauty. Perhaps this was because her looks were entirely natural, unaided, I am convinced, by any of the devices upon which the majority of women rely. There was no make-up, for example, and her greying hair hung rather untidily, I thought, shoulder length. Her clothes too were very sombre and did nothing to focus attention on her. Rather the contrary in fact, but still a great allure was present.

Another former actress I encountered in that part of the world was the erstwhile Grace Kelly, wife of Prince Rainier, a really beautiful princess, now sadly departed following a tragic car accident a few miles from her Palace.

Sir Winston, on each visit to the area, had at least one dinner engagement with the Rainiers at the Palace. In those days I thought that it was also a 'duty' business, but in looking back, I appreciate that Sir Winston did seem to enjoy his evenings with Their Highnesses, especially as there was always a brand-new film after dinner.

The tiny state of Monaco, about as big as Hyde Park in London, encompassing Monte Carlo, had been pretty well run down until Mr Onassis appeared on the scene. He helped get its famous Casino back on its feet, and to play a major role in extending the nearby Hôtel de Paris. One heard many stories to the effect that there was not much love lost between Prince Rainier and Mr Onassis. It might well have been true for it must have been very galling for the Prince to gaze down from his Palace high above Monaco to see Onassis's yacht *Christina* dominating the harbour of Monaco. Nevertheless, it was largely due to the Greek millionaire that the drift of the very rich from Monte Carlo was checked and that the place received a face-lift with an invigorating programme of entertainment, summer and winter, encouraging millionaires to come flocking back.

Prince Rainier seemed to have firm control over the affairs of the tiny state, though, and the Monégasque people were very loyal and proud of their ruling family. The older part of the Principality, with its guards dressed like toy soldiers patrolling the Palace grounds, and the medieval atmosphere and Palace staff always touched off a romantic spark with me, recalling scenes from *The Prisoner of Zenda*. Yet a disturbingly mercenary side to the Royal Family occurred after the birth of Princess Caroline, the first of the three children born to Prince Rainier and Princess Grace. It was an event of international interest, partly owing to the fame of the mother, and partly to the historical fact of there now being a successor to Rainier which meant a continuation of Monaco as a Principality, free from France and French taxation, for at least another half century. The attention of the world's Press was focused on the little state, and after the stories of the birth, the next big event to be awaited was the publication of the first photographs of the infant. In Britain, and probably in most other countries with a royal or quasi-royal family, such pictures would have been issued to all the newspapers at the same time, free of charge. Not so in Monte Carlo, where a large number of representatives of the Press were gathered. There the photographs were examined and haggled over as different newspapers bid against each other for the exclusive right to publish the various pictures. I watched the scene with amazement, having been taken along by Francis Rico of the *Nice Matin*, a good friend, now alas, with us no longer.

22

CHURCHILL THE BACK-BENCHER

SPENDING SO MUCH TIME OUT of England, as he now was, meant that Sir Winston's attention to political matters was less immediate than it had been, though he was still kept very much in touch with affairs of state by the British Government and, whenever we were abroad, a Queen's Messenger would fly in from time to time with official documents for his information and perusal. But he was withdrawing increasingly from public life; in fact one of the last big political meetings he attended was as far back as May 1957, when he took the chair at the Albert Hall for the annual meeting of the Primrose League. On that occasion there was a good deal of destructive heckling by that well-known group of nuisance-makers, the League of Empire Loyalists. Although, even at the age of eighty-three, the Old Man could probably have dealt with normal heckling, there was not much anyone could do against such a sustained attack by the 'Empire Loonies' as they were known. So vociferous were the interrupters that even such a doughty and stentorian-voiced speaker as Lord Hailsham was having difficulty in making himself heard.

So, at a signal from the platform, I called a uniformed policeman, and on behalf of the chairman, he asked the group to leave. They refused his request, however, and a further request by one of the organizers of the meeting, so there was nothing for it but to throw them out. This is actually what happened, and needless to say, there were many photographs of it in the Press the following day, proving quite conclusively that some of the group had left the Albert Hall most unwillingly.

Apparently, so far as the local police were concerned, the camera not only could, but did, lie on this occasion because when I put in my report to the Special Branch next day, my chief asked me if I had seen the report of the incident as recorded by Chelsea police station.

The report, notwithstanding what was written and pictured in the morning papers, concluded thus, 'The group was asked to leave and did so quietly.' There was no point in arguing, so I tore up my own report and typed out a new one, more in line with the 'facts'.

In the early part of 1958 illness, quite serious and prolonged this time, again struck Sir Winston at La Pausa, Roquebrune, going from just a chill, or so it seemed at first, to pneumonia with all the worrying complications that threaten when the victim is aged.

We had been to lunch on the *Christina*, anchored in the Port of Monaco. It was a fine, warm February day and Sir Winston, by this time a firm friend of Mr Onassis, stayed rather longer than usual. After tea, the cards were brought out and a game of chemin-de-fer got under way and it was not until seven o'clock, when the evening air became quite chilly, that the party broke up and Sir Winston returned in a chill, unheated Rolls-Royce driven by his host, Mr Emery Reves, to the Villa La Pausa, at Roquebrune.

Sir Winston had a sleepless night and next day he was not well enough to drive to Nice airport to meet his wife, arriving from London. In fact, he was not even fit enough to leave his bed and outdoor staff were told that he had a stomach chill. However, Dr David Roberts, his local English doctor, spent most of the day at La Pausa and a wire was sent to Lord Moran asking him to come. At the same time a bulletin was issued announcing the fact that Sir Winston was in bed with a slight cold and asking the Press and the public to refrain from phoning the villa.

Such a bulletin was bound to arouse doubts and fears, so it was not surprising that the next day, like vultures scenting prey, the Press began to congregate once more from most parts of Europe. Before long they had made their HQ in the Hôtel de Paris in Monte Carlo. Mr Montague Browne was issuing daily reports at impromptu Press conferences in the Hotel.

By now it was common knowledge that the Old Man had pneumonia. Sir Winston himself became irritable and worried and, as usual in such cases, a difficult patient. He kept a thermometer by the bed and took his own temperature at all times of the day and night, showing alarm at any irregularity. Doctor's orders that he must stay in bed left him restless and fractious, despite the humouring bestowed upon him by his staff and friends. His mood was not improved either by the polite refusal of the Other Club to postpone the date of their next meeting to give him a chance of attending.

After about ten days a portable X-ray machine was procured and a thorough examination permitted his doctors to state that there was no danger. The Press began happily to send out the news and the patient showed signs of perking up a bit. He was by no means out of the woods and his temperature continued to fluctuate but it was very difficult to persuade him to take things quietly and he had almost to be bribed to do so. If he wanted to play cards, a favourite relaxation, Lady Churchill would accept only if he got into bed.

Eventually the pneumonia cleared up but heart spasms gave cause for much concern. All this was of course kept very secret. As far as the world at large was concerned, everything was progressing quite favourably until a portable oxygen kit was delivered. The makers had sent it just in case, without referring the matter to any of the people concerned, and it took quite a while to quell the rumours.

Then came the day when he was able to leave his bedroom, and as I helped him downstairs – a charge I would allow nobody to usurp in a case like this where Sir Winston must be rather frail – he said, 'You have not seen very much of me for a month now,' then with his old chuckle '. . . but you have stopped everyone else from seeing me in a very poor state as well.'

A few days later he got his revenge on his medical adviser for Lord Moran himself had a temperature, opening the way for a little of Sir Winston's impish baiting. On the balcony, after dinner, with His Lordship not looking very happy, his eminent patient advised him, 'Now you get off to bed and take your temperature. Use my thermometer if you like. And let me know if there is anything I can get you.'

It was early April before Sir Winston was finally fit enough to travel back to England. A plane bound for London from Athens – Olympic Airways of course, which belonged to Mr Onassis – was diverted to Marseilles where its passengers disembarked. It was then brought to Nice especially to pick up Sir Winston to carry him safely back to London and home. Even on his return he was still not completely free of the bug and several times during the next weeks he was forced to return to bed with a high temperature.

That illness set him back quite a lot physically and he suddenly began to show the burden of his years, though mentally he could be as alert as ever. Those who did not know him and met him briefly would report that he was on the edge of senility, but this was very far from the truth. If people, or their conversation, interested him, then he would talk as of old. It was certainly a fact that with the advancing years he was tending to withdraw more and more within himself, and paid less attention to those around him, but he could still be as receptive as ever to events. As a matter of fact, he seemed to be intent upon gleaning the uttermost from what life, and nature, had to offer. On the occasions when I would take him out for a drive at Chartwell, as I often did (for it would have been ridiculous to retain a chauffeur for an hour or two each day) he would comment upon the countryside, or talk, with a painter's eye, of the sky and the clouds and the changing moods of nature as if he were determined in his last precious days to miss nothing. Everything was to be noticed, commented on, and stored away in his mind. One day in 1959 we were driving towards the House of Commons, Sir Winston in the back of the car with one of his long-standing friends, Lady Lytton. In Great Smith Street I suddenly saw a former colleague, Chief Inspector George Williams, who had been on protection with Sir Winston when I took up the job. On this occasion, most unfamiliarly, he was wearing a bowler hat, and at first I did not recognize him. When I did, I turned my head to mention it to the Old Man, but he was deep in conversation with Lady Lytton and I refrained from interrupting. A few yards further on he called out to me, 'It's all right, Murray. I saw him.'

On the other hand, in his obtuse moods he could be almost alarmingly remote and absent-minded. We were driving down Constitution Hill one day, en route to Chartwell from Hyde Park Gate, when I glanced into the back of the car and saw that it was full of smoke, so much so, that I could hardly see the Old Man. He was sitting there quite unperturbed, coughing a little but not concerned in any way. He was quite surprised when I told the driver to stop the car and it was not until I pointed out that the seat was smouldering due to a fault in the heater system, that he was in the least aware that something was wrong. As the chauffeur, Joe Bullock, and I could not remedy the fault we had to procure a similar vehicle from Rootes, the suppliers.

Despite illness, despite advancing years, nothing could keep Sir Winston Churchill from the one place which dominated his entire adult life, and which he in turn dominated — the House of

Commons. I, of course, was not in his service at the time of his finest hours at Westminster, but I had plenty of opportunity to observe him as a Parliamentarian, and to appreciate the intensity of the bond which bound him to Parliament. Whenever, in those days, he returned from a holiday abroad, his first thought would be to visit the House of Commons. He especially liked, whenever possible, to attend on his birthday when heartfelt congratulations would come from both sides of the House.

When I joined him in 1950, he was the Leader of the Opposition, and the Tories were harassing the Government under Clement Attlee for all they were worth, with the scent of victory in the wind. That meant, among a lot of other things, a great many all-night sittings. Sir Winston's (he was still Mr Churchill of course then) room in the House of Commons was equipped with a folding bed (it folded back into the wall panelling), and a wash-basin, so that he could snatch at least some rest as his subordinates dragged out the debates in their campaign to wear down the Government. For him, in fact, it was all a bit of good fun, and I never once heard him grumble when I woke him up in the middle of the night to answer the Division bell. For his bodyguard, who had to sit in a chair and remain awake meanwhile, the times were arduous indeed.

As Leader of the Opposition, he used to have two or three meetings each week with the Prime Minister, and then when he again became Prime Minister, Mr Attlee was accorded the same privilege. The conversations were usually confined to a review and denial of the intent of nasty things that might have been said in the House, or the papers, and very often discussion of the situation of the Empire. They would have a Scotch and soda each and often left each other after their reminiscences, with tears streaming down their cheeks.

Going to Westminster was something of a ritual, even to the extent of Sir Winston's attire. His 'House of Commons suit', as it was known, consisted actually of a black jacket, pin-stripe trousers, a white shirt and a dark blue, white-spotted bow tie. Whenever he appeared dressed like that, there was no need to ask the day's schedule. Equally, the siren suit which he had found so convenient during the war and was reputed to have designed himself, was usually worn if a comfortable day with friends around the house was contemplated, while a grey lounge suit normally indicated that visitors, rather than close friends, were expected.

As with most other journeys which he made regularly, Sir Winston knew the time it took to get from his home to the House of Commons almost to the very second. The trip of twelve minutes to the House was facilitated by virtue of the fact that he was one of the very few privileged people to hold a pass to drive across Horse Guards Parade and into Whitehall past the mounted guards. He was very proud of the privilege and never lost an opportunity of availing himself of it when on his way to the Savoy or Mansion House and the City.

MPs' cars are normally parked in Palace Yard, the large area immediately in front of the House between Big Ben and Westminster Hall, but here too, Sir Winston was privileged for he was permitted to pass through Palace Yard and into the Speaker's Courtyard so that he could enter by the Ladies' Entrance and a lift.

Having climbed laboriously from the car and acknowledged the salutes of any policemen in the vicinity, he would invariably extract his watch from his waistcoat pocket and check carefully that Big Ben was correct, then with my assistance he would slowly mount the steps and go through the door, to the lift.

Even on his return to the role of a back-bencher, there were still privileges, and he was given a room conveniently close to the lift and the main lobby. This would be his first port of call for it was there that we kept his hearing aid hidden. It was not known to many members that his seat immediately below the Treasury Bench was specially wired to take it, for it was felt that if it were generally known, all those members with a hearing problem might claim similar facilities. During one particular period, Sir Winston began to complain about his hearing aid, claiming that it no longer functioned properly. I had it tested by one of the engineers at the House who found that it was working perfectly. Just to make sure, however, a member of the firm supplying the instrument was called to Hyde Park to make a new mould of Sir Winston's inner ear – the right one – and from this built a new ear-piece. He tried it at Hyde Park Gate and it was a perfect fit, but on trying it in the House of Commons, he still found that it was faulty. Luckily I had asked the engineer to keep an eye on Sir Winston and his position from the Gallery and he saw that Sir Winston was trying to wear the aid in his left ear. I must say that I had to be very diplomatic indeed in getting him to wear it in his right ear. The next day, in his room at the House of Commons, I said, 'We have another new aid here, Sir Winston, and it may prove better than the other one.'

'Well, let's try it,' he said. Once more he began to insert it in the left ear.

'This one is for the other ear, Sir Winston,' I told him and he tried it. It worked perfectly and there was never any further trouble. Just in case, I placed a notice in the drawer where the aid was kept, to the effect that *this apparatus is for the right ear.*

As a back-bencher, following his retirement as Prime Minister, he still showed great conscientiousness, particularly as far as the Whip and divisions were concerned.

'You might check with the Whips and see whether they want me tonight,' he would say to me when we were away from the Commons when anything important was brewing, and I would phone the Chief Whip's office to find out. Normally he would only be required to attend to vote on important issues. When asked to go he always felt it his duty to respond.

One evening he was being escorted to his car by the then Chief Whip, Mr Edward Heath, after a vote. 'That was a very good majority, Sir Winston,' said Mr Heath by way of conversation, as they went down the steps at the Ladies' Gallery entrance.

'Yes it was, very good,' said Sir Winston.

'It was good of you to come, sir,' continued Mr Heath.

'Not at all,' replied Sir Winston, 'It was very important for the Government, wasn't it . . . very important.'

'Yes, indeed, most important.'

By this time Sir Winston was actually in the car, but just as the door was about to close he leaned forward towards Mr Heath and asked, 'By the way, what were we voting on?'

After giving up his post as Prime Minister, Sir Winston spoke very little in the House of Commons, although there were quite a few people who would have liked to have had him do much more. There was, for instance, a conversation between Sir Winston and a fairly senior member of the Government, at the time of Suez, when Britain's fortunes in the world at large, and especially in America, were pretty low.

'I heard your speech in Paris,' the Minister said, 'You are still the best man to put anything over.'

'But it is very difficult for me to speak in the House,' said Sir Winston.

'Well, why not in America?' he was asked. 'You are the very best person to speak for us in the United States.'

Needless to say, the suggestion was not taken up.

[240]

If his activities in the House declined, his sense of complete assurance at Westminster, the place above all others where he was the master, did not. This sense pervaded his domestic relationships, because although at home Lady Churchill might be the boss, if ever she ventured to the House of Commons her husband would always make it quite plain that this was his territory and he would act and speak as he thought best. It was also demonstrated in other ways as well and I recall a meeting with General Sir Gerald Templer in the Speaker's Courtyard. At the time Sir Gerald was Chief of the Imperial General Staff, but was in civvies – dark suit and bowler hat of course – and although I recognized him, Sir Winston did not. Sir Winston looked at him vaguely on hearing his polite, 'Good afternoon, Sir Winston.' He turned to me as if to say that he had a feeling that he should know this stranger in front of him, some four or five yards away, but who was he?

'General Templer, Sir Winston,' I said quickly.

'Of course,' he replied, trying to imply that he had known all along who it was. They shook hands, and at the door the General stood aside for Sir Winston to enter first, but with a very courteous gesture with his right hand the Old Man waved Sir Gerald in.

'After you, my dear, after you. This is *my* house.'

This story is quoted as both an example of the ex-Prime Minister's sense of proprietorship, almost, with regard to the House of Commons, and also his extreme courtesy which had such a courtly touch to it. He would often march up to a door and throw it open with a theatrical gesture, and bow his companions through with that cherubic smile which illumined his face on such occasions.

I have already suggested that the reason why Sir Winston never accepted the peerage which he could undoubtedly have had was because he did not wish to prevent those of his family who would follow him from succeeding in their turn in the House of Commons. The person he had immediately in mind, of course, was his grandson, Randolph's son, who bore his own name. To bear such a name as Winston Churchill must throw a terrific burden on any successor, and when he spoke in the Oxford Union debates as an undergraduate, for example, young Winston was bound to come up against comparison with his famous grandfather, often to his detriment.

There were other disadvantages too, as the young lad discovered on one occasion when we were at Monte Carlo. He had been invited to lunch on board *Christina* which was anchored, as usual, in the middle of the harbour. Having been swimming before lunch, he asked a boatman to row him from the beach to the yacht, but as he had no money with him – he was in his bathing trunks – he offered to pay when they got to the boat.

'No money eh? Well, who are you?' queried the boatman.

'I am Winston Churchill,' he was told.

'So you are Winston Churchill,' said the man, 'well I am the King of Greece.'

Nevertheless by dint of powerful persuasion, young Winston got his transport to the *Christina*. With such incidents being rather commonplace, life in the south of France was never dull. Apart from anything else, there was always a steady flow of visitors, many of them world-famous. The Duke and Duchess of Windsor have already been mentioned, and Greta Garbo as well, but consider also, some of those who called around the time Sir Winston and Lady Churchill celebrated their golden wedding anniversary, in September 1958. Authors Somerset Maugham and Nigel Balchin head the impressive list, along with politicians Adlai Stevenson and the then Speaker of the House of Commons, Mr W. S. Morrison, M. Coty, President of the French Republic, Lord Montgomery, Lord Derby and Lord Rosebery.

The golden wedding celebration itself passed off quite quietly at Cap d'Ail. Just a few members of the family, including Randolph and his daughter Arabella, then eight years old, and some close friends to mark the occasion. Needless to say, the event did not pass without a good deal of note from the Press of the world. All morning, photographers and reporters had been congregating outside the villa, and after lunch I suggested to Sir Winston and Lady Churchill that they might be admitted to take photographs.

Mr Montague Browne carried a message to me to the effect that five photographers would be allowed in for ten minutes only. I told him that that was rather silly for there were many more than five photographers outside the villa walls and how were we to choose those who could enter. Mr Browne then suggested that I allow five in for five minutes, then another five for five minutes. I then asked what we should do with the television crews and he said he would speak with Sir Winston. He returned shortly saying that Sir Winston would like to speak to me.

'My dear Murray, I leave the matter entirely in your hands. You know best what to do.'

Within fifteen minutes about thirty newspapermen and TV cameramen were happily shooting pictures. At the end of ten minutes or so, I suggested that the cameramen might like to drink to the continued long life and prosperity of the couple. Sir Winston thought it was a good idea and provided the champagne to do it. It goes without saying that one of them did try and take advantage by entering the villa to take something the others did not have, but he didn't get very far. The fierce competition of the Press world throws up plenty of rather unscrupulous characters, especially at the international level, but happily those who desire fair play outnumber the others by far.

For the occasion the family presented Sir Winston and Lady Churchill with a unique gift seen by thousands of visitors to Chartwell throughout the years since. It was an avenue of golden roses in the garden, some fifty yards in length. With this went a book of paintings by a number of prominent people, including some professional artists, each *oeuvre* depicting a type of golden rose to be found in the golden avenue.

This golden wedding anniversary indicated, in my view, the immense strength and satisfaction which Sir Winston had drawn, during the long and troubled years, from that marriage, and the family that came of it.

23

THE FINAL YEARS

As I HAVE PREVIOUSLY MENTIONED, one of my tasks as bodyguard to the Right Honourable Gentleman was to help cope with the Press, which was always something of a battle of wits. Sir Winston himself never had any direct dealings with the Press (even though the big men like Beaverbrook, Rothermere and Harmsworth were all friends and Lord Thompson came on the scene a little bit later on), except to allow the odd photograph on formal occasions, and he never gave interviews. One evening he went to the Savoy for the Other Club dinner and a Press photographer was at the Savoy Hill entrance to meet him and take a picture. I motioned him to wait while I got Sir Winston's permission. 'Who's it for?' he queried irascibly for he had not been mellowed yet by a pre-prandial drink.

'It's for the *Daily Mirror*,' I informed him.

'Not for that bloody rag,' he exploded within hearing of the young fellow in question. I suggested to the latter that he might be inclined to come back to the same place after dinner when he might be more successful. We went in to dinner and had a very pleasant evening as usual.

When we came out, the little photographer was there again and I told Sir Winston, now in rather a cheeky mood, that even the *Mirror* might one day have a good word to say for him. He laughed and turned to face the man with the camera.

Sir Winston was always news, and when he was abroad he was what one could call 'double news' for not only was there the usual corps of British journalists around, but the local newspapermen used to turn out in force too, and they were sometimes more difficult to deal with.

During a visit to La Pausa at Roquebrune in 1958, so much material was getting to the Press, much of it wildly garbled, that Sir

Winston asked me to stop it. I spent several days investigating but it was very difficult to pin anything on to anyone though I was quite sure who was doing the damage. My inquiries and very personal questions to the suspect caused rather a panic and the leakage stopped within days. My report on the investigation to Sir Winston and Lady Churchill concluded '. . . and you can rest assured that in the future, as in the past, as little as possible of the private life of Sir Winston will remain secret and confidential'.

I meant 'as much as possible', of course. It was a slip that gave Lady Churchill a great deal of amusement when she read the report later at Chartwell.

There was no trouble with the newspapers at our next port of call, Marrakesh, at the beginning of 1959, after a delightful, sun-drenched cruise in the *Christina* along the coast of Spain, in the lap of luxury, and up the Quadalquivir to Seville. Here Sir Winston and Mr Onassis, with me perched up in front with the 'driver', went for a fascinating tour of the lovely city in a horse-drawn cab. The trip up the river had been uninteresting for the land on both sides of the river was terribly flat and boring. The passage through the lock into the city was better, then the tour of the city made it really a most enjoyable trip. After dinner, having ensured that the yacht and its access was absolutely secure – with the utmost co-operation of Sir Winston and a gift of money to the police authority by Mr Onassis – I was able to spend the evening ashore with the yacht's radio officer, Erich Reupke. He was a most delightful companion who by this time, together with his charming wife, beautiful enough to have become, had she desired it, the World's Beauty Queen, had become firm friends of my wife and me.

I can imagine some people by now saying, 'What a lovely job this man had. Always close to Sir Winston Churchill, cruises in the Mediterranean, sunshine in mid-winter, comfort, good living.' To a certain extent they would be right, of course, but it was a twenty-four-hour a day job – especially during the last ten years, when I was on my own, and if anything had happened to my protégé, I alone would have been held responsible. Even today, twenty and more years after Sir Winston's death, when dining in restaurants, sitting in bars, or trains, or buses I still only feel comfortable when I can keep an eye on the door and the majority of people in the room there with me. Like Rex Harrison in *My Fair Lady*, 'it's second nature to me now . . .'

When I was with Sir Winston in his car, or when I drove my own or even someone else's car, I always conjured up incidents which could necessitate my having to take immediate action for his protection. I think that I was ready for anything to happen. I felt I owed it to Sir Winston and his lady . . . and to the country. Nothing ever did happen to him, so one can only suppose that my protection was satisfactory − as the Police Instruction Book puts it, 'Only the absence of crime will prove that a police force is efficient.'

In Marrakesh I turned down a very good job and was honoured to receive from the Foreign Legion Old Comrades there an illuminated scroll, 'For services to the Foreign Legion.' It was only the third one ever issued. Sir Winston himself received No. 2.

In 1941, I had spent several weeks in Marrakesh with the Legion, and on going back some fifteen years later after the turmoil of war, I found in and around that city a number of legionnaires with whom I had served, now out of the Legion and prospering for the most part. One man, born in Austria, who had spent fifteen years in the Legion, retiring as Sergeant-Major, was the proprietor of a marmalade factory exporting its products to many parts of the world. Another ex-Austrian had a very flourishing watch repair business, and several Poles had restaurants.

In Britain, I have always tried to retain contact with former members of the Foreign Legion, and in fact, for a number of years just after the end of the Second World War, I was chairman of the Legion Old Comrades' Association in London, covering the whole of the country. One day I was called into the Chief Superintendent's office at Special Branch and told to look at a file, and report on it. I suggested that as protection duties at the time were very strenuous, I did not really have time, but I stopped there for I had seen my own name on the MI5 file. They had discovered apparently that a Mr Edmund Murray was the chairman of an association of ex-legionnaires and it might be in the interests of national intelligence services to investigate him. There was no love lost between MI5 and the Special Branch who usually carried out the dirty work of the former, and my bosses were delighted to have my report a few days later where I admitted that I was the person under investigation, and that I had been in Special Branch for quite a number of years, etc.

Legionnaires, when back in civvy street in England, found themselves doing a wide variety of jobs, and among our own association members were a faith healer with a very wide practice in north-west London, a tic-tac man at the White City dog-racing track, a civil servant who was our Secretary, and a senior travel agency courier. As far back as 1947, when still a recruit in the Force, I gave a fifteen-minute broadcast in the 'World and his Wife' BBC radio programme. It is interesting to note that I was assisted in the preparation of the script at Broadcasting House by none other than the famous poet and writer, Roy Campbell, who had taken part in the Spanish Civil War. We had numerous long, ardent discussions with Eileen Moloney, the producer, on people and war and peace.

With the Secretary of the French Foreign Legion and Comrades Association, John Yeowell, I also appeared on the TV programme 'The Missing Link' when the panel included Peter Noble, Lady Elizabeth Barnett and the lovely Katie Boyle. Although Yeowell was in a suit and I wore a dinner jacket, the panel found the link – the F.L.

On this second visit to Marrakesh with Sir Winston, there were two incidents of note. One of my French Press friends came to warn me that there was a rumour circulating to the effect that the Berbers in the mountains were very dissatisfied with their treatment by the new King and his Government because of their allegiance to the now-dead Pasha of Marrakesh, and were considering abducting Sir Winston, for no nefarious purpose, but just to focus world attention upon their plight. I went to the local police chief and suggested an increase in the number of men at my disposal for protection and he readily agreed to two men permanently in the corridor of the hotel and two men in the gardens of the Mamounia during the rest of the stay. Fortunately nothing untoward happened.

Also during our stay, one evening while I was doing the rounds of the gardens surrounding the hotel, I had returned to the front of the building when I heard a lady weeping, beside a tree. I told her who I was and asked if I could help in any way. She told me that she was Madame X and I then knew that she was at the time intimately involved in an immense litigation case in France where her husband had died and the will was being contested. Part of the family business was the factory at Thionville, in France, where the famous Walther pistol was manufactured – a pistol I was carrying at the time. The whole matter was very much big news in the Press then, and as there were many journalists at the front door of the Mamounia, and in the lobby, she was scared of being mobbed when she went in. I told her not to worry and that, while I spoke with the journalists, a short distance away, she was to crawl through the bushes, making as little noise as possible, to the locked back door and await my arrival. A few minutes later I returned to her side alone and unlocked the door. I escorted her to her room, which happened to be at the outside end of the corridor in which Sir Winston's room, and my own, were, and reassured her that there would be police officers on watch to ensure that no Pressmen came along the corridor. As she opened the door to her room, I saw that she was not to be alone, for inside I recognized one of the reporters of *Paris Match* and he seemed to be very much at home. She told me that he was actually interviewing her on behalf of his magazine . . . he was there several days but as they kept a very low profile, their presence remained a secret.

From North Africa, Sir Winston and his party now cruised south towards the Canaries on the Onassis yacht which we had boarded at Safi, the port of Marrakesh, though a good two hundred miles distant. But just before we left Marrakesh I got another one of those illuminating glimpses of what life is like in the very top bracket of the international set. Mr Onassis had left instructions at the hotel that his wife was to be called at 8 am, and from then on every half hour until she got up, for she was due to catch a plane at 11 am to fly to Casablanca, some 800 miles away, for lunch.

I suppose it was too much to hope for that in such an atmosphere the Onassis family could keep together. It was only a few months later that we rejoined *Christina* at Monaco with the famous Maria Callas on board as well. Her name was then linked to that of Mr Onassis in newspapers throughout the world. Mrs Tina Onassis eventually divorced her husband and in due course married Lord 'Sonny' Blandford, son of the Duke of Marlborough.

However, all that was still some way distant as we steamed serenely towards the Canary Islands in the warm spring sunshine of 1959. As usual there was very little for me to do while we were at sea, and to pass the time I decided to paint a portrait of the Onassis daughter, Christina, who was about ten years old at the time. I always had a soft spot for Christina because, apart from being a very pleasant little girl when treated correctly, I felt that she got left out of things a lot. There was no doubt that her brother Alexander, who was some three years older, was Mr Onassis's favourite. I remember, for instance, when both children went down with measles, it was

[248]

Alexander who had all the fuss made over him, while his sister was almost forgotten. He was a very bright lad, though, and could speak English, French and Greek fluently, which pleased his father very much, but his sister could only manage English and French and was very obstinate in her lack of enthusiasm for Greek. This rejection of her parents' mother tongue did not help matters, but I always felt that her father's obvious preference for her brother made her introspective and sad. Alexander seemed to pick things up very quickly in all fields that he found interesting, particularly of a mechanical nature, and his best friend on the yacht was the chief engineer. He was spoiled by the crew and Mr Onassis's friends and I often told him that a few years' schooling in England would probably do him the world of good. Ultimately he did attend an English school but he found it too tough or restrictive and only stayed a few months before returning to Paris. What a terrible blow it must have been to his family when, aged only twenty-one, he crashed and died in the plane he was flying. He was a real dare-devil from a very early age, driving fast cars and motor-boats to the limit of their capacity. I always found him very respectful of age and superior knowledge and experience and he was always willing to learn new things. It was a terrible tragedy.

I painted Christina's portrait mainly from a small photograph, but I was quite satisfied with the result and when it was completed I presented it to the officers for their mess, for it was there, and not with her parents, that Christina took the majority of her meals. Mr and Mrs Onassis liked the picture and it was still hanging there when last I was on board the yacht, in 1963.

On that trip in 1959, Sir Winston was in great form and he had a very healthy appetite. Most of the time he had rather an Edwardian approach to meals and often had a sort of mixed grill for breakfast, and possibly a glass of champagne with it on special occasions.

But during the winter of that same year, I often had very serious doubts about his survival for it seemed that even the slightest cold or malaise caused him to sink so low that I wondered if he had more than six months to live. The years after 1959 proved how wrong I was.

One of the people entertained by Sir Winston and Lady Churchill at Marrakesh had been Lady Margaret Colville, wife of 'Jock' Colville, Sir Winston's Private Secretary at the time, who had been Private Secretary to Her Majesty the Queen when she was a Princess. Lady

Margaret, née Egerton, had been one of the Princess's Ladies-in-Waiting and not long after we returned from Marrakesh where I had given Lady Margaret a few lessons in oil painting, she repaid the hospitality by inviting the Churchills to the Prince's Theatre to see the D'Oyly Carte Opera Company in a performance of *The Gondoliers*.

Also in the party was Lord Montgomery whose attention throughout most of the evening seemed to be focused more on football than the theatre, for he was a Director of Portsmouth Football Club and they had a very important match that day. Monty had a word with the management before going into the theatre and told them that he wanted the result of the game passed to him as soon as it was known, and this had been agreed. But it so happened that there was a three-line Whip out in the House of Commons and we knew that Sir Winston would have to return to Westminster to vote. Half-way through *The Gondoliers* Sir Winston saw a note brought down the aisle and passed along the row. He immediately arose, assuming that it was his summons to the House – but the note never reached him because it only contained the result of the Portsmouth football match. However, as he was already on his feet, Sir Winston decided that it was time to go and he trooped out, followed by the whole party, including a mystified Lord Montgomery. Needless to say there was no car waiting and we returned to No 10 by taxi.

Although by now Sir Winston was well into his eighties, he was still a very active traveller, and before long we were off again, to the United States.

At New York Airport, called Idlewild at that time, we found President Eisenhower's personal plane, 'Columbia', waiting for us and soon we were in Washington. It was only a short visit of four days, and very much a matter of talking over the good old days as far as Ike and Sir Winston were concerned, because on two successive evenings they dined together at White House stag parties. On the third evening, at the British Embassy, there was quite a big function and among those who gathered there to meet Sir Winston were ex-President Truman, Dean Acheson and General Maxwell Taylor. During this visit, a trip to President Eisenhower's farm near Gettysburg was also made, and I got some rather nice photographs of the President and Sir Winston driving round the estate in a small electric car normally used by the President on the golf-course.

On that visit, I also collected rather an unusual souvenir in the shape of a brick from the original Capitol building. The bricks for this building, according to legend, were taken to America from Britain by Thomas Jefferson who was to be the third President of the United States, as ballast on the vessel on which he crossed the Atlantic. One of these bricks was handed to me by Representative Bill Ayres, of Ohio, as a sentimental gesture, when they unearthed some of the original foundation of the Capitol during redesigning of the entrance steps.

The brick, red and solid, and hand-made, returned to Britain by a very different method – in a Comet of BOAC – and it now forms part of a garden wall I built at our home at the time, in Holders Hill Avenue, Hendon, in north-west London.

Towards the end of July of that year of 1959, came another trip on the *Christina*, a trip which, if it didn't quite shake the world, at least reverberated throughout the gossip columns of newspapers all over the world, and found echoes in café society round Europe and a lot of other areas as well. The reason was that besides the Onassis family and Sir Winston and Lady Churchill and their party, a certain Mr and Mrs Ménéghini were also guests. The latter was none other than the great opera singer, Maria Callas. This was the very first time that the Press began to tie up the names of Aristotle Onassis and Maria Callas together, although from my point of view at the time, most of what they wrote was invented by highly imaginative Pressmen who would have been more profitably and honourably employed writing their fiction in the form of novels. We were all aboard the yacht for three weeks on that occasion during which we cruised in scorching hot weather to the Greek islands and back to Monte Carlo. At no time – and it must be clear by now that I do not go around with my eyes closed – did I see even the remotest suggestion of any liaison or extra-marital relationships developing. In my opinion it would have been extremely difficult anyhow, for Signor Ménéghini never seemed to let his wife out of his sight, and, incidentally, never lost any opportunity of taking photographs of his wife whenever she was in the company of Sir Winston or Lady Churchill.

As for La Callas herself, well, I would never describe her as beautiful, but she always had about her a certain striking quality, an immense fascination conjured mainly I think by her great, expressive eyes and mobile, eloquent hands that were never still. On board the *Christina* there was never about her the aura of the tigress, for which she was noted in operatic circles, but then, she was to a large extent outshone, shall we say, and someone else was at the centre of the stage. I always found her very pleasant in her attitude to myself, and very easy to talk to, in French or in English, for she spoke both with facility, though she had rather an appealing American accent acquired from the fact that the first thirteen years of her life had been spent in New York, where she was born. I think that the overriding impression she gave me was of an essentially very lonely woman, an artiste caught and held by the barriers of a little world she had created around herself, a world in which her intense dedication, allied to the standards she demanded of herself, in some way set her apart from everyone else.

The situation that was supposed to exist at that time between Aristotle Onassis and Maria Callas reminds me of a story Sir Winston had told to some political cronies on our American trip a few weeks earlier. Lord Palmerston, then an old man, was reputed to be having an affair with a woman much younger than himself. Some of his political opponents saw this as a golden opportunity to cause his downfall, and urged Disraeli to expose him. 'Nonsense,' said Disraeli, 'if we revealed that, we would never get rid of him for the people would love him for it.'

This voyage to the Greek islands was a sentimental one for the Onassis family, since we went to the area whence their parents had come; and for Sir Winston, though to a lesser extent, it was a trip of some meaning, since during the cruise we sailed through the Dardanelles. Then to round the voyage off, there was another famous visitor to the yacht – Gracie Fields came to dinner. It was very fascinating to study in the lovely balmy evening at Capri – even from a distance for I was not at the table – these two world-famous women singers. Famous in entirely different spheres, perhaps equally eminent, the one so light and gay and respectfully sparkling in such august company, and the other so overflowing with her glorious, operatic superiority. As far as Lady Churchill was concerned, she was absolutely entranced to meet 'our Gracie' and to listen to her Lancashire humour. She clapped her hands repeatedly and her eyes shone with an enthusiasm I had rarely seen in her, and Gracie undoubtedly enjoyed the situation too, for as she came to the gangway to go down to the motor-boat, she told me that she had had a wonderful evening – the best ever – for she had met Mr Churchill. As she was taken back across the stretch of water separating the yacht from her island refuge, her voice rang out with all the familiar vibrance, 'Come back to Sorrento . . . or I must die.'

This trip, incidentally, was the last one made by Lady Churchill on *Christina*, and though Sir Winston went again, there was no doubt that his wife by her very marked absence in the future, intended to show her disapproval of the rumours about Onassis and La Callas.

Anyway, as far as this voyage was concerned, it seemed to be a compound of heat and boredom, interspersed with high moments when, for example, off Naphlion the Greek Prime Minister came aboard for dinner, and at a later stage, off Prinkipo Island, off Turkey, the ill-fated Mr Menderes, then Turkish Prime Minister, was the guest of honour.

For Aristotle Onassis a voyage through these waters was bound to be intensely stirring since he was born into a Greek colony living in Smyrna, now Izmir, in Turkey. His father was called Socrates and his mother, Penelope, like the wife of Ulysses. In those tempestuous days of 1906 and later, the Greeks and the Turks were the bitterest of enemies and one day he and his parents were imprisoned by the Turks. Onassis himself, as he told me, for he always took great pleasure in talking about the past to anybody he thought was interested, was soon set free but his parents were held for many months until he had accumulated enough money to pay the Turks a ransom.

For Sir Winston there was one particularly evocative moment when we sailed through the Dardanelles. It was at night, deliberately organized by Mr Onassis I am sure to spare Sir Winston's feelings. All that could be seen from the yacht were the signal lights from the shore in recognition of our own identifying flashes from the bridge.

Despite the concern of the others, the nurse was instructed by Sir Winston to fetch me and together we went on deck to watch the dim, distant outline of the shore and the hills, for two hours. We were alone, entirely alone, and invisible except for the glow of his cigar in the blackness. What memories, I wondered, were stirring within his mind? Did he see before him, in that warm night air, the ghosts of the regiments of men who perished at Gallipoli Beach, men who had been just cogs in the vast, ponderous machine that he himself had set in motion? I felt the drama as we sat there, and judging from Sir Winston's reactions then and immediately after, it was an experience which had considerable impact upon him, and during the next two or three days, he was in silent, retrospective mood. On the return journey, the nurse made sure that he slept.

By this stage in Sir Winston's life, eighty-five years of age, retro-spection was becoming of ever-increasing significance as he grad-ually withdrew from public life. Rarely now did he speak either at meetings or at functions. In fact, the last time that he addressed his constituents at Woodford, the pleasant Essex borough on the fringe of London, was shortly after we returned from that memorable voy-age to the Black Sea. It was 29 September 1959, and a General Elec-tion was in the offing with the Tories seeking re-election after eight years in office. Sir Winston found, needless to say, a hall jammed tight from wall to wall, for any speech by him was an event of great moment to the electors of Woodford.

I kept a copy of the speech, seven stencilled foolscap pages with the Conservative and Unionist Central Office title at the top, with a release time of 20.00 hours, underneath.

It was not a speech to compare with those he had made during, and immediately after, the war, speeches for the history books; this one was pretty much the sort of thing Tory MPs and candidates were making all over the country at the time, but it nevertheless did con-tain one paragraph of immense historical significance. This was a reference to the letter he had written to Stalin in April 1945, as the war in Europe was drawing to a close. It was a letter which I had not known of before and which demonstrated to me, and I imagine to his constituents, the great grasp of world affairs and the extreme sagacity he had displayed as an international leader.

He told the meeting; '. . . as the victorious Western and Russian forces were joining hands in victory, I wrote to Stalin: do not, I beg you, my friend Stalin, underrate the divergences which are opening up. There is not much comfort in looking into a future where you and the countries you dominate, plus the Communist parties in many other states are all drawn upon one side, and those who rally to the English-speaking nations and their associates or dominions are on the other. It is quite obvious that their quarrel would tear the world to pieces and that all of us leading men on either side who had anything to do with that would be shamed before all history. Even embarking on a long period of suspicions, of abuse and counter-abuse, and of opposing policies, would be a disaster hampering the great developments of world prosperity for the masses which are attainable only by our trinity. Stalin did not listen,' he concluded.

[254]

Sometimes it was difficult to realize that Sir Winston was one who had literally governed the flow of events affecting the entire world, but on occasions such as this, with just a brief reminder, the full, immense significance of the role he had played for those five desperately vital years came flooding in.

Sir Winston's constituents, whom he had represented in Parliament for forty out of the fifty-six years he was there, decided about this time to erect a statue to his permanent memory on Woodford Green. A total of five thousand pounds was collected, with donations coming from all over the world, particularly America. A Scottish sculptor, David McFall, was commissioned. The work he eventually produced was very controversial, quite as much so as the celebrated portrait by Sutherland presented by Parliament on another occasion. The statue was eight feet high and depicted a pudgy-faced Churchill, a huge head thrust forward, the left hand sweeping back the jacket and the shoulders stooping. One could see that it was Churchill . . . yet it was not he. It was almost as if the sculptor had produced a very good likeness of a Churchill stand-in. It caused much comment, mainly critical, but at the unveiling ceremony, performed by Lord Montgomery, the Old Man took everything without the bat of an eyelid. Whether he had been warned beforehand, or whether his innate and always marked courtesy had simply taken control, I do not know, but either way, there was really nothing to indicate precisely what he felt about the statue. McFall did tell me later, when I, as a fellow artist, gave him my opinion of the statue, that it was to be viewed from the road, not from close up. He had a point, because it was only from some distance away that I found it acceptable. Three years later Sir Winston did tell me what he thought of it. David McFall was also commissioned afterwards to produce a statue of Stanley Baldwin, a former Prime Minister, for the House of Commons, and in due course it appeared in the Members' Lobby.

As soon as it was in place, Sir Winston went to see it and was extremely interested in the work, examining it minutely for quite a time before going to a far wall to lean against it while he studied the statue from a distance. Eventually I said to him, 'It's by David McFall.'

'What?' he asked me.

'I said that it was by David McFall – the man who did your statue at Woodford.'

'Oh! . . . that bloody thing!'

Some men are fortunate enough to retain their full faculties, mental and physical, well on into old age. As far as Sir Winston is concerned, however, there is no doubt that during the last few years of his life he retreated increasingly into a twilight zone. He certainly did not become senile, I hasten to add, but whereas in his seventies he was interested in almost everything that went on around him and never missed an opportunity of making people aware that he was very much *au fait* with those things happening in his vicinity, in his eighties he had to be very interested in the matter in hand or he would lapse into a sort of reverie.

After the first dubious pleasures of retirement, Sir Winston really began to enjoy his travels to foreign climes, taken without any worries as far as he himself was concerned. His biggest job was to smile to the crowds and acknowledge the acclaim he received wherever he went, but as this had been his lot for many years he found it easy. The working classes always appeared to applaud and cheer most spontaneously and he was always ready to respond with his 'V for Victory' sign. This sign, of course, can be misconstrued for in some countries two fingers raised means only one thing whether the palm faces the front or the back, and I nearly always had to consult the local constabulary on the matter should a landing be projected.

Life gradually lapsed into anti-climax . . . he had done it all before . . . and perhaps it was preferable to live with the giants of yesterday rather than with the very ordinary-sized men and women of the moment.

He wanted men around him towards the end of his life, but he did not want them to intrude . . . and I considered myself very fortunate indeed that I was there, and I did not intrude.

In the House of Commons during his last days there, he was content to sit in the Members' Smoking Room sometimes for as much as three hours at a time, a whisky and soda before him, his cigar lit, just to feel the throb of Parliamentary life about him. The Tory Whips always appointed a Member to see him into the Chamber for I could only give him my arm as far as the Churchill Arch, and then he would require assistance when he left the Chamber as well. Once I got him to the Smoking Room there would always be some Member to sit with him for I would only escort him as far as one of the tables, then leave him, for only Members were allowed there. An eminent

Conservative on one occasion told me that he was thinking about proposing that I be made an honorary member of the Smoking Room so that I could accompany Sir Winston there, and remain with him . . . but I fear that it came to naught. Once ensconced in his usual chair in the Smoking Room, there would always be a succession of visitors to greet him, from both sides of the House, but he seldom seemed to be roused by any of them, and appeared to be perfectly happy to sit there in his crowded solitude.

There was always great interest among the Members when he was in the Smoking Room and I was frequently intrigued to watch Lord Boothby's reactions, for example. Boothby and Churchill had been close friends for a longish time and Bob had been his PPS for a while, then for some reason he fell out of favour, and remained out of favour. But often when Sir Winston was in the Smoking Room, Sir Bob as he was then (later, he was given a peerage), would come along the corridor, have a few words about the state of health of his one-time boss or about the weather, go to the door and peer through the glass half-window for three or four minutes . . . then march on, deep in thought . . . but I never saw him go in.

Lady Gammans, wife of the one-time Postmaster-General, was another who seemed fascinated to watch him, and one day, as she stood there looking through the glass, I suggested that she might go in and 'beard the lion in his den' – but she said that she would 'never dare to do that'.

The lady I really wanted to help meet Sir Winston was the recently appointed Member for Finchley, one Mrs Margaret Thatcher. I had met her some time before, when I lived with my wife and three children at Hendon, just a few hundred yards off her 'patch'. In March 1964, one of our daughters, Aileen, who was fifteen at the time and a very sensible young lady, went to visit a friend, Lesley Willson, living in East Finchley. She had been told to telephone me when she was ready to leave her friend and I would collect her by car, but she had not wished to trouble me and decided to run home by herself. When she was approaching a small wood she felt she heard footsteps following her. She turned round and saw a man. She hared off towards home and heard the man running after her . . . just as far as the small wood's end, then he stopped. She ran into a private house where the owner tried to find the man, and his wife telephoned me at home and explained the situation. I dialled 999 and a patrol car was alerted.

I got into my car and sped towards the wood, collecting Aileen en route. I then left the car, dashed into the wood and searched it in the gathering gloom but saw no one. Shortly afterwards I met up with the patrol car but they also had been unsuccessful. They were going to continue their search for another half hour or so but they didn't have much hope of finding the man. They later phoned to tell me that nobody had been picked up and the facts had been recorded just in case. I went and thanked the kind people who had taken Aileen in.

The metal railings round the small wood were in a deplorable state and as it was in Mrs Thatcher's constituency I telephoned her to complain. The very next day I had a letter from her PS, and the day after she came to see my wife and me and was very kind indeed and promised to look into the question of the railings. The next time I went to look, months later, new railings had been erected and the wood was only open during hours of daylight, having new strong gates that were locked at night.

The next time I saw Mrs Thatcher in the House of Commons I thanked her for her attention, and thenceforth we had a chat on each occasion we met in the corridors. Like Lady Gammans, Mrs Thatcher could never pass the door to the Smoking Room, when she saw me standing outside, without looking through the glass of the door to see my boss. I suggested that Sir Winston would be very happy to meet her, but she was also too shy to go in. However, there did come a day when she came along the corridor in front of the Smoking Room when I was there with Sir Winston, just on our way towards the lift and the car. With great pleasure I was able to tell Sir Winston as I introduced him to the lady who was one day to fill the seat he had been so proud to hold as Prime Minister of our great country, that she had helped me in a domestic matter. They shook hands and I felt at the time that Mrs Thatcher was a very happy woman . . . and Sir Winston beamed at her, seeming to indicate that he was also very happy that one of his party could spend time helping one of his friends.

There was one occasion when Sir Winston was in a particularly responsive mood and invited the M.P. delegated to see him into the Smoking Room by the Chief Whip, to have a drink. It was about four o'clock in the afternoon, so the sun was not yet below the yard-arm . . . the M.P. said he would like a cup of tea.

'*Tea*,' snorted the Old Man contemptuously. '*Tea* . . . I am certainly not paying for any tea . . .' Two whiskies were ordered.

On one occasion in the Smoking Room, I had the experience of watching, through the glass window as well, Sir Winston having a drink with Lord Attlee, Mr Harold Macmillan and Sir Alec Douglas Home, three ex-Prime Ministers and the current one, at the same table.

Sir Winston would often remark that I knew my way round the corridors of the Palace of Westminster better than he did, and though that was a nice bit of flattery, I did none the less have a very good knowledge of the place. I have always had a good memory for faces and my wife can cite a hundred episodes in our life together when we have been out walking, or shopping, or in the bus, and I have suddenly told her that I recognized such and such a person near by. Then I would become impossible to live with until I remembered the name of the person . . . and the same thing would happen when I could not find a required word for a crossword puzzle in which I had become involved. I could not get to sleep until the word was found.

Then there was the time when we went to Holland. My wife had won a four-day trip to the tulip fields, for two, in a photographic competition to advertise the Hourmont Travel Agency in Bath, and we went by car to Bristol's Lulsgate Airport, only to find that thick fog there precluded our departure. We were then taken by coach to Rhoose Airport in South Glamorgan where the conditions were much better. Some of the other passengers had driven from that very area in the morning to catch the plane at Lulsgate and it must have been rather annoying for them to drive past their home to take the plane just a short distance away. But the return flight did come back to Bristol. However, on arrival at Schipol Airport, when Beryl and I got on to the waiting bus that was to take us all to the terminal, we found that there were no seats free. A well-dressed gentlemen stood up to offer Beryl his seat, which she gratefully accepted. I looked at the man, paused a moment, then said to him, 'Thank you, Doctor'.

He looked at me in astonishment and asked me if we were acquainted.

I told him that we had never met but I recognized him as one of the medical staff at the Middlesex Hospital and I had seen him passing in the corridor when Sir Winston had been there to have his thigh mended some months previously. He said that that was correct and although he remembered Sir Winston being there, he did not recognize me at all. He laughed when I suggested that he might remember limbs upon which he had operated, for that was his job . . . faces were mine.

It was convenient for Sir Winston to have me on hand, of course because towards the end of his life he sometimes had some difficulty in identifying people who suddenly popped into his line of vision, and I would be able to give his memory a jog in the nicest possible way in order to spare him any embarrassment.

I remember on one occasion when, as we were leaving the Ladies' Gallery entrance, we met Sir Beresford Craddock, the Conservative MP for Spelthorne (Middlesex) at that time. Sir Beresford had always been friendly towards me, and was an old friend of Sir Winston for when Sir Winston was contesting the seat in Dundee, in 1908, and he was a small lad of ten, he actually delivered Tory pamphlets in the locality where he lived. Sir Beresford was duly greeted. He had with him a group of about a dozen Boy Scouts from all over the Commonwealth, and he was in the process of showing them over the Palace of Westminster. I then explained the situation to Sir Winston, and as a tribute to the Commonwealth, he insisted on shaking hands with each of them. It must have made their day.

His need to have people round him towards the close of his life manifested itself very plainly when we returned to Hyde Park Gate after visiting the House of Commons, or the Savoy, or any other place, for as soon as he was out of the car, he would turn to me and say, 'Do come in and have a cup of tea, my dear' . . . then he would lead the way into the drawing-room. I feel that he always suggested a cup of tea for me, just in case any listeners were about, but we always knew that no tea would be asked for. We would sit there, just he and I, in deep armchairs, probably without exchanging a word for minutes on end.

Inside the drawing-room, with the open fire always burning brightly, we would have our whiskies and soda – his very weak – he would still have his cigar between his lips, for we had just come from a public place and he would rarely be seen by the public without a cigar. He would get Norman McGowan or Walter Meyer or the late duty nurse in later years to bring a box of cigars, and then very carefully he would insert the nail of the little finger of his right hand, kept about a quarter of an inch long specifically for this purpose, into the end of the chosen cigar and lift it out of the box to a sufficient distance to permit him to grasp it fully with his left hand – all this in order not to damage his treasured cigars – and pass it to me saying, 'There my dear, one of my very best.'

We used to sit there for hours. I was always reminded of Felicia Hemans' *Casabianca* on these occasions . . . 'whence all but he had fled . . .' despite my frequent reference to the fact that I had a wife and home to go to. If he wanted to talk, he knew that he had an interested listener. When he asked me about the Legion, India, Indochina, my family, my painting, I knew that he really wanted to hear what I had to say. We both felt sort of wanted. For much of the time, he would just sit there and he would be far, far away, the tears occasionally welling into his pale blue eyes as the history which he himself had so largely moulded for three-quarters of a century went drifting through his mind.

Sir Winston would sometimes suddenly burst into 'song' – very often Gilbert and Sullivan pieces that he had not heard for many years – or poems that he had not recited since his schooldays at Harrow. But left alone for just a few minutes, he would nod off . . . and here I stick my neck out, as the saying goes . . . for I was sure at the time that as soon as he opened his eyes and saw me there, devotedly, a look would come into his eyes saying to me, 'Where is my family . . . ? where are my friends? Am I now so unwanted?' and I'd then do my best to ensure that he must realize that time marches on and friends and family had their own lives to lead.

On occasions, Sir Winston and I would arrive back at Hyde Park Gate, I would open the front door with the key I always had, only to see members of the family rapidly disappearing up the stairs so as not to become involved in sitting with Sir Winston in the drawing-room. But perhaps it was better thus, for so often Randolph would have had a drop too much or would have been antagonizing the world in general, and harsh words would be used, or Lady Churchill would have chattered on about the shopping she had accomplished during the day, and the people she had met and how so and so was now sleeping with so and so's wife, and her husband, who loved her so dearly, would listen intently without being really with her, not being able to express an opinion, just intent on regarding her with love in his eyes knowing that his days of adoration were numbered. Not that I would ever stay in close proximity when the two were together . . . but I had alert ears, and eyes.

These were the twilight years, and the manner in which they had imperceptibly taken hold of Sir Winston was brought home to me most vividly as Beryl, my wife, was wrapping the present we had chosen for his ninetieth birthday in November 1964. The present was a book of photographs on African wildlife – towards the end we always gave him picture-type books – and the paper we had selected depicted small pink kittens on a blue background. Beryl had specifically bought this particular paper because she felt that it would please him, but as she wrapped the parcel – and the Swiss are masters of the art of wrapping parcels – I realized that it was the sort of paper one would use to wrap a child's present. Thinking back to his eightieth birthday, when we had given him a silver stand with a methylated spirit heater for a brandy glass, I saw how greatly his tastes and interests, according to Beryl and me, had changed in the passing of a decade.

For Sir Winston's eighty-seventh birthday, in 1961, my wife and I wished to give Sir Winston something unusual – a special number-plate for the car he normally used at Chartwell. I wrote to the Minister of Transport and although they went to a great deal of trouble, red tape won the day. A letter from the Minister dated 26 October 1961 and signed by an Assistant Private Secretary, Mr C. Blake, said that the Minister had tried to see whether he could do anything to help, but the number WSC 1 was issued, and 1 WSC would not be available for at least twelve years. In any case the transfer of a mark between vehicles could not be permitted, for the issue of one would open the floodgates, and the Ministry would be in trouble with the police. The letter ended '. . . I am sorry we have drawn a blank but the Minister is sure you will appreciate that the vehicle registration system is not primarily intended to facilitate the issue of special marks by reasons of sentiment, however worthy the cause may be'.

Not that at the end Sir Winston had become child-like, far from it, whatever others may say – he was a fine actor. He could still be strong-willed and as belligerent as ever when the mood seized him. I recall, as an instance, the row at the time of Princess Margaret's wedding. Sir Winston, never one to much enjoy any function before lunch, even in his younger days, suddenly decided on the morning of the wedding that he would rather stay in bed. This news disconcerted Lady Churchill, and she went very quickly into his bedroom to inform him firmly that it would be most discourteous to the Queen not to attend Westminster Abbey. His deep respect for the

Royal Family finally overcame his objection to the prospect of a tiring wedding service and he duly got dressed. Discreet inquiries by the staff had led to the suggestion that he should wear grey morning dress, rather than the usual black, but when he got to the Abbey he noticed that everybody save himself appeared to be dressed in black. Surprisingly, in view of his eminence, he felt uncomfortably out of place in grey, and was furious to think that he had been advised to wear it. All the way back from the wedding he complained vigorously, 'It was ridiculous, utterly ridiculous,' while Lady Churchill tried vainly to pacify him. Back at Hyde Park Gate he continued to rage like a bear with bees in its fur, giving full vent to his displeasure. To all this I had just been an observer, but I finally saved the day for everyone when I stepped in and pointed out to him that our fellow-Freemason, none other than the Earl of Scarbrough, the Lord Chamberlain and therefore the most senior Court official concerned in the ceremony, was the one other person – and I produced photographs in the evening newspapers to prove it – who was also wearing grey. Sir Winston then felt that protocol had been strictly observed and, after all, it was the several hundred other guests who had been out of step.

Whether or not he had any opinion about Princess Margaret's marriage to Tony Armstrong-Jones I do not know, though he did say to me that he hoped that they would be happy, but I do know that he strenuously opposed the idea of her union with Group Captain Peter Townsend, some five years earlier. It was not that he had any real objection to Townsend, but simply that he feared a repetition of the troubles experienced by her Uncle Edward before her, and that she might be forced to live in exile were she to marry a divorced commoner.

Another, later, occasion when Sir Winston showed himself still very much master of the situation was when he attended the last major social function of his long life, the wedding of his grandson, Winston, the son of Randolph and the lovely Pamela, elder daughter of the 11th Baron Digby, KG, now Mrs Averell Harriman, to the beautiful Minnie, daughter of the late Sir Gerard d'Erlanger, one-time Chairman of BOAC. It was in the summer of 1964 and the reception at the Hyde Park Hotel in Knightsbridge was a memorable occasion. Sir Winston decided not to go there so the bride and bridegroom and close members of the family had a sort of pre-reception at Hyde Park Gate. The famous photographer, Karsh of

Ottawa, was invited to the house to take photographs, but he was so insistent on taking photos of Sir Winston that I was asked by Lady Churchill to see if I could get rid of him, in the nicest possible way. It was very difficult but I eventually persuaded him that it would be in his best interest, and he left. Then Sir Winston suggested that I might like to go along to the official reception at the Hotel and promised faithfully not to leave No 28 for the rest of the day. So I went along to the reception and had a fine time, spending most of the afternoon and early evening in the company of that lovely actress, Valerie Hobson, whose husband, Mr Profumo, was also there among the many guests and kept coming to ask his wife if she was enjoying herself. The two were at that stage under the awful cloud of the Christine Keeler affair and life must have been very unpleasant.

As a wedding present to young Winston and his bride I gave a painting I had done on one of my several trips to Marrakesh with his grandfather. In their note of thanks to my wife and me for the painting, young Winston wrote '. . . it is hanging next to Grandpapa's . . .' He could have said nothing nicer.

During his last years, Sir Winston became more and more reluctant to co-operate with the photographers and I must say that I could not blame him one bit. He was an extremely old man, and in a sense it was harmful to his public image to be seen thus. On numerous occasions I was successful in preventing newspaper cameramen from getting shots when my protégé did not wish to oblige. I have previously related how I once did a deal with *Paris Match* in Bermuda to prevent a particularly unfavourable picture being published. Even so, some pretty cruel pictures did appear from time to time. One especially do I remember, in his ninetieth year, taken on a visit to the south of France. It was a silhouette against the background of a glittering sea, showing him in a Stetson, hunched up in a wheelchair, looking so old and helpless as he was pushed along. It made me quite angry that age should do this to him and the picture should show it so vividly. Technically, it was an excellent photograph, and in consequence it appeared in newspapers in many parts of the world.

I was interested to note, incidentally, that the published plea of Lady Churchill that the Press should regard the burial of Sir Winston at Bladon as a very private ceremony was not completely observed, again by *Paris Match*. I must say, however, that the result seemed hardly to justify the time, trouble and expense incurred. My own responsibility to Sir Winston had ended when I escorted his coffin to Westminster Hall for the lying-in-state, and I was not at Bladon. Had I been there I might well have ended my service on a familiar note . . . in a duel of wits with my friends of *Paris Match*.

For the last six years of his life, Sir Winston was under the regular care of private nurses. Initially there were two, but eventually, to ensure round-the-clock attention, there were four. I suppose that, in a sense, he *was* just another patient, at least, that was how some of them seemed to regard him. I remember on one occasion he had a terrific tiff with one nurse, although, characteristically, he was extremely contrite afterwards. It happened before a dinner of the regiment into which he was first commissioned as a nineteen-year-old subaltern – the Fourth Hussars. The dinner was at Quaglino's restaurant, and though he was not particularly keen to go, Lady Churchill was anxious that he should since she herself was going to the theatre with one of her daughters, and if they were all out the staff could have a night off. When the time came for Sir Winston to get dressed, he was in bed reading *Woodstock* and he decided there and then that he would rather go on reading than get up and dress to go out for dinner. The nurse, however, very mindful of the instructions she had been given by Lady Churchill, determinedly pulled back the bedclothes and made to swing his legs round and out of bed. Not altogether surprisingly, the Old Man was furious and gave her a sharp kick in the stomach. The nurse remonstrated but he pushed her away, saying, 'You're only a hireling and I shall do as I please with you.'

Now this nurse was a rather tough Australian and did not like being pushed about. 'Not bloody likely, you won't,' she growled.

The upshot of it was that when he set out for Quaglino's later he was in a foul temper, but during the ten-minute trip to the restaurant there was clearly time for reflection, and as I helped him out of the car, he said, 'I think you'd better ring Hyde Park Gate and fix it up. Make it all right. Fix it for her to have something to eat. I know you can arrange it all.'

He seemed to have great faith in my powers as a peace-maker, but I duly rang the house, spoke to the nurse and managed to pour some oil on the very troubled waters. Next day, Sir Winston was clearly apprehensive about the whole business and was extremely polite to

the nurse as she went about her chores with very tight lips. He followed her progress round the room from behind the newspapers.
Eventually, as he was dressing for lunch, he said to her in concilia-
tory tones. 'Well . . . we've had a very nice morning, haven't we?'

'Yes,' she agreed, 'but we don't want another evening like last
night.'

'No . . . indeed not,' he agreed with emphasis . . . and then, rather
shamefacedly . . . 'I'm very sorry.'

That was very typical of the Churchill I knew, for he hated domestic dissension of any kind. There was the occasion in the south of
France when Lady Churchill managed to get her husband out of the
Hôtel de Paris without my being there to accompany him. I was only
a few hundred yards away, as a matter of fact, and I had spoken to
Sir Winston about my having lunch with my French colleagues who
were always ready to lend a hand – or a car – when required. He had
agreed and promised me not to move without letting either the
Inspector from the Monte Carlo police who was standing in for me,
or the concierge, know. They knew where I was and that it would
only take me a couple of minutes to get back to the hôtel.

Without telling anyone, Lady Churchill and the nurse on duty got
Sir Winston to the entrance of the lift in his wheelchair. Here they
were joined by the Monégasque Inspector who had no opportunity
to telephone me, and it was only when they arrived at the back door
where a taxi was waiting outside (Lady Churchill had also arranged
this without telling anyone) that the concierge was asked for the key
and then only did he realize that the Old Man was going out. But he
could not keep Lady Churchill waiting so he opened the door, then
used the nearest telephone to inform me. Two minutes later I was at
the back door with my French colleagues in their car. But the bird
had flown, accompanied most correctly by the Inspector who had of
course, more authority than I in Monte Carlo, officially. We dashed
in the most reasonable directions, one after the other, but could find
no trace of the fugitives. They returned about half an hour later and I
met them at the back door and took over my role as protection officer, thanking my Monégasque Inspector sincerely. Sir Winston said
nothing to me while I took him upstairs and handed him over to the
nurse. He went to bed and immediately sent for me.

He told me that he was sorry that he had gone out without me, and
that he realized that it was not my fault that I had not been with him. I
told him that I was most disappointed that he had not kept his promise

to keep me informed of any change of plan and he said he was very sorry. He then handed me a cheque for fifty pounds that he had been able to make out before he got into bed. I threw it back across the bed saying, 'Officers from Scotland Yard cannot be bought.'

Tears welled up into his eyes as he asked me to please accept the cheque and he was so despondent that I said, 'I will only take it to spare you the pain you appear to be feeling, if I may use the telephone by your bed to ring my wife and suggest she comes here for a few days on the strength of the fifty pounds.'

'Do, by all means, my dear.' He seemed very relieved. I spoke with my wife in Hendon and she agreed to come down to Monte Carlo as soon as possible.

The next morning, a Sunday, about eleven o'clock, Sir Winston and Lady Churchill came out on to the balcony to have their aperitifs as I stood patiently at the other end surveying the surrounding blocks of flats being built at that time.

Lady Churchill approached me, with her drink in her hand. 'Well, Sergeant Murray, if you cannot be there when Sir Winston requires you, why don't you just buzz off back to England?' she said acidly.

'Lady Churchill,' I replied, 'with all due respect, the Home Secretary of Her Majesty's Government in his wisdom, decided that I was the person most suited to protect Sir Winston, at home or abroad, and until the Home Secretary decides to replace me, I shall remain here, and with perhaps a little co-operation from those persons who may be occasionally closer to Sir Winston, I shall fulfil my duties to the satisfaction of everyone.' That was the last I heard about the matter.

Beryl quickly made arrangements for the three children to go to friends for a few days and then flew down to Nice, arriving there more than five hours late because of fog at Heathrow. The late Francis Rico, a reporter on *Nice Matin*, volunteered to collect Beryl at Nice and brought her post-haste to the Hôtel de Paris. I gave her just about one hour to have a cup of tea (very essential where Beryl is concerned), to bathe, and dress, before whisking her across to the brand new Scotch Club, just opposite the hotel. There we officially opened the Club and had a wonderful evening. It was Tuesday, 3 February 1960, and my wife and I enjoyed the few days she was there very much indeed and Sir Winston insisted on having a chat with her. As usual when they met, he apologized for keeping me away from home such a lot.

One particular evening during those few wonderful days, I took Beryl to the Casino and we spent most of the night sitting at the bar reminiscing with Dame Margot Fonteyn and her husband, though the latter did leave us occasionally to play the tables. Early in the morning when we all decided to call it a day and go to bed, Dame Margot, or Madame Arias as she was known outside professional circles, declared she had had a most enjoyable time. Her husband was then Panamanian Consul to Britain. Later he was to be disabled by a terrorist shooting incident.

Sir Winston was always solicitous of the well-being of those with whom he was connected, and I knew that he was prepared to listen if I had a grumble. I believe that only on two occasions did I take such a step – once was the time I have just talked about when he left the hotel with Lady Churchill without my being with him and the other time was when we were on board *Christina* in the Caribbean, moving from island to island. I discovered that everyone seemed to be in the picture as far as our movements were concerned – except me, and I thought that, as I had to liaise with local police in all those places where the Old Man decided to go ashore, I should be kept *au courant*. I told Sir Winston that I was not very happy about the situation and he took it up with his Private Secretary at the time, Mr Montague Browne, and told him that I must be kept better informed. That night, in the ship's cinema, he beckoned me over his shoulder and said, 'Have you had it out with him yet?' in a deep conspiratorial whisper. When I told him that things had been settled he seemed most relieved, and as he went into his stateroom later on, he shook me warmly by the hand, saying, 'Good-night, my dear Murray, good-night'.

At that moment I was reminded in a strange sort of way of a picture that used to hang in my parents' bedroom in County Durham when I was a lad. It portrayed a woman on her knees in front of a crucifix, and underneath were the words, 'In Thee do I put my trust'.

Mind you, life was not all sweetness and light, for Sir Winston could be very trying. For one thing he was extremely stubborn, and if he could not have his own way he would become thoroughly obstreperous. At Chartwell, in the closing years, he liked to be pushed around the grounds in a sort of *chaise-longue* with wheels and handles at one end. It was made of cane and quite light. One of his favourite places was by the side of the pond wherein swam the golden orfe. The grounds are very steep in places and it wasn't always possible to manhandle the chair with its heavy passenger up the steeper inclines. But if he found himself being taken in some different direction to that ordained by himself, he would get furious and would sometimes insert his walking-stick into the wheel-spokes to stop it.

Occasionally he would admit to his stubbornness, as the time in the south of France when I tried to explain to him the difference between the old franc and the new franc, which had just then been introduced. For some reason he would not accept that the new franc was worth 100 times more than the old one. We were on our way to the Casino at the time and eventually, just before the car stopped I said in exasperation, 'You are sometimes a little obstinate.'

'Yes,' he replied, preparing to leave the car. Then, once on the pavement, 'I'm even bloody obstinate.'

The frequent trips we made to the south of France in his last years undoubtedly did him good. His appetite on such occasions was extremely healthy, and I recall the surprise of the hotel staff at the amount of food he used to get through even when he was a very old man indeed. His breakfast usually consisted of orange juice, eggs in various forms, buttered toast, jam, stewed fruit and plenty of very hot coffee. Other meals were of similar proportions with plenty of red meat and vegetables, and there was always a sweet.

I remember an occasion so well once at the Hôtel de Paris. It was the 'glorious twelfth' – the opening of the grouse season in Scotland. Now most people know just how important it is to eat grouse on the opening day – but not too many people realize that one cannot export fresh meat. As far as Sir Winston was concerned on this particular *séjour* in Monaco, arrangements were made for the Savoy in London to have a certain number of birds flown down by special plane from Scotland and picked up at London Airort. Then by car to the Savoy where they were plucked and cooked for just two minutes when they became 'cooked' meat and could be legally exported. All actions were timed to coincide with the departure of a flight to Nice where the birds were collected and brought to the Hôtel de Paris in order to be on the evening's menu. Sir Winston loved the procedure. Young Winston, his grandson, was staying with him at the time and the guests at dinner that evening also included Sarah, his daughter, Mr Onassis, and Mr

Montague Browne. It was an odd number and as they had half a grouse each from the three birds at their disposal there remained half a bird. Monsieur Albert knew that I was dining in the Grill Room, just a few yards from Mr Onassis' private room, and he hurried to me and suggested that I might like to have the remaining half grouse. I told him to offer it to Monsieur Broc, the general manager, but Monsieur Albert, who was the restaurant manager and a famous name in the hotel trade, told me that Monsieur Broc himself had told Albert to offer it to me. I declined and added that it might be a good idea to put it into the fridge.

The next day when Sir Winston sat down to lunch, Albert gave him the menu, but was very surprised when the Old Man said, 'I believe that there still remains half a grouse from yesterday – I would very much like it cold.' I told Albert that I had a nose for that sort of thing.

It was about this time that my wife and I had a wonderful night out in London. During my frequent stays in the south of France, I had made the acquaintance of a renowned sculptor. He was a Polish count and as his name was almost impossible to pronounce, I regret that it has faded from my memory. He had a lovely property near Eze, just along the Grande Corniche from Monaco, and had sculpted many famous people including Prince Rainier. He had promised to look me up when next he came to England and in May 1962, he rang me in Hendon to invite Beryl and me to dinner at the Pigalle, now the Piazza, in Piccadilly. He was accompanied by a delightful young French girl and after a wonderful dinner, we went underground, through the kitchens and up some stairs to a rather exotic night-club, lit by candles. We sat at a table with about a dozen men and women. There were many bottles of wine opened already and the party was in full swing and the principal guest had just rung up to say that he was on his way. It turned out to be none other than the famous controversial Russian poet and writer, Yevgeni Aleksandrovitch Yevtushenko who was in London to give a recital of some of his poems at the Royal Court Theatre. He and the Polish Count were apparently old friends, and vodka soon replaced the wines on the table as stories were told, poems recited and Russian songs sung.

Then as soon as Yevtushenko learned that I was with Sir Winston Churchill, he called for paper and wrote a longish letter in Russian for me to present to the great man. He was a great admirer of

Churchill, and though deprecating his militancy on occasions, he realized that his was a fight for the freedom of peoples throughout the world. His secretary-cum-interpreter at the time was a delightful English girl, Jan Butler, and my wife and I were aware of their feelings for each other though the poet was married at that time. I promised to get the message to my boss as soon as possible and next day I had it translated at Scotland Yard and then handed it to Mr Montague Browne for treatment as a message from a VIP. The message contained nothing untoward and was quite laudatory with regard to Churchill and stressed the importance of co-operation of the leaders of the world to ensure peace and freedom from tyranny.

Yevtushenko had been born in the Irkutsk region of Lake Baykal, not far from the Mongolian frontier, on 18 July 1933, and his work reflected the thoughts and feelings of the younger generation. His poems, particularly, usually denounced the cold and calculatingly ascetic outlook of Russian bureaucracy and were charged with human thoughts and emotions. I thought that evening that he resembled somewhat the angry young men of our own country. The year after his visit to England he produced two epic poems, the second of which was circulated only as typescript, both criticizing Stalinism, bureaucracy and the failure of the older generation even to try to understand the younger. Nikita Krushchev, in his turn, criticized the young man severely for his work.

That evening was a most memorable one for Beryl and myself and the young English translator was kept very busy interpreting our conversation with the poet. Yevtushenko divorced his first wife in Moscow in 1961 and married his young interpreter in Moscow's Central Palace of Weddings in April the following year. She had studied Russian literature at the State University, Moscow, and it was during her employment with the State Pioneer publishing house that she met Yevtushenko and began to help him in his work. Since The Krushchev days, the poet has drawn much closer to the Soviet establishment and the only trouble he has had with the authorities during the past few years was when he was censured for his defence of the dissident author Alexander Solzhenitsyn.

The next day after that wonderfully exciting evening, our Polish friend returned to the south of France and on my next visit to Monaco, I heard that he had died suddenly.

As I have mentioned before, Sir Winston was always extremely courteous, but this trait led to a rather amusing mix-up on one French trip. During the longish spell on the Riviera, on that occasion when I had 'missed the boat' and my wife had joined me for a few days on the strength of the fifty-pound cheque, she had returned to England before we did, and on our return flight, which was heavily booked, Sir Winston noticed that I was seated next to a lady to whom I chatted, naturally enough, during the journey. On arrival at London Airport, Sir Winston and his small group, as usual, were the first to leave while other passengers were requested to remain seated. As he passed down the gangway, Sir Winston paused and raised his hat to my utterly mystified travelling companion, and said, 'Did you have a nice holiday? I do hope you enjoyed yourself.'

She gulped hard and muttered something, and Sir Winston passed on holding my arm, happily convinced that he had exchanged pleasantries with Mrs Murray.

The next time we went to the south of France we left Hyde Park Gate at 09.15 and got to London Airport before the appointed time mainly because we had the usual jeep police escort as soon as we arrived at the turn-off from the A4 to the Airport and there was not much traffic. We drove towards the departure building for Europe and came to a stop at the entrance to the VIP lounge. Airport police and staff materialized out of nowhere, but Sir Winston decided that he was not getting out of the car. There were audible groans of disappointment which altered nothing and after about fifteen minutes we drove on to the apron where the Elizabethan class RMA 'William Shakespeare' was waiting. I introduced the Airport Manager and my friend, Inspector Buswell, in charge of the Special Branch group at the airport, to Sir Winston, while the fuelling was completed and the Press cameras clicked furiously. Then we went on board. There were no other passengers as yet and Sir Winston was made comfortable in a foursome seat while Mr Howells, the male nurse, and I took the six-seater opposite determined to hold it for ourselves and the paraphernalia and boxes that always went with the Old Man.

I went to thank the Manager and Inspector Buswell for their help and bid a more or less gracious farewell to Miss Gill Mathurin, one of the secretaries. Returning inside I found that Mr Montague Browne had now joined Sir Winston. He asked Mr Howells for the newspapers. Sir Winston stretched his neck and asked me if I had his box. This was a black dispatch box inherited from his days at No 10 and contained important official documents for the most part. He alone had the key. I assured him that 'I was sitting on it' (figuratively of course). Even before take off he asked for the cards to be laid out for bézique which he would play with Mr Montague Browne. His next order was for whiskies all round. As the plane climbed his glass kept slipping towards his chest and Mr Montague Browne said, 'Shall I move it further away from you?' and made to move it.

'No!' shouted Sir Winston and raised his hand as if to smack the offender, then relaxed, blushing, with his mouth puckering, his eyes gleaming while his spectacles slipped slowly down his nose. He beamed as only he and Puck could do. Then he lit a cigar and got down to the task of playing bézique, not missing a trick . . . as did his companion.

The Captain came to report on two occasions as we made our way over the English Channel and over France. Sir Winston also required Mr Howell's assistance on two occasions to make his way to the toilet, bowing to passengers on his way.

Then everybody had lunch – except Sir Winston and Mr Montague Browne, for they were in the middle of the third game. The stewardess told me, 'It's chicken.' The game ended. I called across to Sir Winston that we were having chicken for lunch. However when I came to taste it, I found that the chicken was in fact, duck. I told the stewardess that her chicken had been saying 'Quack, quack' all its life.

A plate was eventually set in front of Sir Winston and he examined it carefully. Mr Montague Browne said, 'Duck! duck! duck!' – for Sir Winston did not always respond the first time. Sir Winston looked blank . . . and then suddenly 'ducked' his head, removing his hat, but replacing it quickly when I told him it was 'quack-quack' and Mr Montague Browne repeated that it was 'quack-quack'.

'Ah!' said Sir Winston taking up his glass of Moët et Chandon, 'we are having duck for lunch.'

Arrived in Monte Carlo, we rejoined the yacht *Christina* and left for what proved to be a last meeting with another famous war-time leader, an old friend of Sir Winston's despite his political convictions, Marshal Tito. We took our time sailing down the coast of Italy, offshore and without stopping, just enjoying the fine weather and the peace, and then up the Adriatic to Venice, where Dr Arias and Dame Margot Fonteyn left us. After a gondola and motor-boat tour of the canals by Sir Winston and Lady Churchill, accompanied by a host of members of the Press who were rather a nuisance, we sailed to Split on the Adriatic coast, where the Yugoslav leader had his summer residence.

We arrived there early in the evening and took one of the yacht's launches to a small jetty where the President, his wife, and a few senior officials were waiting. The two leaders were glad to meet again and embraced warmly – though embraces on both cheeks were not among Sir Winston's favourite pastimes unless they were feminine or family – and after a few moments we walked down the garden path, Tito holding one arm of his friend, and I supporting the other, while Yugoslav seamen flanked us on either side. In the lounge of the superb villa, we were attended by Sir Winston's party including Mr and Mrs Montague Browne and the British Ambassador, but also by the Yugoslav Chief of Staff and the Security Chief for whom I had obtained the setters in London. Glasses were filled and as they were raised, Sir Winston said to the Marshal, 'I look at you and I remember the dark days of war. It is nice to meet again after all the troubles and storms.'

Glasses clinked all round . . . indeed more than once, and Sir Winston continued, 'which days do you think were the darkest?'

'They were all dark days, sir,' said Tito, 'all very dark I think . . . but those of 1942, when we were surrounded by the enemy, were probably the darkest of all.'

'I am now very happy that things are good with you,' said Sir Winston, with tears in his eyes. In a throaty voice, the Marshal said, 'Things are still not very clear, but I am not a pessimist in these things.'

We returned to the ship and the next day the Yugoslavs came aboard for lunch.

Those meetings were in 1960, when Sir Winston was eighty-six, and Tito, born Josip Broz, was sixty-eight, and as they said goodbye, I felt that they knew they would never meet again on this earth.

Early in March 1961, we were due to cross the Atlantic to tour the West Indies and the idea was for us to go aboard at Gibraltar. However, then as now, make no mistake about it, the weathermen do their best but someone, somewhere, had more control over the wind and the rain than the poor weathermen. We came in to land at Gibraltar where the landing-strip is just that, a strip of land jutting out into the Mediterranean. The winds were blowing at gale force and the pilot was finding it very difficult to control the plane as he swept in towards the Rock. Lady Churchill came to sit beside me, next to the window so that she could keep her eyes towards the inside, while she clung to my arm, as her husband opposite calmly smoked a cigar that should have been extinguished a long time ago, and peered out of the window. We left it to a tactful stewardess to relieve him of the cigar eventually, knowing how he was very often susceptible to the charms of a lovely young lady.

Three times the pilot tried to land – for he was aware of the fact that *Christina* and its owner were waiting for us there – but eventually he had to give up and radioed the Rock to inform them that he would try Tangier where the weather was considerably better. Even there the wind was high and whirling dust made landing hazardous, but there was much more room to manoeuvre in Tangier than in Gibraltar and the pilot made it seem very easy. We spent the night in one of the excellent hotels in the free city which made a pleasant change, while *Christina* and its passengers made a night crossing of the Mediterranean. Except for the fact that the Atlantic was not in a very pleasant mood, and the stabilizers installed on the yacht did not work efficiently, and ninety per cent of the passengers and crew kept to their bunks or beds, the trip was uneventful and I spent most of my time eating and drinking and being blown about as I surveyed the tempestuous scene from the bows. Once we were in the Caribbean the weather changed and Trinidad welcomed us on 21 March 1961, with brilliant sunshine and blue skies.

Jane, daughter of Mr and Mrs Montague Browne, and I had our luncheon together in the officers' mess beneath my portrait of Christina who, with her father and young Alexander, we were to collect after Guadeloupe, our next port of call. Jane liked to hear my stories of life with the Murrays, a family life quite different to her own. We decided that it would be nice to have a birthday party in the afternoon as it was my younger daughter Yvonne's birthday. It was a great success with Jane and I acting as hosts and receiving the guests. Sir Winston, Lord and Lady Moran, Mr and Mrs Montague Browne, Madame Patrouniklas (Christina's *gouvernante*), Professor Garoufalidis, two nurses and the Captain turned up for tea and cakes on the poop-deck. The French chef, Monsieur Miral, made a fine birthday cake which everybody, except Yvonne, tasted.

At Trinidad, Sir Winston did not go ashore but I was allowed off to have dinner with the Chief of the Special Branch of Trinidad Police.

It was very enjoyable but I always worried when I did not have Sir Winston in my sight and I got back to the yacht as soon as I decently could without hurting any feelings.

We stayed off Guadeloupe for four days while an engineer flew down from New York to mend the gyroscope that had gone wrong in mid-Atlantic. Sir Winston, Mr Montague Browne and I went to the Governor-General's Residence for the garden party where twelve hundred guests were expected. Mr and Mrs Macmillan were also there. It poured with rain and the Governor-General, Lord Hailes, was chasing everywhere and was soaking wet. He declined to obey Lady Hailes' order to change his suit and shoes, so she came and asked me, on the strength of our long acquaintance, to see what I could do about it. He was like a lamb and immediately I suggested that it would be silly to catch the flu and pass it on to his guests, he dashed upstairs to change. Lady Hailes told me that I was wonderful, but it really had not been very difficult. The next day we went to anchor off Regina Island where Sir Anthony and Lady Eden were wintering and they came aboard for a meal.

Then came a very short visit to Jamaica, and after that Puerto Rico where Sir Winston and company made a tour of the capital and hinterland.

The *Christina* did not stay very long at Palm Beach, the next stop, but it was very exciting cruising up along that distant sandy shore to get there. Sir Winston did not go ashore, and in fact stayed in bed for three or four days with a slight cold. This permitted me to go ashore with Norman McGowan, the valet. We went to the Yacht Club where we had dinner with a government accountant from Fort Lauderdale and his friends. So many people wished to entertain us that we forgot the time and when the Club closed down for the night, the last boat out to the yacht had gone and we had to wait on the steps of the Club, through a very cold, wet night, absolutely freezing, till the first boat the next morning – actually it was not only the first boat, but the last one, and as soon as we were back on board, Mr Onassis gave the order to weigh anchor, and off we went up that long sandy peninsula towards our final destination, New York.

Once anchored in the East River, there was no holding Sir Winston – he wanted to go home, and the *Queen Mary* was almost due to leave, but there were gale force winds to cope with first.

Now here I must explain how Sir Winston used to get off the yacht.

The gangway to the main deck would be raised by means of wire ropes attached to its extremity and a manual winch on the sun-deck above. This was done by either the second or third officer, indicating the importance of the operation. When the gangway was horizontal, I would precede Sir Winston along the length of it and place a chair at the end, so that he could sit in it with his face towards the direction whence he had come. The huge bosun, the Greek Achilles, would stand just in front of him while I, with my back towards the front of the yacht, would hold the wire rope, the stanchions, and the chair by hands, arms and legs, for should the chair move just a couple of inches on the platform, the chair and its passenger could have fallen in the water.

Then the whole platform and gangway would be slowly winched down to the level of the motor-boat's gunwale. The bosun would climb through the supporting wires to enter the boat and assist me in the final disembarkation of the Old Gentleman, down two or three movable steps, and into a deck-chair. This was the procedure whether we were in Greece, Spain, the West Indies or anywhere else when the *Christina* was at anchor and Sir Winston decided to go ashore. The bosun and I had completed the operation hundreds of times without incident, though occasionally the seas had made it a very tricky job. On that occasion on the East River, in New York, where it was imperative we descend in order to catch the *Queen Mary*, it seemed an impossible task. The ship's launch was winched off and brought alongside, but the rise and fall of the huge waves threatened to smash the launch against the side of the vessel, despite the Herculean efforts of the crew and the Master who started the engines and tried to manoeuvre the yacht to give us some lee. We decided, despite Sir Winston's calls that we could manage it by trying just once again, to abandon it and proceed to the normal dockside, miles away, which would take hours. Then I espied a big police launch and hailed it to come alongside. After numerous attempts it finally managed to stay with us long enough for me and the bosun to swing the Old Man bodily into the arms of the waiting policemen . . . and off we went. Looking back I am fully convinced that I should never have let *us* do it.

By 6 June 1961, we were again in Monte Carlo after a very fast drive from Nice Airport with three police motor-cyclists in front and the French 'Voyages Officiels' Facel-Vega, and another motor-cyclist behind. The weather was dull and overcast and Sir Winston not very happy with it. He remarked as he got out of the car, at the Hôtel de Paris, that *Christina* should have left New York on Saturday and should be in Bermuda today. I think that he missed the beautiful sunshine of the West Indies – though we did also have a lot of downpours there.

For my own entertainment while sitting in front of Sir Winston's door on this occasion, instead of a jigsaw where every Tom, Dick and Harry could steal a piece just to annoy me, Beryl had hidden a model aeroplane in my luggage, complete with sharp knife and glue that I would require. I love putting aeroplanes or ships together so it really was fun.

On 9 June we went for a drive up to 'La Tête du Chien' above Cap d'Ail and Sir Winston got quite cross with a French TV photographer who came too near, and menaced him with his walking-stick.

The next day I had my dinner in the Grill Room because Sir Winston had stated his intention of going to the Casino later on. At 10 pm he sent one of the waiters to fetch me and I joined him and Mr Montague Browne in the salon. They were drinking the special brandy.

'My dear, good evening . . . pull up a chair.' I did and then he said, 'I shall not be going out . . . oh! I beg your pardon, I'm sure you'd prefer some of this brandy to anything else.' He took a water glass and said, 'It's quite clean and unused – not many people drink water round here.' Mr Montague Browne had already asked the waiter to bring a brandy glass, but Sir Winston could not wait and poured a real legionnaire's portion into the water glass. I then transferred it to the brandy glass which had just arrived. He stretched his glass towards mine. 'Good health and happiness,' said that Old Gentleman, to a very happy man.

We talked of many things, Mr Montague Browne joining in on occasions, then Sir Winston refilled my glass and even wanted me to have another refill about half an hour later. I declined. He told me that we would be returning to London by French 'Caravelle' in a few days' time. He then asked me to escort him to his bedroom where the nurse was waiting.

Shortly afterwards there was another memorable cruise on the yacht *Christina*, with only a brief stop on the Ligurian coast to have lunch with the future King Juan Carlos I and his fiancée at the beautiful home of an Italian friend of Mr Onassis. Then down through the Tyrrhenian Sea and across to Tripoli where we had a quick trip ashore before continuing along the Libyan coast stopping at the renowned Bengazi (Banghazi), the chief seaport of the Province of Cyrenaica and joint capital with Tripoli of Libya. The city still bore signs of the damage caused during World War II when it changed hands no less than five times, being finally taken by Montgomery and the British Eighth Army in November 1942. Sir Winston landed to visit the British cemetery there. His son Randolph was one of the guests on the cruise, but was behaving atrociously towards the other people on board, particularly the ladies, and Mr Onassis and Sir Winston got their heads together to see what they could do about it – mere words were having no effect.

We were by then en route for Tubruq (Tobruk, ancient Antipyrgos). It was common knowledge that the King and Queen of Greece were to visit England in a few days' time so it was suggested to Randolph that Mr Onassis should phone the King to fix a meeting in advance of the state visit. Randolph could then be landed at Crete and flown to the Royal Palace on Corfu, from Iraklion. Mr Onassis quickly made the necessary arrangements for Randolph, who was with the London *Evening Standard* at that time, and the yacht made a detour to drop him off. The *Christina* seemed to echo to the sighs of relief when he'd gone. When Randolph was busy on an item for a newspaper, for instance, he was a most charming character with a vast knowledge of people and life in most countries of the world . . . but if he was at a loose end, which was not very often, he was just impossible, and 'hit the bottle rather hard'.

We then continued to Tobruk which, like Bengazi, had also changed hands five times during the war, falling to the Eighth Army on 13 November 1942. The city has a wonderful harbour, able to accept vessels of any size or draft, but at that time, and it is probably still so today, there was no fresh water; it had to be brought by sea from Bengazi, or by road from Bardia, more than two hundred miles away. The party landed at Tobruk to visit King Idris I (Mohammed Idris el-Mahdi es-Senussi), the last King of the United Kingdom of Libya, at his desert residence which was just a collection of mud forts. It was a very pleasant interlude but soon we were back on board the yacht heading for . . . nobody ever knew where we were heading for, really . . . but on this occasion we arrived at Beyrouth (Beirut), then a very lovely city. Some months before I had made the acquaintance of the First Secretary at the Lebanese Embassy in London and had been to a cocktail party at the Embassy and Jean

Riachi had made me most welcome. We met on several occasions afterwards and he had told me often that his brother would always welcome me should I ever go to Beyrouth. So here we were and I immediately asked the local police to get me the telephone number of Jean's brother.

Christina had to take on fuel, and as we were not alongside the quay but anchored offshore, the fuel had to be brought to the yacht in barrels. These were attached to each other in a long chain and towed alongside to be hoisted aboard by derrick. I remember that the last barrel swung so much that the rope broke and it took the Lebanese oil-men about an hour to recapture it. But all this, and permission from Sir Winston, of course, allowed me to contact Jean's brother, and after a long sightseeing tour by Sir Winston and the guests, I was picked up by car on the quayside and driven several miles outside the city, through the hills where the famous cedars of Lebanon spread their branches and perfumed the sweet, dry air, to a fine residence where Jean's mother and beautiful sister gave me a wonderful lunch. The reader will notice that I am using a number of superlatives with regard to my visit to Beirut and I must say that they were justly used. The memory of those most happy hours spent in the company of such beautiful people remains a really treasured corner of my life and when I see and hear of all the awful things that are happening in that once superb city and country, I shudder, and feel a great sense of shame that the human race can be guilty of such abomination.

As we returned towards Monte Carlo, we passed Stromboli, the 'Lighthouse of the Mediterranean' and the top of it burned red in the dark night. Mr Onassis, however, thought that it was not bright enough and had fireworks set off to get Sir Winston out of the rather dismal mood he had been in for the past few days.

Off Glyfada, where we were to disembark for the trip to the airport, it was decided to go by boat to a nearby cove where a friend of Professor Garoufalidis was building a new house on the cliff over-looking the cove which was very rocky, with very deep water. There was a concrete jetty with quite a large space beside it and when we arrived there for a barbecue, this space was prepared with numerous tables and chairs and parasols. Wide steps led from the area up the side of the cliff to the new residence above. They were quite steep. Half-way up, on the right, a goat path, to which there was no normal access, led across the side of the cliff to a sort of rocky natural plat-form on which were cooking, supervised by a couple of chefs in white uniforms and white hats, a huge round of beef on a vertical spit 'à la Turque' with a fine wood grill, a whole lamb and a whole sucking-pig and numerous chickens which were being turned over a fine wood fire.

From his seat on the landing-stage, Sir Winston could see the other guests walk up the steps, climb over the wall and go carefully along the goat-path, negotiating a huge boulder in the middle of the path, and help themselves to slices of meat, from the grills. Sharp knives were there for the purpose. I could see Sir Winston watching as people came back licking their chops. Calling to me he said he would like to go up the steps and sit on a chair. He would have a better view of everything, he said. Once at the spot where the others, now all apparently satisfied, had climbed over the wall, he told me that he would like to visit the barbecue.

I told him that that was quite impossible – there was no way that I would help him along that narrow path – I was even scared of it myself. He was only a step from the wall, on his chair. As I stared in the opposite direction, I suddenly heard a movement and turned to find the Old Gentleman half-way over the wall. I grabbed him and pulled him back, sitting him once again on the chair.

'I shall go there,' he told me rather acidly, 'I shall see what is hap-pening along there at the fire.'

'Over my dead body,' I said. 'There is a fall of over sixty feet down to those cruel rocks below. I am not prepared to risk our lives for such a futile cause. At the barbecue, beef, pork, lamb and chickens are cooking and within a few minutes we shall all be sampling them.' He was not happy and I knew that he would do his best to get over that wall . . . and would certainly fall into the sea. I was not going to risk that and so, placing myself behind the chair, I lifted it and him, and carried them down to the lower platform to sit him in front of his drink.

The meal came immediately afterwards, together with secreta-ries, nurses, guests and Mr Onassis . . . but no word came from Sir Winston. He was mute for the next two or three hours. The meal passed in awful silence and whispers, then we got into the launch to return to the yacht which then steamed back to Glyfada. I got him off the yacht into the launch again, still in silence, and we landed at a jetty where a car was waiting. Then into the car, with Mrs Montague

Browne sitting beside him and off to the airport. (Mr Montague Browne remained on board, for later that day he was apparently going on leave somewhere in Switzerland.)

At the airport, the car slowed down for the reception committee, which included a Greek Admiral and the British Consul-General from Athens. 'I shall go direct to the plane,' came the firm sound of Sir Winston from the back.

'Pull in to the reception area,' I told the driver, and I got out to open the back door.

'Sir Winston, you must say good-bye to the Admiral and the British Consul-General . . .' and I stepped aside to let the two of them incline themselves to salute Sir Winston, who gave them each a quick shake of the hand, and a short smile. He was still not happy. I closed the door and shook the hands of the two gentlemen, got into my seat, and we drove to the Olympic airplane waiting for us. The other passengers for the flight to London were already there and they gave quite a cheer as he took his seat. Mrs Montague Browne sat beside him as we took off. After a few moments, I looked in his direction. He was watching me . . . I returned to my book.

Shortly afterwards, Mrs Montague Browne touched my arm. 'Sir Winston would like you to sit here,' she said.

'I am not sure that I wish to sit there,' I replied and considered the matter for a few minutes, then I got up and we exchanged seats. I turned my head to look at him. He returned my stare for a while then I said, 'It was not very nice, Sir Winston, was it?'

'Bloody awful,' he said grimly. Then, with a lovely smile, 'I am very sorry . . . you probably saved my life and I am most grateful. Remind me to give you a cheque when we get back.'

'No reward is necessary,' I said, 'I was doing my duty.' That was the end of his silence and after I had resumed my seat and Mrs Montague Browne hers, life returned to normal.

Back in England, for some weeks afterwards, I thought about his mention of a cheque, but it was two months later when he was sitting with Mr Montague Browne at a cane table on the lawn at Chartwell that the whole thing was resuscitated. I was sitting on the garden wall, some thirty yards away, when I thought I heard my name mentioned, and Mr Montague Browne saying something about it 'being a lot of money'. It was about five o'clock and almost time for me to go home to Hendon. Suddenly there was a shout – 'Murray!' from Sir Winston and I went to the table. As I got there,

Mr Montague Browne got up saying to Sir Winston, 'I shall say goodnight then. Good-bye, Sir Winston.'

'I wonder if you would ask Mr Montague Browne to stay for a few minutes, Sir Winston?' for I had seen the cheque-book on the table and I suspected what was going to happen.

'I am going home, Sergeant Murray,' said the Secretary.

'Do sit down for a few minutes,' said the Boss, and he sat down.

Sir Winston stretched his arm across the table, his hand holding a cheque for five hundred pounds. 'My dear Murray, that is the cheque I promised you in Greece, when you prevented me from doing something very foolish indeed – just to say thank you.'

'This is very kind of you, Sir Winston,' I said, 'but as I was just doing my duty when everybody else had left the ship, with your permission I shall return this cheque to the secretaries, so that they can cancel it. Nevertheless I am most grateful for your consideration. I think Mr Montague Browne can now go home.'

Mr Montague Browne left, but by the time I had entered the house and was going along the corridor towards the office, I saw him, in the salon, with Lady Churchill. Knowing full well that I was the subject of the conversation, I entered the drawing-room and as I approached Lady Churchill I heard her say, 'Well, this is most embarrassing, Sergeant Murray.'

'I can understand it being a bit embarrassing for me, Lady Churchill, for a Detective-Sergeant in the police force does not get a lot of money, but with all due respect, I cannot see how any other persons should be embarrassed. Perhaps, Lady Churchill, you would be kind enough to see that the correct action is taken with this cheque,' and tearing it half-way across, I handed the cheque to her, saying 'Good-night, Lady Churchill . . . good-night, Mr Montague Browne.' I turned and went to my car, then drove off.

The cheque was never mentioned again.

Many friends bidding Sir Winston farewell in those days must have wondered whether they would ever meet again, but resolutely he survived. Even when he broke bones, as he did in his thigh, he still came through without any of the dangerous complications which so frequently cause death in the aged. I must say though, that when he broke his thigh in July 1962, I feared the worst. This accident happened at Monte Carlo, and it was the result of his having a lower bed than the one he used at home. In the night he wanted to go to the lavatory, so not wishing to disturb the night nurse who was in an adjacent room, he got out of bed on his own. He staggered and reached back for the bed, but the bed being much lower than usual, was not there, shall we say, and he fell back on to it somehow breaking his thigh in the process. He lay there, helpless and in great pain, for about half an hour before anyone heard him.

He certainly did not turn out to be a model patient on that occasion and after a couple of days of torture for everyone, though he was in the care of a very competent staff and his usual doctor David Roberts, he was flown back from Monte Carlo, his thigh in plaster, in a plane of the Royal Air Force, and driven in an ambulance to the Middlesex Hospital.

The specialists were Mr Yeoman and Mr Newman and at 5.30 pm he was being lifted out of bed to be X-Rayed. 'I am a Member of Parliament,' he called out to the doctors. 'I refuse to allow any more of it.'

They came and asked me to help as they could do nothing with him. I went in and found Sir Winston in bed, glowering.

'Murray, my dear Murray,' he said, 'I'm a free man. Why are they pushing me about like this. I have never seen anything like it. Look, Murray, I'll leave here before dinner tonight. All we've got to do is get out of here and across the Park. I never saw anything like it.'

'They do know what they are doing, Sir Winston,' I told him. 'They are like everybody else in the streets outside. They want to get you on your feet again. One thing's quite certain – if they say you have to stay, you can't get up and walk out.'

Later as I helped Mr Newman to lift him back into bed, I told him, 'Put your arms around our necks and pull yourself up as we lift you.'

He looked at me as we lifted him. 'I never imagined *you* would become associated with this atrocious manhandling, Murray,' he said, with tears in his voice.

The very next morning, Mr Newman and Mr Seddon, consultant orthopaedist, came to say a brief goodbye to Sir Winston. 'You are so well now,' said Mr Seddon, 'I'm sorry that you no longer require us.'

A broken thigh must be painful at any age, but at eighty-seven one is really less well equipped to bear that sort of pain. He 'sacked' the doctors after the first few days in the hospital, but they took it in their stride, and pretty soon Sir Winston began to recover some of his old verve. When he saw that one of the nursing sisters kept going to the door to look down the corridor, he eventually asked her what she was looking for. 'I want Sergeant Murray, Sir Winston,' she said.

'Well, you cannot have him, you ought to know,' he said, 'he's married and has three children.'

At 3.30 pm on Saturday, 14 July 1962, Miss Powell, one of the nurses, came to me and said, 'Sir Winston wants "the man who looks after me".'

I went in. We were alone together.

'Do you stay here all day?' he asked.

'Nearly all day, every day,' I replied.

'How good of you and I'm most grateful. I called you in, did I not, to ask you to do something for me . . . and now I cannot remember what it was. I am so stupid now. I have to try very hard.'

'Never mind, Sir Winston, I'll come back when you have remembered, and I shall take some time off when you're out of hospital.'

He laughed, down, down low in his chest . . .

'I'll never come out of hospital.'

'Don't be silly,' I said, 'you're the only one who thinks that. Everyone else thinks that you'll be out very soon.'

'Out of bed, perhaps . . . but not out of the hospital.'

'We shall soon have you out of here and down at Chartwell, feeding the swans,' I told him. But he laughed again, in disbelief.

'In any case,' I continued, 'I shall be just outside if you want me.'

'Look in to see me when you want to go home, my dear, dear, Murray.'

'I shall do that, Sir Winston. Au revoir.'

'Au revoir, my dear, au revoir,' and he returned to his book.

Later Lady Churchill brought him some large cigars, but he called for me. 'I should like one of those small cigars,' he said, 'That's what I wanted to ask you before.' I gave him one of the cigars from the case I always carried and hoped that Lady Churchill was not put out by his preferring my cigar to hers.

We realized that he was on the mend when he began to have champagne sent to the hospital from Hyde Park Gate. Each day a small bottle would arrive for him and was kept in the hospital fridge. Also, from the moment he had entered the hospital, masses and masses of flowers kept arriving for him. His own room was full till they were distributed to all the other wards and rooms, but still they came, right until the day he left. The Pressmen at the entrance sent him a box of cigars.

But we all knew that the end had to come one day, for this is something none of us can evade, and when I walked with him out of the House of Commons for the last time, upon his retirement in July 1964, I wondered then whether it could be very far off.

There was no official ceremony in the Commons to mark Sir Winston's departure, the feeling being, I was led to understand, that they did not want him to attempt a farewell speech in case it proved too much for him. However, when the party leaders came to 28 Hyde Park Gate to present him with an illuminated scroll, his brief, informal words of thanks were so felicitous that the three leaders, Sir Alec Douglas Home, Mr Harold Wilson and Mr Jo Grimond together with Sir Thomas More and Mr Emanuel Shinwell who made up the specially appointed committee, appeared to be sorry that they had not staged the occasion in the House of Commons after all.

The tribute, printed on vellum, read:

'That this House desires to take this opportunity of marking the forthcoming retirement of the Rt Hon Gentleman, the Member for Woodford, by putting on record its unbounded admiration and gratitude for his services to Parliament, to the nation and to the world; remembers above all his inspiration of the British people when they stood alone, and his leadership until victory was won; and offers grateful thanks to the Rt Hon Gentleman for these out-standing services to the House and to the nation.'

The visitors then toasted the former Member for Woodford in champagne and there was not a dry eye in the room on this, probably the saddest day in the life of Churchill.

Then came the last days. Four days, I was told, was the most that Sir Winston could be expected to survive, but he defied all the expert predictions. For the next nine days I stood guard, mostly for as long as eighteen hours a day, there in front of that house in Kensington where the public and the world Press began to congregate in their hundreds.

While I was standing one day outside the house at Hyde Park Gate, I was handed a note by a member of the Press. The letter inside was from a 'friend' of many years standing, with Associated Press. It was dated 19 January 1965. 'Dear Ed,' it began, 'Between us, some-one has given me a tip that if the end should come, you will emerge from No 28 wearing a red tie. Should there be anything to the story, will you please tell the bearer – who incidentally knows nothing of the contents of this note – to tell me 'yes' or 'no'. With best wishes and kind regards.' I hope he is still waiting for my answer. *Red* tie, indeed.

During those last days I found that I had friends in most of the houses around, especially the Pearson and Wyndham families opposite, who missed no opportunity of asking for news of the great man and asking me to convey their best wishes to Lady Churchill. On the top floor of one house, a flat was rented to three young ladies, including the daughter of the Rt. Hon. Norman St John-Stevas, the Conservative member for Chelmsford. They invited me to have tea with them one day, and made sure that I was able to keep an eye on the front door of No 28 while I relaxed in their very pleasant company for about half an hour.

An old friend of my Legion days in Indochina, Jean Stokman, came to visit me at Hyde Park Gate at this time to present the good wishes and concern of the Paris Office of the Association of the Old Comrades of the French Foreign Legion. On a previous visit I had been able to present Jean to Sir Winston and it made him a very proud man. Stokman and I had completed both the Corporals' and NCO's schools together at Tong, in Indochina, and as he was sent to the Third battalion and I was with the Second, we did not see much of each other, except when we faced each other playing football. Beryl and I were to see much more of Jean and his dear wife, Madeleine, in later years, on the outskirts of Paris.

At one time it looked as if he might defy all the predictions, and pull through, for on the fourth day he rallied slightly.

I had myself been in to see him that morning, as usual, and as I stood beside his bed he seemed to be unaware of my presence and made no response when the nurse, Roy Howells, announced me. Then gently I placed my hand in his right hand as it lay on the counterpane, and at once his fingers curved round mine in a firm grip. At that moment the nurse, seeing the rebirth of interest, offered a glass of orange juice to the invalid, and for the first time in four days, he sipped from the glass.

His complexion improved, losing the bluish tint of past days, and optimism grew. Young Winston came into the room, then followed me into the lounge when I left.

'He'll do it on them yet, Sergeant Murray,' he said with a hint of excitement in his voice as he offered me a Scotch.

But of course, it was not to be, and on a grey Sunday morning that chill 24 January 1965, at five minutes past eight o'clock – seventy years to the day after his father, Lord Randolph had passed on – Sir Winston Churchill finally let go his hold on life. I saw him shortly afterwards, his features composed, and firm, and at peace.

Soon afterwards, Lady Churchill discovered that there were no suitable candles to place in the room where her husband lay and she asked me if I could find some. It was Sunday, and in those days the shops were closed. My wife and I had Swiss friends who owned the Montana Hotel in Gloucester Road, just around the corner, and I hurried there only to find that Mr. Bonvin was not there and he had the keys to the store-room with him. I telephoned to the Savoy Hotel and Mr Contarini, joint general manager at the time, was as always, very co-operative and promised to send some suitable candles to the Montana as soon as possible. It would only take about ten minutes. I waited outside, in Gloucester Road.

A few seconds later a small car, driven by an elderly lady, drew up beside me and the side window was wound down. The lady asked me if she might have a word with me, and thinking that she wished to be directed to some place, I approached and bent down. She grasped my hand. 'Thank you for all you did for Sir Winston. God bless you.' Then she slowly drove off towards Chelsea.

The candles duly arrived, brought by a porter from the Savoy in a taxi, with the compliments of Mr Contarini and a request that I present personally to Lady Churchill, the sincere condolences of himself, the management and staff.

I took the candles back to Lady Churchill with the message from the Savoy, and once they had been placed and lit, she asked me to sit with her for a while, there at the side of that humble bed in that small downstairs room at No 28 Hyde Park Gate.

That great man who lay there, who was no longer with us, had brought Britain through the greatest struggle in its long, exciting history. His had been the voice, his the spirit and the determination, the courage and the strength, though he did admit to me on one occasion that God had been on his side. He had taken Britain and Britons to the highest peak of glory they had ever known. He had inspired men and women, in this country and in other countries as well. He had inspired us all. So, from a balcony in Whitehall on 8 May 1945, the descendant of the Duke of Marlborough was able to stand forth, in the presence of a vast multitude including his King and Queen, to say, 'God Bless You All. This is your victory, everyone . . . man and woman, have done your best.'

Erich Reupke, one-time radio officer of Mr Onassis on the *Christina*, after hearing of the death of Sir Winston, wrote . . .

'Dear Eddie, when the younger Pitt died, Sir Walter Scott wrote
  Now is the stately column broke,
  The beacon light is quenched in smoke,
  The trumpet's silver sound is still,
  The Warden silent on the hill . . .'

What more is there to say about this episode in my life.

EPILOGUE

ESCORTING LADY CHURCHILL TO WESTMINSTER HALL for the lying-in-state was a most painful experience. Lady Churchill bore her great loss with superb dignity and courage throughout. On 22 June 1965 she sent me the following letter:

My dear Sergeant Murray,

I feel I should have written to you before this, but I am sure you will understand how occupied I have been in the past weeks, and excuse me.

I would like now to thank you for all you did for Sir Winston over the years, and for the many services you performed for him which were beyond your duty. I feel you would like to have something to keep as a memento of him, and I am sending you one of his pictures with my good wishes.

Yours sincerely

Clementine Spencer-Churchill

The very thought of returning to the Yard and Special Branch appalled me. I would now be far behind in the promotion stakes and fifteen years of loyalty and devotion on *'service commandé'* would not be of much account. The day after the funeral, on 30 January 1965, I returned to Scotland Yard, went to my office, looked reverently across the roofs to Big Ben, a few hundred yards away, and typed out my resignation to terminate my service with the Force, effective from the end of the month. Eighteen years after all had been a very long time for me to stay in one job.

During the days and weeks following Sir Winston's death, I received more than a hundred telegrams and letters from friends like my old colleagues of the Foreign Legion, General Alessandri, General de Cockborne, Jean Stokman, and their families; from people I had met in the United States, particularly those in the Secret Service with whom I had been connected on protection duties; from members of the French *'voyages officiels'*, Lejeune, Gauthier and others; and from so many members of the public who had read about me in the newspapers, or heard of me on radio and television programmes. There was even a very touching letter from Miss Nicol, living in Jesmond Dene, near Newcastle-upon-Tyne, who had been my English mistress at Stanley so long ago. There was also a cable from my old friend Bill Ayres, Congressman for Ohio. It read: 'Our deepest sympathy is extended to you. Have arranged for a flag to be flown over the Capitol in memory of the late Sir Winston to be delivered to Ambassador David K. E. Bruce. Hope the Ambassador directs the same to you.' I often wonder what happened to that flag.

On the last day of my duties as a Police Officer I walked to the Yard, but at the gate I was accosted by a reporter from the *Daily Mail* who informed me that the well-known author, Elleston Trevor, who wrote *Flight of the Phoenix* and many other novels under his own name and also the pen-name of Adam Hall, had invited me to go to Cannes for a fortnight, staying, at his expense, at the Hotel Martinez. He wished me to open a new school of painting he had organised. He agreed when I suggested that my wife should accompany me at my own expense, and so we made the necessary arrangements to have the three children looked after, and off we went to Cannes where we had a wonderful time. We were met by Jean-Pierre, the son of Elleston and his wife Jonquil, but his parents had, regrettably for us, been called to Hollywood to supervise the filming of *The Flight of the Phoenix*, and so we did not meet my benefactors at that time.

Back in London I began to search for work and, influenced by friends in the catering business, we decided to buy a small very interesting hotel in mid-Devon and looked forward to life in the country. The Burton Hall Hotel had been purchased by Fulford Vicary, owner of numerous mills in the south-west, in 1871. Originally a private, timber-built house in Norway, the house was taken to pieces where it stood, each piece of timber being individually numbered, and, together with five local builders, the whole lot was shipped, in two men-o'-war (Vicary had a cousin who was one of the Lords of the Admiralty at the time) to Exmouth, in Devon.

Thence the consignment went by barge up the canal to Exeter, by rail from Exeter to Yeoford, and the rest of the way by horse and cart, to be erected at last on Bouchiers Hill, North Tawton. It remained as a private residence for many years before being turned into a private hotel and club.

One good customer of ours was the recently-nominated Poet Laureate, Ted Hughes, who lived at an old manor-house in the town, and who used to come up at all hours of the day and night with his friends, including authors Henry Williamson and Alan Sillitoe and a number of others. They knew that they were always welcome at Burton Hall and that the red wine was always good and *'chambré'*. Ted used to have a couple of goats and on one occasion, as he was going away for a few days, he asked us to look after them. I tried to curb their activities with ropes, with chains, by putting them behind bars, but nothing could stop them devouring everything they could touch.

I used to run a snooker club at Burton Hall which was great fun, for it was something the town lacked, and the bar adjoined the snooker room which was very practical. Assisted by our son, William, I made another bar in the main cellar and folk-singers came from all over Devon to entertain our guests there.

In 1969 I was pleasantly surprised to be invited to be the Curator of a Churchill Exhibition in the Isetan Superstore in Tokyo, during the British Week organised by British Overseas Fairs Ltd, and sponsored by Mainichi Shimbun, one of the leading Japanese newspapers. I gave the matter considerable thought because I imagined there might be some danger for a person who had been a small thorn in the sides of the Japanese during the War and had fought so assiduously in Indochina. However, all my doubts were set aside by the arrival of three of the managers of the Isetan store at our hotel to examine *me* as to my suitability for the job. They were a delightful trio and the very first evening we had fun in the bar when they asked persmission to use the kitchen, brought out a collection of dried foods and proceeded to delight out guests with Japanese hospitality.

So Beryl and I flew to Japan and had a wonderful time. The highlight of the Exhibition was the visit of Princess Margaret and Lord Snowdon. It was a lovely experience to take the Princess round the exhibits; I had not spoken with her since her visit so long ago to Chartwell with her sister, now Her Majesty The Queen. Meanwhile

Beryl, at the request of the Directors of the store, had the pleasant privilege of taking Lord Snowdon around. All in all it was a most successful exhibition.

Back home in Burton Hall we continued to enjoy our life in the catering business but by 1971 the Hotel was not having the financial results we could have expected from the work we put in. So, after the celebrations for the hundredth anniversary of its being brought over from Norway, we decided to sell, with great regret. Without a job, without a house, we were rescued by Ted Hughes, who let us store our belongings in his mansion at North Tawton. Beryl and I took a flat in the town for a few weeks while I looked for work.

Shortly afterwards I was offered the job of Curator of the fabulous Titania's Palace, at Wookey Hole Caves, near Wells, in Somerset. But in 1972 the owner, Mrs Hodgkinson, decided to sell the Caves to Madame Tussauds and to take her Titania's Palace to Jersey. Such a move was of no interest to Beryl and myself so I sat an examination and went to the Ministry of Defence at Bath where I enjoyed a Top Secret job connected with nuclear submarines, until I retired at the age of 65.

The concept of a 'European Community' was an abiding vision of Sir Winston's and something we often discussed. If there were 20 million people in England who had three or four friends in France, that, to my mind, would be a 'community'. If there were the same number being friendly in Italy, Germany and all the other European countries, that would at last be the beginning of a United Europe as envisaged by Sir Winston Churchill.

'Politics,' he said to me thoughtfully one day, 'is a dirty business, but it is the way to obtain power . . . and power is the thing necessary for extending our principles of good will to all men wherever they may live.'

I have tried to give the reader, in my chapters about my life with Churchill, an idea of the innate goodness of the man, of his lack of those things that smaller men think are necessary in great men – jealousy, malice, envy and thoughtlessness for others, for throughout those fifteen years, I saw only his kindness and consideration, his devotion to those he loved, and a simple, sincere trust that with his leadership, and God's help, all would come right in the end for Britain.

'When I get to Heaven,' wrote the great man, 'I mean to spend a considerable portion of the first million years in painting and so getting to the bottom of the subject. I expect orange and vermillion will be the darkest, dullest colours upon my palette.'

When I myself go to Heaven, I trust that there will be fishing, and that the trout will be just a little bit more willing to take the fly; that the jack will find itself just a little closer to the bowls I throw up; that the little white ball I have just driven beautifully some 300 yards will not hide itself in a sandy bunker, behind inhospitable trees, or in the rough, but sit there bright and smiling in the middle of the fairway; that slugs and snails and wood-lice will not enter the vegetable garden to make Beryl cross; that there will always be friends and relations to enjoy my Saturday bake of fresh rolls, bread and perhaps Danish pastries or chocolate éclairs, and my home-made elderflower wine; that the sun will shine most of the time to permit Sir Winston and myself to sit at last side-by-side with our easels and paints and brushes; and that my dear wife, Beryl, will be there to share with me, with love, all those joys forever.

INDEX

Butler, 'RAB', 155, 156-7

Callas, Maria, 217, 248, 251–2;
situation between M.C. and
Aristotle Onassis, 252
Campbell, Lady, 66
Campbell, Roy, 247
Camrose, Viscount, 147
Carbonnel, Major,
Commander of Military School
of Son Tay, 32
Carey-Foster, Major, 129, 220
Casablanca Conference, 95
Cecil, Sir William, 122
Chenillot family, 22, 25–6
Chenillot, Lucienne, 22–6
Chequers, use of by Prime
Ministers, 119
Cherwell, Lord, 95, 99
Chevalier, Maurice, 20
Chiang Kai-shek, 31
Churchill, Arabella, daughter of
Randolph, 242
Churchill Centenary Trust, 224
Churchill International Society, 86
Churchill, John, 1st Duke of
Marlborough, 199
Churchill, John, nephew of W.C.,
86, 188
Churcill, Lady, 85, 94, 95, 107;
assists W.C. in election
preparations, 118; her passion
for croquet, 120; an ardent
book-reader, 134; great charm
of, 137; accepts life peerage,
171; publishes plea for Press to
regard burial of Sir W.C. as
private ceremony and ignoring
of by Paris Match, 264–5
Churchill, Lady Randolph, 164,
200; sterling qualities of, 164
Churchill, Lord Randolph, 138
Churchill, Randolph, son of W.C.,
117, 138, 242
Churchill, Sarah, 138–40, 224,
226–7, 269; a highly-strung
disposition, 139–40, 158

Churchill, Winston, grandson,
138–9, 241, 269; wedding of,
263
Churchill, Winston Spencer, 61,
67–8, 74, 84; his absorption
with painting, 86, 151–55; his
attitude to protectors, 87; to
Denmark to receive Order of the
Elephant and Danish Resistance
Medal, 88; returns to London,
90; attends Conservative Party
Conference, Blackpool, 90–1;
his politeness and courtesy
towards secretaries, 91; to
Marrakesh, 95–106; becomes
Knight of the Order of the
Garter, 102; recipient of many
gifts, 115; held in high esteem,
115–6; his thorough
preparations of pre-election
speeches, 116–8; his love of
horses, 129; an avid
newspaper-reader, 131–4;
favourite authors, 134; his great
enjoyment of works of Gilbert
and Sullivan, 134; interested in
films and cinema, 134–5; enjoys
theatre-going, 135–6; his great
love for wife and reliance on
her, 136; places wagers for E.M.,
141–2; congratulates HM Queen
on horse-racing success, 142;
immense passion for gambling
in casinos, 143, 201; shocked at
news of King George VI's death,
145; his emotion at funeral of
King, 145; immersed in
painting, 153–4; takes deep
interest in E.M.'s paintings, 157;
made Honorary Mayor of Cap
d'Ail, 158; subjected to trouble
with Press, 160–168; his real
liking for President Tito, 169;
knighted by Queen, 171; reason
for refusing peerage, 171; suffers
stroke, 172–3; convalesces at
Cap d'Ail, 173–4; paints at Cap

THE FOLLOWING TITLES ARE AVAILABLE FROM
GOOD BOOKSHOPS OR IN CASE OF DIFFICULTY BY
CONTACTING THE PUBLISHERS:

WH ALLEN & CO PLC
44 HILL STREET
LONDON W1X 8LB

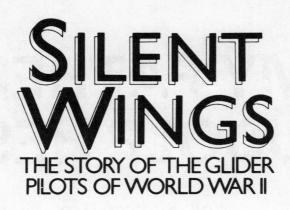

SILENT WINGS

THE STORY OF THE GLIDER PILOTS OF WORLD WAR II

Gerard M. Devlin

Glider pilots are a special breed of men and during World War II they were among the most uninhibited individuals in the fighting forces of either side. Their uniquely perilous situation – flying a fragile, unpowered machine on assaults into heavily guarded enemy positions without parachutes – has not yet been fully appreciated in the history of the last war. This volume sets out to remedy that omission.

Opening with an account of the early pioneering days of aviation and the pre-war build-up by Germany of its glider force, the book gives a blow-by-blow account of every glider assault during the war, and vividly recreates the outstanding part played by gliders and their pilots on both sides: from the first gliderborne assault in the history of warfare – Hitler's air offensive against Belgium – to the Allied victory in the battle for Sicily, a turning point in the war, but at the cost of almost 20,000 casualties; to Operation Overlord where over 1,000 Allied gliders spearheaded the invasion of Normandy; to the vital part played by gliders in the taking of Burma. The author also gives a detailed account of 'Operation Eiche', Hitler's spectacularly successful use of gliders in freeing Mussolini from his hotel-prison on the highest peak of the Abruzzi Mountains.

Based on extensive interviews with the men who participated in these actions, Gerard Devlin's history is alive with fascinating personal anecdotes. Although a totally factual account, the book incorporates within the context of a military history all the excitement of a first-rate war novel.

Hardback, 234 × 153mm, 528 pages, illustrated, ISBN 0–491–03134–3

MY FATHER RUDOLF HESS

Wolf Rüdiger Hess

In the history of the Second World War and the post-war period, Rudolf Hess's flight to Britain stands out as one of the most mysterious and controversial events in modern international politics.

Hess, Deputy Führer of the Third Reich, was arrested just outside Glasgow after his Messerschmitt 110 crashed there on the night of 10 May 1941. After the war he was found guilty of conspiracy to commit war crimes at the Nuremberg trials and was sentenced to life imprisonment. Since 1966 Hess has been the sole inmate of West Berlin's Spandau Prison — 'the loneliest prisoner in the world'.

Why did Hess fly to Britain in May 1941? Was it the 'fanatical deed of crack-brained naïvety' that Churchill belittled in his memoirs? Was it the peace mission that Hess himself claimed? If so, what was his peace plan and why did the Allies so effectively shoot it down? Most importantly, why have the four Occupying Powers, but especially the Russians, found it so necessary to silence Hess forever, by making sure he never leaves Spandau alive?

This book reveals a previously unknown peace plan, brought by Hitler's deputy to Britain. It proves beyond doubt that the whole of Germany was at that time seeking peace. So why did Churchill fail to go along with this initiative? Did he wish to weaken Hitler by the loss of prestige and to use Hess to put pressure on Stalin, goading him into war? The book analyses the foundations of the policies of the British Prime Minister and the American President: to eliminate Germany as a power factor once and for all by the longest and bloodiest of all wars.

**Hardback, 234 × 153mm, 436 pages, illustrated,
ISBN 0–491–03772–4**

BODYGUARD OF LIES

OF LIES

Anthony Cave Brown

From top secret information the author has assembled a cruel triumph of revelation. Swept through with dramatic stories of plot and counter-plot, lies and deceits, deadly cat-and-mouse games with the Gestapo, this book shows us just how D-Day worked, how Churchill decided not to warn Coventry that it was about to be destroyed . . . Explosive stories of code-breakers, plots and ruses at the highest levels make up this monumental book.

Critical Acclaim for Bodyguard of Lies

'It is rich in the spicy minutiae of the world of secret services and clandestine operations, but its major revelations will reverberate around Whitehall for years . . . Sensational'
SUNDAY TIMES

'A work of real and considerable stature and a high adventure to read'
THE NEW YORKER

'There has never been such a veritable encyclopaedia of skulduggery'
BIRMINGHAM POST

'Sufficient intrigue and action to keep a generation of spy writers busy'
MANCHESTER EVENING NEWS

'Spell-binding'
DENVER POST

Paperback, 197 × 135mm, 976 pages, illustrated, ISBN 0–86379–064–X

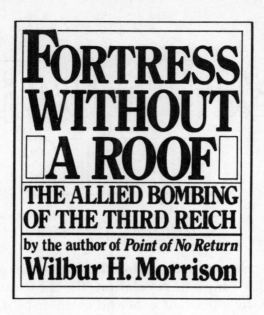

FORTRESS WITHOUT A ROOF

THE ALLIED BOMBING OF THE THIRD REICH

by the author of *Point of No Return*

Wilbur H. Morrison

An epic saga of crisis and victory – through the eyes of the generals and fliers who were there.

'Hitler built a fortress around Europe, but he forgot to put a roof on it' Franklin D. Roosevelt

In this instructive, provocative and fascinating account of the British and American bombing of the Third Reich – an effort born of crisis and shortage in the face of an overpowering airforce that ended in triumph for the Allies – Wilbur H. Morrison takes us up with the planes into the air battles, with heroic tales of what the pilots endured and overcame in the skies over Hitler's 'Fortress Europe'.

It is also an account of the agonising top-level decisions made behind the scenes on both sides of the Atlantic. As well as the obvious cooperation there was inevitably much infighting amongst the generals – the huge debate over daylight versus nighttime bombing, for example, went on throughout the war.

The author, himself a Second World War air combat veteran, has used exclusive, unpublished writings and interviews with such top generals as Jimmy Doolittle and Ira Eaker, who have given fresh accounts of their private conversations and debates with Winston Churchill, Dwight D. Eisenhower, Franklin D. Roosevelt, George C. Marshall and Sir Arthur T. Harris, to name a few. Morrison, with great insight, discloses the reasons behind their decisions, and their second thoughts today.

Hardback, 216 × 135mm, 352 pages, illustrated, ISBN 0–491–02878–4

KLAUS BARBIE
The Untold Story

Ladislas De Hoyos

**An exclusively researched assessment of war criminal
Klaus Barbie from the French perspective**

Much has been written about former SS Hauptstürmfuhrer Klaus
Barbie since his extradition from Bolivia in February 1983.
However, this account of his life by the distinguished French journalist Ladislas de Hoyos sheds new light on the whole affair by virtue
of its French viewpoint and the author's access to previously
untapped sources. These include the personal archives of Simon
Wiesenthal, new testimonies to Barbie's activities in Amsterdam,
and the circumstances surrounding the arrest of Resistance leader
Jean Moulin, and exclusive interviews with, among others, the
former head of the Gestapo in France, the French ambassador to
Bolivia and Barbie's French daughter-in-law. The book contains a
number of previously unpublished photographs and documents,
including the transcript of Barbie's first cross-examination by the
French Special Police in Germany in 1948.

*In 1972 Ladislas de Hoyos won an award at the Cannes Television festival
for a televised interview with Klaus Barbie alias Altmann that stunned the
French nation. He is currently the Chief Crime Reporter for French Channel
One and following the Barbie case closely.*

**Hardback, 216 × 135mm, 336 pages, illustrated,
ISBN 0–491–03043–6**